An Introduction to Research, Analysis, and Writing

SAGE was founded in 1965 by Sara Miller McCune to support the dissemination of usable knowledge by publishing innovative and high-quality research and teaching content. Today, we publish more than 750 journals, including those of more than 300 learned societies, more than 800 new books per year, and a growing range of library products including archives, data, case studies, reports, conference highlights, and video. SAGE remains majority-owned by our founder, and after Sara's lifetime will become owned by a charitable trust that secures our continued independence.

Los Angeles | London | New Delhi | Singapore | Washington DC | Boston

An Introduction to Research, Analysis, and Writing

Practical Skills for Social Science Students

Bruce Oliver Newsome
University of California, Berkeley

Los Angeles | London | New Delhi
Singapore | Washington DC | Boston

Los Angeles | London | New Delhi
Singapore | Washington DC | Boston

FOR INFORMATION:

SAGE Publications, Inc.

2455 Teller Road

Thousand Oaks, California 91320

E-mail: order@sagepub.com

SAGE Publications Ltd.

1 Oliver's Yard

55 City Road

London EC1Y 1SP

United Kingdom

SAGE Publications India Pvt. Ltd.

B 1/I 1 Mohan Cooperative Industrial Area

Mathura Road, New Delhi 110 044

India

SAGE Publications Asia-Pacific Pte. Ltd.

3 Church Street

#10-04 Samsung Hub

Singapore 049483

Printed in the United States of America.

A catalog record of this book is available from the Library of Congress.

ISBN: 978-1-4833-5255-8

This book is printed on acid-free paper.

MIX
Paper from
responsible sources
FSC® C014174

FSC
www.fsc.org

Acquisitions Editor: Helen Salmon
Editorial Assistant: Anna Villarruel
Production Editor: Bennie Clark Allen
Copy Editor: Rachel Keith
Typesetter: C&M Digitals (P) Ltd.
Proofreader: Rae-Ann Goodwin
Indexer: Robie Grant
Cover Designer: Scott Van Atta
Marketing Manager: Nicole Elliott

15 16 17 18 19 10 9 8 7 6 5 4 3 2 1

Contents

Preface

This book is an introduction to the practical and applied skills required to complete a project of research, analysis, or writing.

This book is intended to be an accessible, introductory, step-by-step guide through the project, from identifying a topic to writing a report or dissertation. It is intended to introduce students to the complete skill set, including planning, design, analysis, argumentation, criticizing theories, building theories, modeling theories, choosing methods, gathering data, presenting evidence, and writing the final product.

I was motivated to write this book because of my experiences as an undergraduate student of the social sciences, with complacent professors who did not teach me these skills. I resorted to taking courses in hard sciences and management sciences. Since then, I have worked as an interdisciplinary social scientist by training and profession. I needed to apply these skills as a research policy scientist, advising governments (from national to local) on current issues and on what do about them. One of my motivations to leave full-time research behind, in favor of teaching, was to bring these useful skills to students.

The best time to open this book would be when you enter higher education as an undergraduate student. Most books on research or analysis are written for advanced graduate students or professionals, but in reality almost everybody, at almost any level, in almost any position, needs to understand the overall process of research, analysis, and writing. Any education benefits from research, analysis, and writing skills from the start. A few decades ago, academics started to oppose these skills for perpetuating traditional "power" structures and repressing creativity and self-discovery, but this fashion went too far. Social scientific skills are fundamental to verifiable knowledge about societies.

Some books and courses on research concentrate on few skills within the skill set, such as statistical analysis or writing, but leave the student struggling to fill in the other stages of the process.

This book provides a practical guide that takes the reader through the full spectrum of skills required for the whole project—from idea to delivery.

This book is likely to be required for:

- Courses on research (e.g., praxis, thesis methods, historical methods, qualitative methods, scientific methods, research skills)

- Courses on writing (e.g., "writing across the university")

- Courses on analysis (e.g., environmental analysis, foreign policy analysis)

- Preterm and introductory classes at the start of professional degrees (e.g., business intelligence analysis courses)

- Senior theses or capstone projects at the end of programs of instruction

Employers demand these skills. Perhaps you are a professional who has been asked to explain something or to report on an issue. You could be in commercial or official work, tasked with producing regular reports on what is happening. You might be tasked with analyzing what other people think is happening. You could be the person who undertakes to decide which of the reports and analyses is most accurate or useful. You may even consider a full-time career in research.

You will find in this book:

- An emphasis on skills, including planning, scoping, analysis, argumentation, theory building, theory modeling, methods, data gathering, evidence presentation, and writing, and on how to apply these skills practically

- Reviews of the options and alternatives available to you when you approach a particular step in the process of research

- Practical exercises to help you to develop and produce your research

- Comparisons between concepts, to help you understand one in relation to the other

- Research in the Real World boxes to illustrate the decisions and choices that you will face

- Practical Advice boxes to guide you throughout the process, from idea to delivery

- End-of-chapter questions and exercises for content review and fact checking

- A complete glossary of terms used throughout the book.

The research, analysis, and writing skills in this book are generally accessible, meaning that almost anyone, after some dedication and application, could acquire them. This book should be useful to anyone who needs to research, analyze, or write, at any time, in any position, at any level.

Acknowledgments

Helen Salmon at SAGE Publications has opened a portfolio of practical student-focused books of this type, and has encouraged and guided the development of this book in particular, with my thanks.

This book has benefited from the many students to whom I have taught these skills in the last eight years, and who have helped me to refine my teaching, on which this book is based.

I want to praise two exceptional employers: Frank Plantan, PhD, who directs the International Relations Program at the University of Pennsylvania; and Alan Karras, PhD, who directs the International and Area Studies Program at the University of California, Berkeley. Both have developed rigorous programs focused on applied knowledge and practical skills, against the many trends and incentives in the opposite direction. I and my students have benefited from their responsible attitude.

Additionally, I would like to thank the following SAGE reviewers for their feedback and suggestions: Jennifer P. Anderson, University of Southern Mississippi; Vivian Chin, Mills College; Andrew M. Essig, DeSales University; Randy Gainey, Old Dominion University; and Sébastien G. Lazardeux, St. John Fisher College.

About the Author

Bruce Oliver Newsome is Assistant Teaching Professor in International Relations at the University of California, Berkeley. Previously he served as a consultant to governments on security and risk while being employed by the RAND Corporation in Santa Monica, California. He earned his undergraduate degree in war studies with honors from Kings College, London; a master's degree in political science from the University of Pennsylvania; and a PhD in international studies from the University of Reading.

CHAPTER 1

The Way Ahead

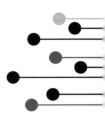

The Goal of This Book

This book is a practical introduction to the skills required to complete a project of research, analysis, and writing—a guide to the whole process, from scoping out your topic to writing a report or dissertation.

To understand this preview, you should learn now that:

- **Research** is the process or product of acquiring knowledge

- **Analysis** is the process of disaggregating, categorizing, and relating something in order to better understand it

- **Writing** is the process of recording what you mean to communicate

This book teaches research, analysis, and writing as a complete skill set. Why should you care? As explained in the following five sections, this skill set is useful to you, useful at all levels of higher education and business, applicable throughout the research project from start to finish, practical, and scientific.

Useful to You

This book is aimed at students in higher education (i.e., optional formal study as an adult). The best time to open this book is when you enter higher education as an undergraduate student. Realistically, you are most likely to open this book around the middle of your

Learning Objectives and Outcomes

At the end of this chapter, you should be able to:

1. Understand the goal of this book

2. Realize your needs as a reader of this book

3. Consider your roles as a researcher

4. Conceptualize the process of research from start to finish

5. Conceptualize the different levels of research

6. Differentiate the practical and theoretical skills that you would need to complete a research project

7. Understand what is meant by "scientific skills"

8. Know what to expect in the rest of this book

Source: ©iStockphoto.com/PeopleImages.

degree, when students typically get around to completing the skills requirements for their academic degree.

If every student and professor thought ahead to all the research projects that are required during coursework, he or she would realize the value of opening a book like this at the beginning of any higher education. Any higher education demands research, analysis, and writing from the start, so it is amazing how rarely the skill set is taught. Just a few years ago, a fashion emerged for opposing these skills on the grounds that they repressed subjective creativity and experiences and perpetuated traditional "power" structures, but these are fundamental skills without any agendas of their own.

Fortunately, more and more institutions of higher education are requiring their students to demonstrate some research skills. Many schools now require students to pass at least one approved course in such skills. Many degree programs now demand a final research project (a thesis or dissertation or capstone project) from all students before they can be awarded a degree.

More and more employers are demanding these skills. More of us are being employed as **knowledge workers**—people whose main value is their knowledge, such as consultants, analysts, and lawyers. Perhaps you are a professional who has been asked to explain something or to report on an issue. You could be in commercial or official work and tasked with producing regular reports on what is happening. You may be expected to analyze what other people think is happening. You could be the person who undertakes to decide which among a group of reports and analyses is most accurate or useful. You may even be considering a full-time career in research (see Research in the Real World Box 1.1).

Whatever the course or project, you will find this book useful.

All Levels

This book is meant to guide you at every level of your career, from your undergraduate degree to your professional employment. A *level* is a relative position or rank in a hierarchy. *Hierarchies* have levels from the lowest to

Research Occupations Recognized by the U.S. Department of Labor

Source: ©iStockphoto.com/bo1982.

"*Research Associate*: A term applied to persons who conduct independent research in scientific, legal, medical, political, academic, or other specialized fields. Individuals working at this level are required to have a graduate degree."

"*Research Engineer*: Conducts research in a field or specialization of an engineering discipline to discover facts, or performs research directed toward investigation, evaluation, and application of known engineering theories and principles. Plans and conducts, or directs engineering personnel performing, complex engineering experiments to test, prove, or modify theoretical propositions on basis of research findings and experiences of others researching in related technological areas. Evaluates findings to develop new concepts, products, equipment, or processes; or to develop applications of findings to new uses. Prepares technical reports for use by engineering or management personnel for long- and short-range planning, or for use by sales engineering personnel in sales or technical services activities. Classifications are made according to discipline. May use computer-assisted engineering software and equipment."

Source: U.S. Department of Labor, http://www.bls .gov.

the highest. Institutions of higher education issue degrees at different levels: undergraduate, and postgraduate or graduate, including master's and doctoral degrees. Businesses also have levels, from the most junior employee to the most senior, accountable, or responsible.

Most books on research or analysis are written for highly specialized graduate students or professionals, but in reality almost everybody, at almost any level, in almost any position, needs to understand the overall process of research, analysis, and writing.

Although this book is useful at all levels, people tend to need or learn these skills at particular levels, so this book is aimed at:

- Advanced undergrads as they consider longer research papers

- Lower-level professional students, such as candidates for a master's degree in business administration or public administration, who are asked to apply their new knowledge in order to explain or advise

- Commercial analysts, official analysts, and staffers who report to superiors

This is a book that you can reference throughout your higher education and your career. It will get you started, remind you of what you should be doing, show you more advanced techniques when you need them, and remind you of what you have learned. This book is the guidance you can call on whenever you need it, from the start of your career to your next challenge.

From Start to Finish

A process is a series of activities or steps by which something occurs or is produced.

This book is intended to be an introductory but comprehensive guide to the complete process of research, from start to finish. It is a practical guide through all the steps of the project, from choosing the topic to delivering the final written product.

Most books on research concentrate on parts of the process, such as statistical analysis or how to write better. These books leave readers struggling to fill in the other stages of the process. This book does not teach statistics, although it explains how to make methodological choices and search for more advanced help. Instead, it aims to be a practical, accessible, step-by-step guide to anyone intimidated by the overall process of research, analysis, and writing.

To help you imagine what you will learn in the rest of this book and what you should be able to do by the end of the book, consider the following steps in a typical research process:

1. Design a research project

2. Review the existing literature or knowledge

3. Analyze the phenomena

4. Develop a valid, sound, and cogent argument

5. Build a theory

6. Deduce or induce hypotheses

7. Model key processes

8. Test hypotheses

9. Deliver a coherently written product, such as an undergraduate thesis or professional report

The scale of the product does not matter; whether you are writing a short memorandum or a publishable document, this book contains skills to help you.

Practical

This book is meant to be practical. Something is practical if it can be applied, rather than remaining purely **theoretical**, that is, explanatory but perhaps impractical. **Practice** involves doing things, while **theory** is used to explain facts (as you will learn in more detail in Chapter 8).

You need to learn practical skills before you can start doing things. You may not know where to start, or you may just want to improve your skills. You may be one of the many people who enjoys reading about a subject but does not know how to evaluate sources of information. You may like writing but not know how to organize your knowledge. You may know what you want to say but have difficulty writing it down.

Some people would lead you to believe that research, analysis, and writing are skills that you are either born with or not, but be skeptical of such claims. Many people were never taught these skills, so they naturally view such skills as exotic or vague; other people have acquired these skills but would rather claim that they have exceptional, inaccessible talents than admit how hard they had to work and how many mistakes they made along the way to greatness.

The research, analytical, and writing skills in this book are generally accessible, meaning that almost anyone, after some dedication and application, can acquire them.

Scientific

This book teaches you scientific skills. The modern word **science** is derived from the ancient Latin word *scientia*, meaning "knowledge," which indicates how fundamental science is to knowledge.

The word *science* here refers to a replicable way of verifying knowledge, which you will learn more about in the next and subsequent chapters. In practice, this usually involves carrying out observations, developing theories that could explain the observations, and looking for evidence to support a theory—all in a replicable way.

Some researchers do not think of themselves as scientists and are critical of what they see as narrow scientific approaches. Indeed, science is not necessarily appropriate in creative, interpretive, or philosophical endeavors. Genuinely original creations are usually protected (ethically and legally) from replication. Subjective interpretations or experiences are not perfectly replicable. **Philosophy** (the reasoned study of fundamental issues) is not necessarily replicable or even factual.

However, you can apply science wherever you want to be replicable or evidence-based rather than merely creative, interpretive, or philosophical. You do not need to be a hard scientist to use scientific skills; you were developing scientific skills as a child when you tested how different objects interact, and you have demonstrated scientific skills whenever you have presented evidence during an argument or pondered how to explain the world around you.

Scientific skills are demanded in professions and endeavors that contain no explicit reference to science. For instance, managerial skill sets now routinely include "performance measurement." Much research is now differentiated as "evidence-based." In each case, the approach is fundamentally scientific; if we could not replicate it, how would we know whether performance is being measured effectively or whether the research is truly evidence-based?

The **hard sciences**, or *natural sciences* (such as physics, chemistry, and biology), are easier for laboratory experimenters, but science can be applied anywhere. Most of the **applications** in this book are *social scientific*, a term which here refers to the application of science to the study of human society. Most formal professions and academic disciplines fall within the scope of this definition, including the formal **social sciences** (economics, politics, psychology, sociology, anthropology), some of the **humanities** (academic disciplines that study human culture, such as history) and **liberal arts** (the traditional core disciplines, such as philosophy and literature), and the professions (such as law and business).

The professions and social sciences dominate the 10 most popular majors in America (see Table 1.1).

Table 1.1 The 10 most popular and 10 least popular undergraduate majors in the U.S. in 2010

Popularity rank	Major	Students (percent of all majors)	Ratio of females to males (percent of all students in major)	Full-time employment rate (percent)	Earnings (median full-time, full-year salary, 2010, US$)
1	Business management and administration	8	44:56	90	58,000
2	General business	5	39:61	90	60,000
3	Accounting	5	52:48	89	63,000
4	Nursing	4	92:08	77	60,000
5	Psychology	4	71:29	79	45,000
6	Elementary education	4	91:90	80	40,000
7	Marketing and marketing research	3	51:49	88	58,000
8	General education	3	76:24	84	42,000
9	English language and literature	3	67:33	80	48,000
10	Communications	3	58:42	83	50,000
162	Precision production and industrial arts	<0.01	11:89	93	(not available)
163	Geological and geophysical engineering	<0.01	27:73	97	(not available)
164	Nuclear engineering	<0.01	9:91	96	(not available)
165	Soil science	<0.01	24:76	83	(not available)

(Continued)

Table 1.1 (Continued)

Popularity rank	Major	Students (percent of all majors)	Ratio of females to males (percent of all students in major)	Full-time employment rate (percent)	Earnings (median full-time, full-year salary, 2010, US$)
166	Geosciences	<0.01	36:64	91	(not available)
167	Educational administration and supervision	<0.01	53:47	79	(not available)
168	Pharmacology	<0.01	56:44	69	(not available)
169	Astronomy and astrophysics	<0.01	27:73	86	(not available)
170	Military technologies	<0.01	7:93	90	(not available)
171	School student counseling	<0.01	94:06	93	(not available)

Data sources: Carnevale and Cheah, 2013; Carnevale, Strohl, and Melton, 2011.

One of the reasons that social science majors are so employable is that social scientific skills are widely useful (see Table 1.2).

In this book, you will not find detailed discussion of particular laboratory methods, statistical methods, mere storytelling, purely philosophical discourse, or the arts of obfuscation so popular in legal and political settings, although you will learn to identify them. You will learn enough about the research, analytical, and writing processes in general to get you rolling through most projects. You will learn enough about your options that you could make informed choices about supplementary texts in more specialized areas.

A Preview of the Rest of This Book

This book will guide you through the entire process of research, from choosing your topic to writing the final **product**.

Table 1.2 Employment rate and earnings in the main social scientific, liberal arts, and humanities majors (in alphabetical order) in the U.S., 2010

Major	Ratio of females to males (percent of all students in major)	Full-time employment rate (percent)	Earnings (median full-time, full-year salary, 2010, US$)
Anthropology and archaeology	61:39	78	45,000
Area, ethnic, and civilization studies	70:30	74	45,000
Art history and criticism	85:15	76	50,000
Composition and speech	60:40	80	45,000
History	40:60	84	50,000
Humanities	61:39	77	48,000
Intercultural and international studies	65:35	78	44,000
Liberal arts	60:40	82	48,000
Criminology	42:58	87	48,000
Economics	34:66	90	70,000
General social sciences	56:44	80	49,000
Geography	30:70	89	54,000
Interdisciplinary social sciences	70:30	80	48,000
International relations	60:40	85	50,000
Miscellaneous social sciences	54:46	78	51,000
Political science and government	41:59	86	59,000
Psychology	71:29	79	45,000
Sociology	68:32	82	45,000
Statistics and decision science	51:49	81	67,000

Data sources: Carnevale and Cheah, 2013; Carnevale, Strohl, and Melton, 2011.

The following chapters discuss the major steps of the process in the order that you would proceed through them in an ideal linear process. Realistically, as described in Chapter 2, you might move nonlinearly between steps, just as you might move among chapters of this book out of order.

Chapter 2 explains research: the different purposes of research; the different products of research; the different approaches to knowledge, including those in the humanities and the social sciences; and how to manage the project's life cycle.

Chapter 3 explains ethics and laws related to research: how to ethically and legally handle subjects, data, permissions and licenses, intellectual property, and supporters, and how to avoid misrepresentation and plagiarism.

Chapter 4 helps you to define the scope of your research: to identify a topic that is interesting, employable, important, improving, challenging, or novel; to justify its feasibility and to prepare the things that are necessary to make its achievement more likely; and to develop a proposal or design for the project.

Chapter 5 explains how to start reading about and reviewing your topic: how to evaluate and choose sources, how to manage your sources, and how to describe your review to others.

Chapter 6 explains analysis: the purposes of analysis, the different types of analysis in different domains, the different levels of analysis, and how analysis should be implemented.

Chapter 7 explores how to argue and explain. This chapter will cover desirable forms of argument, such as valid, sound, and cogent arguments, as well as undesirable forms of argument, including fallacies and biases. The chapter concludes with practical advice about how to describe and critique other arguments.

Chapter 8 explains theory, hypotheses, models, variables, constants, relationships, and boundaries; how to trace processes; and how to model trickier processes, such as contradictions, cycles, and nonlinear processes.

Chapter 9 explains methods, methodologies, and tests; the choice between control and naturalness; how to research history; how to research in the field; case studies; surveys; participant and non-participant observation; and experiments.

Chapter 10 explains the difference between observations, data, and evidence; the difference between correlation and causation; the value of empiricism and objectivity; how to classify data; how to produce data judgmentally; how to find objective correlates; the application of triangulation, multiple measures, and meta-analysis; and the differences and trade-offs between quantitative and qualitative data.

Chapter 11 explains the creative and technical process of writing: structuring your whole document; getting started; disciplining your creativity; and raising the quality of your writing by structuring each section, paragraph, sentence, clause, and phrase; using subjects, objects, prepositions, adverbs, verbs, adjectives, and nouns appropriately; and writing more succinctly, precisely, and literally.

CHAPTER SUMMARY

This chapter explained:

- The goal of this book

- Your needs and roles

- All the levels of research that this book covers

- The process of research from start to finish

- This book's focus on the practical skills you will need to complete a research project

- The scientific skills that this book will cover

- What to expect in the rest of this book

KEY TERMS

(For definitions, please see the Glossary in the back of this book.)

Analysis 1	Liberal arts 6	Science 6
Application 6	Philosophy 6	Social science 6
Hard sciences 6	Practice 5	Theoretical 5
Humanities 6	Product 8	Theory 5
Knowledge worker 2	Research 1	Writing 1

The Research Process

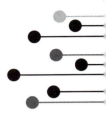

Opening Vignette: Great Writers' Habits

Source: ©iStockphoto.com/gpointstudio.

What habits should you adopt to be a great researcher? Oliver Burkeman, who writes for a living from his home in New York, recommends these six:

1. Get up early: Great writers get up early and start work early, no later than 7 a.m., when the mind is fresh and disturbances are low.

2. Keep the day job: William Faulkner worked at a power plant, T. S. Eliot at a bank, William Carlos Williams as a pediatrician. Day jobs give you structure and teach self-discipline and focus.

3. Take walks: A walk is a way to literally step away from focused work and rest and consider for a while.

4. Stick to a schedule: Do not accept the conventional wisdom that you should wait for inspiration to strike. Hard work is just another form of creativity.

5. Abuse coffee.

6. Learn to work anywhere: Do not pretend that you need special conditions. Agatha Christie used to say that all she needed was a table that would hold her typewriter.

Source: Campbell & Porzucki, 2013.

Learning Objectives and Outcomes

At the end of this chapter, you should be able to:

1. Explain what research is

2. Understand the purposes of research

3. Understand the objectives and products of research

4. Compare different approaches to research

5. Foresee a project's life cycle

6. Foresee the process of research

7. Manage the steps of research

8. Manage your skills

9. Manage your motivations

10. Manage your effort

11. Manage change

What Is Research?

Research is a word with two main meanings: (a) the process of acquiring knowledge, and (b) the product of the research process. This chapter is about research in the first sense—the process. The final chapter explains how to write the product of this process.

The aim of research can be described on three main dimensions, as described in the next three sections: (a) its purpose or utility, (b) its objectives or products, and (c) its approaches.

What Are the Purposes of Research?

Research has three main purposes:

1. **Basic research**, or **pure research**, improves knowledge about something, such as how organizations have been managed in the past. Basic/pure research overlaps analysis. *Analysis* is the examination of something without any other necessary agenda. Indeed, basic/pure research may be known as **analytical research**. As Chapter 6 explains, all research must involve some form of analysis, even though many researchers remain unaware of analysis.

2. **Applied research**, or **practice research**, improves practical solutions to a problem, such as how an organization should be managed.

3. **Action research** improves understanding of how to implement change, such as how to change the leadership or the culture of an organization.

What Are the Objectives and Products of Research?

Research can be described by its objectives and products, of which this section introduces eight:

Exploratory research aims to find a new research project. You will engage in some exploratory research before choosing your research project. Any research is exploratory if:

- A final project has been chosen but not yet fully defined, or

- Several options remain for a final project.

Conclusive research aims at something conclusive, such as an answer to a question, a proof, a recommended policy, or a recommended practice. Just because someone aims to be conclusive does not mean that his or her research will be conclusive. Some researchers honestly report that they failed to find the conclusion they had aimed for. Some researchers might claim to offer something conclusive but be criticized by others for inconclusive research. In fact, research is rarely absolutely conclusive, due to imperfect information or contested interpretations. Scientists tend to regard all research as inconclusive—a contribution to knowledge, but not the final word (see Practical Advice Box 4.2).

Prescriptive research aims to conclude with a prescription. A **prescription** is advice, guidance, or even an obligation regarding how something should be done. For instance, prescriptive research could start with concerns about how to import goods legally or ethically.

Descriptive research aims to produce a description of something, such as the material composition of ancient pottery or the process by which a plant reproduces.

A **case study** aims to explain one case in particular. The case could be an event (such as a crime as experienced by the victim), an action or activity (such as the crime as perpetrated by the criminal), or an actor (such as the criminal).

Survey research aims to assess many things, such as the behaviors exhibited by a particular species of animal, the attributes of a building, or the attitudes of a group of people.

Historical research aims to produce knowledge about things from the past, typically past events (such as elections), past persons (such as former presidents), or past organizations (such as the now defunct Pan Am airline company).

Ex post facto is a Latin phrase that means "after the fact." **Ex post facto research** literally means research into something after it has happened, but it is conventionally used to mean research into the variables within experiments that have already occurred, without repeating the experiments. The *variables* are those factors that can change. Ex post facto research would be necessary if an experiment produced data with unexpected variance, without collecting other data that could explain this variance. For instance, we might have tested the reactions of people to crime by showing each of them in turn some photographs of crimes being perpetrated. Our data might show an anomalous peak in the subjects' self-reported sensitivity to these photographs on one particular day. Ex post facto research into events outside the experimental setting could test whether their increased sensitivity was due to a news report the previous night about a particularly horrific crime.

What Are the Approaches to Research?

An approach is a way of reaching something. An approach to knowledge is a way of achieving that knowledge. Many approaches exist. Some might not be accessible to you, perhaps because they do not apply to your particular project or just because you do not yet understand them well enough. Some people have preferred approaches because they are ignorant of superior alternatives.

Ideally, every researcher would learn the alternatives and understand and describe the approaches that other people use.

The subsections below describe these different approaches. Some of these approaches have been categorized over millennia of philosophical and scientific investigation, so some of the terms below might seem parochial or intimidating. I find that the best way to understand these different categories is as a series of opposing pairs. Think of each pair as poles at opposite ends of a spectrum.

The contrast between dissimilar things should help you understand their boundaries. In practice, much research does not perfectly fit any one of these things, but partially fits lots of these things at the same time, so you might find that you could describe research as a bit of several approaches. For instance, research that is experimental is inherently empirical too; a positivist approach is inherently observational.

The pairs that are compared in the subsections below are:

- Experimental versus field

- Empirical versus theoretical

- Deductive versus inductive

- Subjective versus objective

- Philosophical versus positivist

- Relativist versus replicable

- Metaphysical versus physical

- Traditional versus behavioral

- Phenomenological versus observational

- Ontological versus epistemological

Experimental Versus Field Approaches

In Chapter 9, you will learn more about methods, but methods are so defining of many approaches to research that some of those methods need to be introduced here. **Experimental research** is performed under controlled conditions (often termed "laboratory conditions"), while **field research** is performed in less-controlled, more natural conditions (often termed "field conditions"). For instance, in order to study human competitiveness, we could ask people to compete in a game of our own design—the game is an example of controlled conditions. If we asked them to do so in a controlled space, like a room, we might describe the space as a laboratory. Alternatively, we could observe people going about their natural behaviors, perhaps at home, which would count as research in the field.

Empirical Versus Theoretical Approaches

Empirical research focuses on replicable observations of the real world in order to gain knowledge, while **theoretical research** focuses on explaining facts. For instance, if you pick up a book that describes observations of food consumption and obesity in a city, you have picked up the product of **empirical** research. A theoretical book could attempt to explain why obesity is increasing. Theoretical research is entirely theoretical until it refers to observations of the real world. Many academic works are both theoretical and empirical; they might theorize about why something occurs, then present data as part of a test of their theory.

Deductive Versus Inductive Approaches

Inductive approaches start from observations of the real world. Deductive approaches start from other premises, such as unreal assumptions. For instance, a book that proposes to explain why humans consume foods that are bad for them could start with observation of people consuming food—the resulting argument would be inductive. An argument that starts with an assumption about human needs would be a deductive argument. Chapter 7 has more to say about deductive and inductive arguments. Here we need to note a choice between deductive and inductive research—a choice that would affect other approaches to research. Purely **deductive research** would be purely theoretical research, because deductions are made from premises for the purposes of developing theory. By contrast, **inductive research** would be both theoretical and observational, because inductions are based on real observations. For instance, a book that observes a high rate of obesity in a particular city might compare it to the obesity rate in a different city and find differences in behavior to explain the differences in obesity; this explanation is now an inductive theory.

Subjective Versus Objective Approaches

Subjective research is based on personal experiences and judgments, while **objective research** is not. Subjective approaches are usually easier and may offer more detailed observations. Objective approaches are usually more replicable. If someone were to write a recommendation for reforming a police force based entirely on his or her experiences in the police, then the project would be entirely subjective. Someone else might write a recommendation for reforming the police force based on independent data on police activities and crime; this would be a more objective approach. The subjective approach might be considered superior because of the author's credibility. The objective approach might be considered superior because of its independence. Chapter 9 will explain more about subjective and objective methods.

Philosophical Versus Positivist Approaches

In the past, the term *philosophy* meant almost the same as research, because philosophy was understood as an approach to all knowledge. The modern word comes from the Ancient Greek *philosophia*, which means "love of wisdom." Indeed, some of the early philosophers founded science. Today, *philosophy* is closer in meaning to reasoning about fundamental issues, such as ethics, rights, aesthetics, and reasoning itself. Modern philosophical reasoning is usually not empirical, although some of the reasoning may be based on inductions.

Modern philosophy developed a schism between traditional philosophizing as reasoning and an early modern alternative known as positivism. **Positivism** denied that anything could be known unless it could be observed in a replicable way. Absolute positivism is dissatisfying because it does not allow for things that cannot be observed replicably, such as possibilities, past experiences, future trends, and subjective experiences (see Research in the Real World Box 2.1). **Antipositivists** criticized absolute positivism and allowed for knowledge derived from largely subjective or other similarly unreplicable observations. The social sciences include research that spans the full spectrum from absolute positivism to traditional philosophizing.

Relativist Versus Replicable Approaches

Scientists insist on replicable observations. For instance, some researchers refuse to present any data other than data collected by automated instruments that anybody could use—this is a positivist position. By contrast, others (known as **relativists**) criticize any claim that any person's or culture's observation could be replicated by another; thus, they offer their own observations or intuition as personal and unreplicable (see Research in the Real World Box 2.1).

Metaphysical Versus Physical Approaches

Another schism in philosophy is between metaphysical and physical approaches. **Metaphysics** is a late ancient branch of philosophy examining the physical world—in this sense, metaphysics includes much of early science. However, science later separated from metaphysics, leaving metaphysicists to reason about the physical world in largely nonempirical ways. Thus, **metaphysical approaches** are largely nonempirical claims to understand the physical world, while **physical approaches** are based on observations of physical things. For instance, as shown in Chapter 7, a common metaphysical approach is to imagine each thing as a clash of two opposing things (the dialectic approach). This is usually purely conceptual or theoretical, without any attempt to observe the two opposing things. A physical approach would be to examine something as a system of material parts and physical processes.

Many theorists conceptualize more abstract things, without admitting or realizing that they are being metaphysical. For instance, traditional sociologists, political theorists, and historians conceptualize human groups as exercising "power" or seeking "power," but critics reject the concept of power as too abstract, and instead focus on observations, particularly of tangible behaviors, such as trade. In turn, traditionalists complain that their critics engage with only tangible things and neglect other things just because they are more difficult to measure.

Traditional Versus Behavioral Approaches

Traditional research and philosophical **instrumentalism** view theory as useful in itself, without needing to explain anything real. This is justifiable if the aim is to be prescriptive but becomes confusing when traditional research claims to be theoretical, descriptive, or normative. A prescription does not need to be descriptive—one could prescribe an ideal society without observing anything like it. For research to be theoretical, it must explain some facts; in other words, it must be descriptive. Traditional research is described inaccurately as **normative** research because it often aims to explain what people normally should do or would do. However, prescriptive research does not need to be normative; we could prescribe an ideal society without expecting any such society to materialize.

Traditionalists are opposed by anyone who focuses on observational approaches, such as experimenters, empiricists, positivists, and physical researchers. A new category of researcher to introduce here is the **behavioralist**, who focuses on behaviors as the most tangible things to study. **Behaviors** are activities or actions, such as enforcement of the law, mechanical movement, biolocomotive travel, production, feeding, reproducing, and so forth.

You should realize that this contest overlaps many of the other pairs already described above. Both traditionalists and their critics could be attempting to understand the same activity, but the traditional approach is likely to be more theoretical, deductive, subjective, prescriptive, and philosophical, while the nontraditional approach is likely to be more empirical, inductive, objective, descriptive, and scientific.

Phenomenological Versus Observational Approaches

Phenomena are things that are observable. **Phenomenology** is a branch of philosophy focused on how observations are interpreted by humans. **Phenomenological approaches** attempt to explain how something is interpreted by humans. For instance, a phenomenological approach to crime would investigate how people think about crime in general or how they think about crimes that they have experienced.

Observational approaches attempt to understand something as it is without interpretation. In this sense, observational approaches are trying to achieve objective observations, while phenomenological approaches study how observations are interpreted.

Ontological Versus Epistemological Approaches

Ontology is a branch of philosophy dealing with existence. Traditionally, it developed ways to classify things; thus, modern **ontological approaches** develop ways to classify the objects of the research—that is, to decide in which class each object should be placed. In this sense, ontological approaches are analytical. For instance, an ontological approach to a transport system would classify the vehicles, loads, routes, delivery times, and so forth.

Epistemology is a branch of philosophy dealing with how knowledge is understood. **Epistemological approaches** aim to understand what is understood. For instance, an epistemological approach to a transport system would explain how we came to know what we know about that transport system. In this sense, epistemological approaches are knowledge reviews.

Research in the Real World Box 2.1

"Bad Philosophy" Versus Quantum Physics

Source: Cprmstock/iStock/Thinkstock.

"The culprits were doctrines such as logical positivism ('If it's not verifiable by experiment, it's meaningless'), instrumentalism ('If the predictions work, why worry about what brings them about?'), and philosophical relativism ('Statements can't be objectively true or false, only legitimized or delegitimized by a particular culture'). The damage was done by what they had in common: denial of realism, the commonsense philosophical position that the physical world exists and that the methods of science can glean knowledge about it. . . . Things have been gradually improving for a couple of decades, and it has been physics that is dragging philosophy back on track. People want to understand reality, no matter how loudly they may deny that. We are finally sailing past the supposed limits on knowledge that bad philosophy once taught us to resign ourselves to." (Deutsch & Ekert, 2013)

The Life Cycle of a Project

The Project

A **project** is a particular process for achieving something. Your research project starts on its journey when you scope out your topic, as described in Chapter 4, but first you should appreciate the project as a whole, so that your expectations are more realistic and you are better prepared to manage the project (see Practical Advice Box 2.1).

Any project has a *life* from beginning to end. Projects have a **life cycle** in the sense that as one project ends, you are free to start another project. In practice, we may be involved in many projects at the same time, each at different stages of the life cycle.

Managing your project's life cycle is an important part of your skill set as a researcher. You should be prepared to manage:

- The steps
- Your skills
- Your motivations

- Your effort
- Your productivity
- Unplanned changes

What Is the Process of Research?

A **process** is a series of activities or steps by which something occurs or is produced. For instance, the first step in your research is realizing your topic. As Chapter 4 will show, you should realize your interests, find something important within your interests, and so forth, until you find a justifiable topic for your research.

In this book, you will learn practical social scientific skills that can be applied to any project. These skills include the following, as ordered in a suggested process:

1. Realizing the topic
2. Designing the project
3. Finding sources
4. Evaluating sources
5. Reviewing literature
6. Reviewing knowledge
7. Analyzing phenomena, situations, and issues
8. Reviewing arguments
9. Evaluating and building theories
10. Modeling causal and other processes
11. Generating hypotheses
12. Designing a methodology
13. Choosing methods
14. Conducting tests
15. Gathering data
16. Evaluating evidence
17. Drawing conclusions
18. Structuring your report
19. Writing your report with clarity and style

Source: Anna Berkut/iStock/Thinkstock.

"Whether you are preparing to write about current events, interpret a newly collected set of data, explore emerging trends, or look into the future, your plan for research and production showcases what you are learning and the quality of your analytic skills and tradecraft. Here are some important things to keep in mind:

- Write down your plan and change it as needed rather than researching without a strategy, plan, or structure. Your plan and your products are the yardstick by which your analysis will be measured. An explicit strategy becomes particularly critical when you are engaged in a lengthy, high profile, or multi-organization project.

- Plan for multiple products to highlight your progress. Research aids can provide valuable waystations as part of the process for producing a longer analytic product. Short pieces on new developments help you develop the expertise needed to produce long papers on difficult, evolving, or more complex issues.

- Keep a list of your key assumptions, intelligence questions, and multiple hypotheses to be explored. Keep in mind that you are looking for evidence to disprove or eliminate a hypothesis. Review these lists as you complete the final draft of your paper or presentation.

- Search for the best information in the time you have available. Keep the ratio of time spent in research and production in balance. This is particularly useful if you can contact experts in government, academia, or private industry, or levy requirements on field collectors rather than being a prisoner of your inbox.

(Continued)

(Continued)

- Beware of the most common analytic pitfalls:
  - o Not defining the problem or issue correctly.
  - o Jumping to a solution before analyzing the problem.
  - o Not involving people who know most about the problem.
  - o Not having an open mind.
  - o Using the wrong criteria.
  - o Mirror imaging or assuming others think or act as you would.
  - o Assuming actors have more control or power than they do." (Pherson & Pherson, 2013, pp. 54–55)

Two alternative types of research processes will be considered in the subsections below: (a) critical thinking and (b) intelligence.

The "Critical Thinking" Process

Critical thinking is a process of clarifying knowledge by critical consideration of the arguments and evidence. Critical thinking is really another term for a scientific process or a commitment not to accept whatever we are told. "Much of the literature on critical thinking processes and models focuses on the logic and argumentation thinkers use to make their points. But successful analysis is part of the larger process of inquiry, research, reasoning, and communication" (Pherson & Pherson, 2013, p. 43).

Some people would conceptualize the critical thinking process as limited to how we think about arguments. Others think of the critical thinking process as a complete process of research, which would follow at least the following seven steps:

1. Identify your research question

2. Identify your assumptions

3. Review potential answers to your research question

4. Derive hypotheses

5. Test the hypotheses with data

6. Analyze the results and derive findings

7. Deliver your findings (cf. Pherson & Pherson, 2013, p. 45)

The "Intelligence Process"

Intelligence is analyzed information. It is widely demanded in commerce and government; in these domains, much research aims to produce intelligence. In the productive sense, it is "processed information" (Volkman, 2007, p. 7). In more nuanced use, it "is knowledge acquired through collection, evaluation, and interpretation of all available information concerning a possible or actual competition operation. It is information that has been processed by the intelligence section, it is a finished product" (White, 2005, p. 4). In official use, intelligence is the "product resulting from the collection, processing, integration, evaluation, analysis, and interpretation of available information concerning foreign nations, hostile or potentially hostile forces or elements, or areas of actual or potential operations. The term is also applied to the activity which results in the product" (United States Department of Defense, 2012, p. 152).

In official circles, the *intelligence process* or *intelligence cycle* "refers to the steps or stages in intelligence, from policy makers perceiving a need for information to the community's delivery of an analytical intelligence product to them" (Lowenthal, 2011, p. 57).

The U.S. Central Intelligence Agency's (CIA's) official "intelligence cycle" has the following five steps, where the last returns to the first (Lowenthal, 2011):

1. Planning and direction

2. Collection

3. Processing

4. Analysis and production

5. Dissemination

Mark Lowenthal is a former CIA employee who has offered this critique:

> Although meant to be little more than a quick schematic
> presentation, the CIA diagram misrepresents some aspects and

misses many others. First, it is overly simple. Its end-to-end completeness misses many of the vagaries in the process. It is also oddly unidimensional. A policy maker asks questions and, after a few steps, gets an answer. There is no feedback, and the diagram does not convey the possibility that the process might not be completed in one cycle. (Lowenthal, 2011, p. 68)

The Federal Bureau of Investigation's official intelligence cycle adds "requirements" at the start (Lowenthal, 2014):

1. Requirements

2. Planning and direction

3. Collection

4. Processing

5. Analysis and production

6. Dissemination

The U.S. Department of Defense (2012, p. 152) defines the intelligence process with "evaluation and feedback" at the end:

1. Planning and direction

2. Collection

3. Processing and exploitation

4. Analysis and production

5. Dissemination and integration

6. Evaluation and feedback

Mark Lowenthal recommends the following process:

1. Identifying requirements (priorities)

2. Collection

3. Processing and exploitation

4. Analysis and production

5. Dissemination

6. Consumption

7. Feedback

However, Lowenthal wants users to visualize the process not as a linear series of steps but as a "multilayered process," as shown in Figure 2.1.

Managing the Steps

Nominally, a project proceeds step by step in a linear order, where each step builds on the last. For instance, we should review all the theories before we decide which theory we prefer. In practice, we are likely to work on some steps out of order or at the same time (see Figure 2.2).

This is likely because of, first, imperfections in our own execution of a plan. Even if we set out to proceed through our plan linearly, we are likely to return to

Figure 2.1   The "multilayered" intelligence process

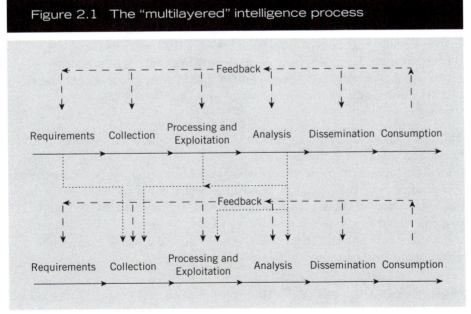

Source: Lowenthal, 2011, p. 69.

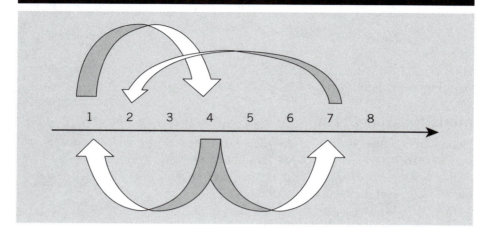

Figure 2.2 Linear and nonlinear progress through eight steps of a notional project

an earlier step as we remember what we missed. For instance, we may think we have reviewed all the theories and are ready to move on to the next step, only to discover a new theory later.

Second, we work nonlinearly because of the imperfect availability of resources, such as books. We are likely to work on several steps at once as we wait for the resources needed to finish any step. For instance, we might simultaneously review the theories and review the methods by which we could test the theory, without finishing any of these steps, while we wait to receive books on the rarer theories or methods.

Third, in working on one step, we will from time to time discover things relevant to another step. For instance, when reviewing theories, you should be thinking mostly about the section of your product where you would describe the competing theories to the reader. Evaluating these theories includes evaluating how well they were proven—this evaluation will influence the methodology that you would choose to test your theory. In turn, when you review different methodological options, you are likely to discover a new way to evaluate the evidence for the theories that you reviewed earlier.

Managing Your Skills

Skills are learned abilities. **Knowledge** is acquired awareness and understanding. Knowledge may help you acquire skills, but knowledge is insufficient. You may be able to declare how something is done (a knowledge), but you need to be able to do it (a skill).

In the subsections below, you will think about your basic skills, advanced skills, and strengths and weaknesses.

Basic Skills

Any research project requires basic skills. Your acquisition of this book is one step toward improving your skills, yet you must also read it, understand it, apply it, and stay committed to what you have learned. You would help yourself further by seeking an instructor or a mentor in the skills. You would help yourself too by allocating enough time and resources for the acquisition of the skills and by adopting a learning attitude.

Advanced Skills

Beyond the basic skills, you face some choices about the more advanced skills. The more advanced the skills, the fewer the people who have the capacity to learn them. This is not necessarily a competitive situation—you could excel in one part of the skill set while someone else excels in another part. Both of you could contribute to knowledge in different ways. Indeed, research, analysis, and writing are increasingly performed in teams—one member might lead the building of the theory, another the development of the test, another the gathering of the data, and another the analysis of the data.

If you are working alone or are at the start of your career, you will likely need to acquire a wide set of skills at a basic level without having the right or opportunity to work in a team. Most student research must be performed alone as a test of personal skills.

Beyond basic skills, you still face some choices about advanced skills. For instance, if you are confident in your mathematical capacity, you could promise to acquire an advanced statistical skill to test a theory in a new way. If you are uncomfortable mathematically, you should aim to excel in other methodological skills.

Weaknesses and Strengths

When thinking about your capacity, you should be mindful also of your own weaknesses and how you must respond. For instance, most researchers early in their careers realize that their writing could improve. If you are least confident about your writing skills, you should prepare to improve your writing skills and seek a tutor, reviewer, or editor.

A common mistake would be to focus all your attention on something that you are good at because you enjoy it or find it easy, while neglecting an essential skill, without which the whole project will fail. On the other hand, do not forget your most enjoyable or admirable skill—when other things are going wrong, going back to that skill will remind you of your strengths, motivations, and rewards.

Managing Your Motivations

Motivation is the conscious or unconscious stimulus for action toward a desired goal.

You may be the most skilled person, but without motivation you will not achieve anything.

The subsections below will consider your planning, self-discipline, navigation of technical flaws, ambition, and self-efficacy.

Planning

Your motivation is open to management. A realistic awareness of what to expect during the forthcoming process of research will help you to prepare your motivations. For instance, be aware that your motivations are likely to be high at the start, when you are fresh and excited, but may fall toward the middle of your project, when the tasks become more difficult and outputs are low.

Planning is a structured way to prepare yourself. If you plan for what you want to achieve, you are more likely to achieve it. Setting goals is critical—if you plan to achieve some part of the research in a certain way and by a certain date, you are more likely to direct yourself toward that goal. You should plan to curb your bias for action at the start, stoke your motivations in the middle, and sustain the same level of effort to the end. A good way to manage the midway trough in your motivations is to set a midway goal, such as delivery of the literature review.

Self-Discipline

Planning is one thing; holding yourself accountable for delivering on your plan is another. Thus, a critical factor in motivation is self-discipline. *Self-discipline* means making yourself do what you should be doing. Some parts of the research are less enjoyable, feel more tedious, demand more difficult skills, last longer, or were imposed by some stakeholder with whom you disagree. You will be less motivated to work on these parts, so practice self-discipline.

Some of the best researchers do nothing more insightful or advanced than the average researcher—they are just methodical, reliable, careful, and self-disciplined enough to deliver what was expected. Stakeholders often prefer the reliable researcher to the brilliant researcher.

Think about your role as you study this book. The skills in this book are not magic or dependent on faith. They are tangible and within the capacity of most people. The more self-disciplined you are, the easier the skills will be to acquire.

You should plan to give yourself breaks from intense self-discipline. This is not an excuse to avoid work—you need to have worked intensively to deserve a break from work. Breaks give you time to rest and to reflect on the project and to catch up with other needs in your life.

Navigating Technical Flaws

You need to finish the difficult as well as the easy parts, with one caveat: The difficult part may reflect some technical flaw in the research. Dogmatic self-discipline is admirable, but it can force people to finish the wrong task, so always search for the best way to do something; otherwise, you will waste your self-discipline on unnecessary difficulties.

For instance, your plan may include an unnecessarily difficult test, when an easier and equally valid test is available. If you are experiencing difficulties motivating yourself to complete the difficult task, consider whether the task is flawed. This realization may be subconscious; you may be uncomfortable with the task and feel undermotivated—until you realize consciously what the flaw is, or someone points it out to you. The solution is technical, not motivational.

As you may imagine, this caveat is easy to abuse. You may be struggling with a task because you are feeling lazy at the moment, not because the task is flawed. Many researchers abandon a task because they decide it is too difficult or does not work, even though with a little persistence they would have finished something valuable.

Ambition

Your motivations make up part of your capacity and thus influence your ambition. Ambition is the desire to achieve something valuable or difficult. If you are interested in your research, or are naturally a self-disciplined person, you can promise more than the disinterested or lazy person. Feasibly you can gather more data, review more literature, and write more than someone who is less motivated or self-disciplined. This will make you valuable: A risk-averse stakeholder will sponsor the reliable researcher and reject the flighty researcher.

You can use ambition to motivate yourself. You could choose an easy project without being pressed to raise your ambition. By raising your ambition, however, you are effectively setting yourself a higher goal. Remember that goals are effectively motivating in themselves; also, ambition offers the chance of improved rewards, such as promotion or payment, which in themselves should motivate you.

Self-Efficacy

The concept of **self-efficacy** captures the belief that the self controls destiny and thus that the self can achieve something. In general, the higher your self-efficacy, the higher the likelihood that you will achieve what you have in mind. Self-efficacy helps you to pursue something without doubting yourself. Lack of self-efficacy tends to undermine your motivations. Self-efficacy improves your moods and emotions—confidence is a good feeling, while self-doubt is a bad feeling. Someone could be brilliant and her project well within her capacity, but a lack of self-efficacy could persuade her that it is not within her capacity; this would be a tragic waste of her abilities.

In everyday speech, self-efficacy is partly captured by terms such as *optimistic*, *positive*, and *hopeful*. **Optimistic**, or positive, people expect the best. Optimistic people use situational factors to account for failure rather than blaming an enduring dispositional trait. **Hopeful** people think they can improve. They show less depression and anxiety. They are more likely to reassure themselves, find new approaches, and break down their goals into manageable steps.

Unfortunately, most people do not consider themselves particularly high in self-efficacy, optimism, positivity, or hope, although they would like to be. Yet self-efficacy is sticky—by adulthood it does not change much, but largely reflects the temperament with which you were born and your formative experiences in childhood.

One solution is **stoicism**—a philosophy of accepting the way things are. This is useful for diverting yourself from self-blame, but could err into fatalism—the belief that everything is beyond your self-control (this belief is the opposite of self-efficacy). Another solution is **mood purism**—the decision not to challenge your moods. This is useful because at least you will not suffer the stress of challenging your moods—but most people want to improve their moods.

Most people struggle to realize their own moods, so they cannot intercept them, but you could practice self-efficacy by staying alert to self-doubt and replacing it with self-efficacy. You should try to surround yourself with people who improve your mood and self-efficacy, because moods and attitudes are contagious.

In the long run, you will gain self-efficacy from learning, experience, and achievement. Learned competencies add to self-efficacy, because competency helps to make achievement more feasible. In turn, self-efficacy helps you make the best use of your skills. Experience helps you to apply your declarative knowledge and to practice your skills. Achievements are evidence of your own capacity:

Once you have achieved something, repeating it will seem less intimidating. By completing this book, you will improve your skills and thus your self-efficacy too.

Like most things, the prescription for self-efficacy has a caveat: Unbounded self-efficacy, which typically arises when outsiders praise you without warrant or without reminding you of humility and responsibility, leads to arrogance and unrealistic expectations.

Managing Your Effort

Effort is the strain of doing something. You may naturally visualize the process of your research as a ladder, stairway, or road that you climb steadily from beginning to end, until you reach your goal. If you see it this way, you are likely to view your effort as consistent, as if you make the same effort at all times.

Rather than visualizing a steady effort along an unbroken and consistent path, you should visualize a path with some cracks, or a stairway with some broken steps, but do not let them intimidate you. Part of being realistic in your expectations is being prepared to fix those obstacles along the way—to invest more effort when the going gets tough, so that you can return to easier going.

Your effort is likely to vary with your own internal motivations and the availability of external resources. Sometimes you will be distracted, disillusioned, lost, or just plain lazy. Such difficulties are normal in any project, so you should be realistic enough to expect these difficulties and to be mindful of them throughout your project. Such mindfulness will help you realize the difficulties and manage them, rather than deny them and let them ruin your project.

In practice, your effort is likely to cycle between peaks and troughs. In the peaks of effort, you may need to save energy for the long haul. In the troughs, you may need to kick yourself into more effort. At all times, you should try to be aware of your own effort and hold yourself responsible.

We know enough about normal effort during projects to make some forecasts of typical effort over time (see Figure 2.3). At the start of the project, everything may seem intimidating, so you may experience difficulty getting going, but after some investigation the project should seem fresh, exciting, and full of opportunities. Frankly, you also may be fairly naive about the challenges. Your effort in the early part of the project is likely to rise healthily.

However, at some point, having made the easy choices and fulfilled the easy tasks, you must move on to the more difficult or less pleasant tasks, such as

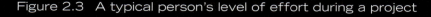

Figure 2.3 A typical person's level of effort during a project

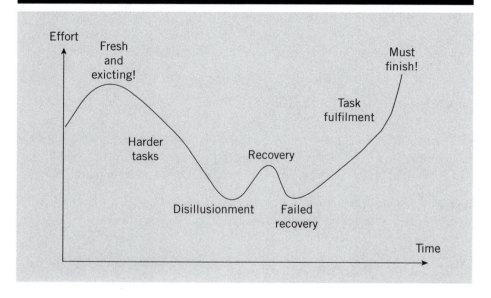

reading badly written theories or learning a difficult methodology. Here your intrinsic motivation will fall. At some point, difficult tasks, frustrations, and obstacles may overwhelm you, at which point you may stop work entirely.

Extreme difficulties of motivation are typical about midway through the project—midway between the first excitement and the final deadline. Consequently, one principle of project management is to schedule delivery of some part of the final product by midway through the project, so that the researcher is accountable for delivering something when his or her self-motivation is likely to be weakest.

Whether forced by a midpoint deadline or reinvigorated by a new approach, your effort is likely to recover after the first trial, but be prepared for some false recoveries too. Your new approach may not work or you may be distracted by something else. Yet eventually you should find your final approach.

As you make progress, your effort would be stoked by the pleasures of achieving and fulfilling your tasks. Toward the end of the project, you will be more conscious of the final deadline. The exciting prospect of finishing or anxieties about finishing in time should motivate you to make a final enhanced effort.

Most humans are procrastinators, so almost all projects end with a final gallop to the finish line. Some people find the final part of the project exhilarating because of the focus that it brings, but others find it sickening. Some people know the final part of a project as the "final crunch"—when you are squeezed between the final deadline and your own tardiness. A final crunch is somewhat unavoidable, given that some obstacles are unexpected, but most final crunches would be avoidable if only people would be self-disciplined enough to make a constant effort throughout.

Managing Productivity

Productivity, too, is likely to peak and trough. **Productivity** is a measure of how much you are producing; it is related to effort, but it is not the same. You should prepare for times when your effort is high but your productivity is not. You may invest a lot of time in reading different theories but struggle to work out which theory you prefer. You may design the perfect test of your theory but be denied access to your intended subjects.

The product is the final **output**—the result of productivity. Outputs imply **inputs**—the things you must invest in order to be productive. You must invest your effort, skills, other resources, and time as inputs; outputs do not appear out of nowhere.

The imbalance between effort or inputs and productivity or outputs has a somewhat predictable profile within project time (see Figure 2.4). Generally,

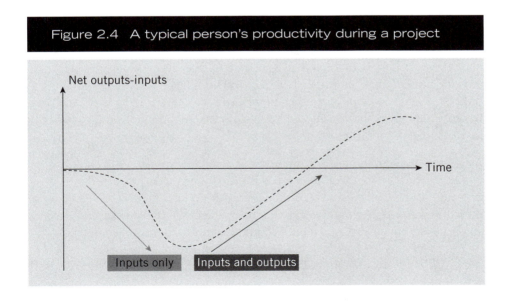

Figure 2.4   A typical person's productivity during a project

Source: ©iStockphoto.com/AngiePhotos.

your effort in the first half of the project produces less of the final product than in the second half, because at the start you expend more effort working out what to do, while toward the end you expend more effort delivering on your plans. The early imbalance between inputs and outputs can be alarming for the uninitiated, as they pass project time working hard but delivering little of the final product. This early imbalance is something you need to accept, although you should not use it as an excuse for procrastinating on delivery of the final product.

Managing Change

A naturally optimistic vision of your journey through the project is of a clear straight path from your start to your goal, with nothing unforeseen or unexpected, everything within view, and one clearly superior way to get there.

A more realistic vision of your project is of an uncertain way to your goal. Imagine that you are standing on top of one hill and you can see the top of the hill that is your destination, but you must cross a valley in between that is hidden by fog. Alternatively, imagine a set of roads ahead, all of which lead in the general direction, but whose going becomes vaguer with distance—some may lead into dead ends, some may lead you back to where you started, some offer a straighter route or better going, some offer less efficient going.

You can be certain that you are starting a journey, you may be certain of what you want to produce, and you may be certain of a deadline by which the project must be finished, but the way is always uncertain. The going will become more difficult or time-consuming at some points; you may get lost; you may even need to scrap the route you have chosen, retrace your steps, and find another way. You may even need to redefine your destination.

Again, do not be intimidated by these realistic visions; your feelings should be realistic but not defeatist. Realistic expectations help you prepare, and preparations help you toward fulfillment of your project. An obstacle could leave the unprepared person shocked, so that he or she gives up. You cannot foresee all obstacles, but at least you should accept that you will encounter some.

Uncertainty implies change. Change is an alteration, and you must expect change in your knowledge, skills, motivations, effort, and plan; you must expect too that something in the situation or environment could change, beyond your control, perhaps in very dramatic and consequential forms, such as a war in the country that you had intended to visit, or a sponsor who withdraws funds.

Change is entirely normal in a project, so you should be realistic enough to expect change. People are normally averse to change, particularly when they feel personally invested in their own project.

Be mindful of the dilemma of choosing between the effort of trying to fix the current way and the effort of searching for a better way. Truly you should not scrap your project at the first obstacle if you could pass that obstacle on the most effective way to your goal. Since all situations are unique, you must learn how to evaluate each situation as a trade-off between potentially wasting more effort on a hopeless cause or potentially scrapping past effort on a salvageable cause. When you start your project, you should expect change and prepare yourself for some tough choices, such as abandoning work or struggling on with a chosen path.

You should realize the different implications of change at the start of the project versus change toward the end. At the start, change is most effective, because you still have plenty of time to adapt and you have little to lose, but later in the project you will be on a path that is increasingly difficult and costly to change, with less and less time available to implement change (see Figure 2.5).

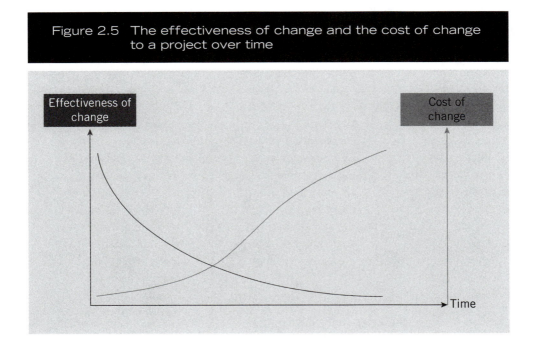

Figure 2.5 The effectiveness of change and the cost of change to a project over time

CHAPTER SUMMARY

This chapter explained:

- What research is: the purposes of research, the objectives and products of research, and different approaches to research

- The life cycle of a project

- The different processes of research, such as the critical thinking process and the intelligence process

- How to manage the steps of the process efficiently but also realistically, given the availability of resources and unforeseen discoveries along the way

- How to manage your skills, from the basic to the advanced, and from your weaknesses to your strengths

- How to manage your motivations—by planning, self-discipline, technical corrections, ambition, and self-efficacy

- How to manage your effort through the project, given what we know about when your effort will rise and fall

- How to manage your productivity throughout the process, given what we know about the lag between effort and productivity

- How to manage change so that you do not make changes unnecessarily, but also so that you *do* change things that are not working, and so that you make the changes as early as you can to increase their effectiveness while minimizing their cost

KEY TERMS

QUESTIONS AND EXERCISES _____

Select a book or article that you have read already.

1. Summarize its purposes and objectives.

2. Is its research best described as exploratory or conclusive?

3. Is its research best described as prescriptive or descriptive?

4. Does it contain a case study or a survey?

5. Can you separate any historical research from nonhistorical research?

6. Can you separate any experimental research from field research?

7. Which parts are more empirical or theoretical?

8. Can you identify any deductions or inductions?

9. Can you identify any parts that are more subjective or more objective?

10. Describe an imaginary approach that would be more:

- philosophical
- positivist
- metaphysical
- physical
- traditional
- behavioral
- phenomenological
- observational
- ontological
- epistemological

Research Ethics and Laws

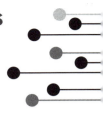

Opening Vignette: The Gaddafi Regime and the London School of Economics

http://commons.wikimedia.org/wiki/File:Muammar_al-Gaddafi_at_the_AU_summit.jpg.

In 2004, a foundation—funded by the autocratic regime in Libya led by Muammar Gaddafi—pledged £1.5 million over five years to the London School of Economics (LSE). Meanwhile, LSE Enterprise contracted for £2.2 million to train Libyan officials.

In 2003, LSE's department of philosophy admitted Saif al-Islam Gaddafi, Muammar's son, into its doctoral program. In 2008, it awarded him the degree.

In February 2011, a revolution started in Libya, leading to increased student protests and external scrutiny of the LSE's relationship with Libya. (By then, the Libyan foundation had paid £300,000.) On March 3, 2011, the LSE's director, Sir Howard Davies, resigned, admitting "errors of judgment."

The LSE asked former Lord Chief Justice Harry Woolf to investigate. He reported that the LSE had made errors of judgment that had damaged the LSE's reputation; that Saif had been admitted on idealistic expectations that he would improve Libya, even though he had been rejected by other LSE departments on academic grounds alone; and that Saif had "duped" his academic supervisors by receiving extensive outside help in preparing his thesis. The LSE accepted Woolf's report in full.

Learning Objectives and Outcomes

At the end of this chapter, you should be able to:

1. Explain what ethics are and why they matter

2. Properly handle the subjects of research

3. Properly manage data

4. Understand when to seek permissions and licenses

5. Properly handle intellectual property

6. Manage supporters

7. Avoid misrepresentation

8. Avoid plagiarism

At the time, a separate University of London panel was investigating allegations that Saif's thesis had been plagiarized and written by paid contractors.

Source: Stuart Hughes, 2011.

What Are Ethics?

Ethics are considerations of what is right or wrong. **Research ethics** are considerations of what is right or wrong in the conduct of research.

The study of ethics is usually aimed at deciding what is ethical. Something is *ethical* if it is judged to be right or at least more right than some alternative. For instance, is it ethical to research a topic that started as somebody else's idea?

Ethical prescriptions are not necessarily laws or rules, so usually the ethics are uncertain and contested or even left up to the individual to decide. Sometimes a behavior is not illegal but is still considered unethical, such as plagiarism. Some behaviors are illegal in some jurisdictions, but still considered ethical in other jurisdictions, such as protest against illegitimate governments.

The following sections explain why ethics matter, the ethical and legal treatment of the subjects of research; data; permissions and licenses; intellectual property and other stakes; how to treat supporters; how to avoid misrepresentation; and how to avoid plagiarism.

Why Do Ethics Matter?

Ethics matter because unethical choices might make you uncomfortable, taint otherwise good research, ruin your career, or expose you to civil or criminal legal actions.

Sometimes unethical behaviors are criminalized. For instance, some jurisdictions criminalize misuse of the resources that you might access to help with your research, particularly resources with high public access, such as hospitals.

Sometimes the ethics are expressed in a contractual form, in which case you are obliged to follow these ethics or you could be punished in civil law. Sometimes an employer or sponsor may require you to sign a formal document acknowledging that you have read and understood their expectations of how you will behave. Such a signed document carries the weight of a contract in civil law. If you were to fail to comply with the contract, the other party could sue you in civil court. Some behaviors, such as theft, would likely expose you to an indictment in criminal law.

Ethics vary by the authority. Some ethics are left up to the individual person, without any consequence beyond the actor's conscience. For instance, some universities allow **vivisection** (experimentation on live animals), but within such a university one employee may choose to participate in vivisection while another may not.

Many institutions set ethics without drawing your attention to them, leaving you responsible for seeking them out and reading them. Today, most universities publish ethical guidelines that apply to all staff and students, undergraduates included.

Sometimes the ethics are set by the government, the employer, the profession within which you are working, or the sponsor of your research. Sometimes you are subject to each of these stakeholders, even if their ethics do not agree.

Ethics can vary by level. For instance, the ethical guidelines for faculty may be written differently than the guidelines for students.

Ethics can vary by role. For instance, the guidelines for the medical researcher would focus on patients and biological subjects, whereas the guidelines for the archival researcher would focus on the proper treatment of archival material.

Ethics can vary over time. A century ago, medical research routinely proceeded without patient consent or awareness, but informed consent is now a normative and legal expectation. In the past, archives were accessible to rare researchers with sufficient free time, interpersonal connections, and money; researchers often referred to their supposed discoveries in archives without citing anything in particular; and some researchers cited things that subsequently could not be found; but now archival research is supposed to be generally accessible and replicable.

Subjects of Research

The **subjects of research** are the things that you study. Some subjects deserve legal and ethical protections, especially humans and other animals.

Human Subjects Research

Human subjects enjoy special ethical protections, such as expectations of informed consent. Indeed, all institutions of research should offer ethical guidelines for human subjects research. Extra ethical guidelines are often written for some classes of humans, such as children and those with learning disabilities.

In the U.S., the National Research Act of 1974 created the National Commission for the Protection of Human Subjects of Biomedical and Behavioral Research. The commission fulfilled this responsibility by preparing and releasing the Belmont Report in 1979 (U.S. Department of Health and Human Services, 1979), which identified three fundamental ethical principles for conducting research with human subjects:

1. Respect for persons. This includes "two ethical convictions":

   o "Individuals should be treated as autonomous agents."

   o "Persons with diminished autonomy are entitled to protection."

2. Beneficence. This includes two expectations:

   o "Do not harm."

   o "Maximize possible benefits and minimize possible harms."

3. Justice, meaning fairness and equity in the selection of participants and the distribution of benefits.

In 1991, the U.S. government adopted the Department of Health and Human Services' (USDHHS's) core regulations for the protection of human subjects in research studies as the Federal Policy for the Protection of Human Subjects, known as the Common Rule. The **Common Rule** is a federal policy for the protection of human subjects. It is followed by most of the federal departments and agencies that sponsor research with human subjects. Three of the central requirements in the Common Rule are:

1. Any research supported or conducted by any federal department or agency must ensure compliance with the policy.

2. Researchers must obtain written informed consent from human subjects.

3. Institutions must have an institutional review board (IRB) in place to review and approve research with human subjects. The IRB requires that researchers (including students) submit an IRB application for approval before any recruitment procedures are enacted, any contact with potential participants is made, or any data are collected. (Bui, 2014, pp. 77–89)

Additional to your obligations to avoid harm are the implications of offering benefits. For instance, when surveying people, you could improve response rates by offering payment or by passing the survey through somebody who has authority over the respondent, but these options could bias the results and ultimately harm some people. If you offered payment, perhaps more needy people would respond to a survey about the effectiveness of local government and these people would respond more positively in the hope that they would be selected for another paying survey in the future. These falsely positive responses are biased and could be used to suggest that public services are serving the needy better than they really are, thereby justifying reductions in services.

On the other hand, if you use humans as subjects, take up their time, or rely on their volunteerism, perhaps you should compensate them. A solution to this dilemma between fair compensation and unfair corruption is to offer compensation that does not corrupt. Perhaps you could compensate after the survey, without promising any compensation at the start. You could compensate all respondents but check whether compensation is encouraging some sort of self-selection bias, in which case you should select respondents to maintain representativeness.

Other Animals

Other animals are less protected than humans, but they still are especially protected. Even plants, especially if rare and exotic, can be specified as subjects with special protections. Generally, living subjects should not be harmed in the course of research, although some ethics allow for harm in return for a greater good (**utilitarianism**).

Utilitarian arguments are common in favor of vivisection. Harm in general is proscribed, but harm to animals is commonly justified on the grounds of human benefits, such as improved medical treatment of humans. In some cases the subjects are bred solely for a lifetime of distressing or painful experiments where the only benefits are to human cosmetics. The line between commonly justified vivisection (such as experiments with cancer-fighting drugs) and commonly repellent vivisection (such as testing of cosmetics) is subject to increasing public exposure. Some people oppose all vivisection.

In the U.S., the Animal Welfare Act of 1966 requires researchers to provide animals with minimum standards of care and treatment and criminalizes behaviors inconsistent with these standards. The U.S. Department of Agriculture's Animal and Plant Health Inspection Service (APHIS) is the main federal authority responsible for inspecting, investigating, and enforcing the Act.

Most experimentation on animals is justified as medical, and the National Institutions of Health is the main federal funder of medical research. Recipients of its funding must comply with regulations issued by the National Institutes of Health.

Data Protection

You should protect some types of information gathered from subjects, such as private information about a human subject's sexuality or finances.

Since the 1980s, official standards, regulations, and laws have increased the responsibilities and liabilities of organizations for securing data and for granting freedom of access to data by those whom the data concern. In 1980, the Organization for Economic Cooperation and Development (OECD) issued its seven "Guidelines Governing the Protection of Privacy and Trans-Border Flows of Personal Data":

1. Notice: Data subjects should be given notice when their data is being collected.

2. Purpose: Data should only be used for the purpose stated and not for any other purposes.

3. Consent: Data should not be disclosed without the data subject's consent.

4. Security: Collected data should be kept secure from any potential abuses.

5. Disclosure: Data subjects should be informed as to who is collecting their data.

6. Access: Data subjects should be allowed to access their data and make corrections to any inaccurate data.

7. Accountability: Data subjects should have a method available to them to hold data collectors accountable for following the above principles.

Source: Guidelines on the Protection of Privacy and Transborder Flows of Personal Data, © OECD, 2013 http://www.oecd.org/internet/ieconomy/oecdguidelinesontheprotectionof privacyandtransborderflowsofpersonaldata.htm.

Given the OCED's seven principles, in 1981 the Council of Europe agreed to the Convention for the Protection of Individuals With Regard to Automatic Processing of Personal Data. This convention obliges the signatories to enact legislation concerning the automatic processing of personal data.

In 1995, the European Union (EU) adopted the Data Protection Directive (officially "Directive 95/46/EC on the Protection of Individuals With Regard to the Processing of Personal Data and on the Free Movement of Such Data"), which adopted the OECD's seven guidelines and directed member states to regulate the processing of personal data, effective 1998. Under an amendment of February 2006, EU law requires Internet and telephone service providers to retain data on the location of and parties to each communication for at least 6 months and no more than 24 months, but not to record content. On January 25, 2012, the European Commission unveiled a draft European General Data Protection Regulation that supersedes the Data Protection Directive by extending the scope to all foreign companies processing data of European Union residents. This is expected to come into force at the start of 2016.

Britain responded to European legislation with its own Data Protection Act of 1998, which requires organizations that hold data about individuals to do so securely and only for specific purposes. Section 55 specifies as offenses any attempts to obtain, disclose, or "procure the disclosure" of confidential personal information "knowingly or recklessly" without the consent of the organization holding the data. The Act also gives individuals the right, with certain exemptions, to see personal data that relates to them. The Freedom of Information Act of 2000 entitles people to receive information from any organization unless the organization faces high burdens in gathering the information or the information is protected on the grounds of privacy, commercial sensitivity, or national security.

The United States has not followed with a data protection act, but it had previously enacted strong criminal laws against economic espionage and violations of intellectual property, and strong civil laws against defamation and slander, all of which help to control misuse of private information. In U.S. jurisdictions, organizations face severe legal and commercial risks for violating data privacy (although they are also incentivized by commercial advantages). For instance, in 2005, after the U.S. Federal Trade Commission accused an American consumer data broker (ChoicePoint Incorporated) of improperly securing confidential data from theft, the broker admitted that the personal financial records of more than 163,000 consumers in its database had been compromised and agreed to pay $10 million in civil penalties and $5 million in consumer redress, while millions of dollars were wiped off its stock market value.

The International Organization for Standardization (ISO) and the International Electrotechnical Commission (IEC) have issued international standards (ISO/IEC 17799:2005 and ISO/IEC 27001:2005) for information security, including expectations for technical and organizational controls on unauthorized or unlawful processing of personal data (Newsome, 2014, pp. 275–276).

Permissions and Licenses

Sometimes a researcher uses resources that are allowable only with permission or license. A **permit** or **license** is a formal consent, such as a permit to report what someone told you in an interview, or a license to operate a particular type of machinery.

Some archives, data, and software are not viewable or usable without a license or permit. Much of the software useful to a researcher, such as data mining software or statistical software, is licensed to a user. Some software is freeware, meaning it is distributed without financial cost, but often still with expectations for use, to which the user must agree.

Intellectual Property and Other Stakes

In law, intellectual creations that are claimed by some stakeholders are known as **intellectual property**. Intellectual properties can be identified by such conventions as declaring or registering authorship, copyright, trademarks, or patents.

You would normally expect to own the knowledge produced by your research or at least to claim authorship. However, if another entity, such as your employer, provides support that contributes to your product, it has a stake in your research—it becomes a **stakeholder**. A **stake** is some interest in something—this stake gives the stakeholder rights to some part of your intellectual property. Employers or funders of researchers normally expect full ownership; they can claim ownership while acknowledging your authorship. To clarify ownership, you and any stakeholders should agree in contractual form who owns what. Note that some stakeholders may fail to assert their claims or renounce any claims, while others may pursue their interests aggressively.

If you pay someone else for material, data, or software, and you abide by the conditions they place on you, normally they cannot claim any stake. However, the payment may be contracted in such a way that the other party retains their rights.

Be aware that plagiarizing content is a form of theft of intellectual property, as described in the section on plagiarizing below.

Supporters

Note that someone may offer to support your research without expecting you to do anything unethical, but your acceptance of their support could be considered unethical just because of who the supporter is. For instance, the supporter may be associated with an illegitimate government or with harmful research elsewhere (see this chapter's opening vignette).

Note that while paying for data or software is usually ethical, paying for someone else to write or otherwise produce your research is usually unethical, at least if you do not admit their full role.

Avoiding Misrepresentation

Researchers should accurately represent their research activities. Any inaccurate representation is **misrepresentation**. Researchers should make no errors of omission or commission. An **error of omission** is a failure to share information that the consumer needs in order to understand what you did. For instance, if you reported someone else's opinions but did not report the source, a consumer could reasonably assume that you had received those opinions directly.

An **error of commission** is an action that misleads. For instance, a researcher might falsely claim to have interviewed a human source. This error can be seductive for ambitious researchers, but can ruin the reputation of even the most famous researchers (see Research in the Real World Box 3.1). Similarly, a researcher might pretend that somebody else's research is their own (this is also plagiarism, as described in the next section).

Scientific standards of replicability imply that an author should fully represent everything that another researcher would need to know in order to replicate the author's research.

Sometimes our publications are constrained in space so that we cannot accurately report all our research, just a summary. Some researchers then refer consumers to a website or some other repository where the full information can be found. This is common where a researcher has space to publish the analytical results but not all the data. Under the scientific principle of replicability, consumers might request your data in order to replicate your results.

In order to accurately report your research, you should accurately record your research activities. Records are useful as:

- Reminders of what you did, so that you do not duplicate research unnecessarily

- Evidence of what you did, in case someone else doubts what you claim

- Repositories of the data that you produced, so that someone else could use the same data

Research in the Real World Box 3.1

A Famous American Historian's Misrepresentation of His Research

Source: http://www.history.navy.mil/photos/images/ac10000/ap16071.jpg.

Dwight D. Eisenhower

When Stephen Ambrose died in 2002, he was America's most famous and popular historian, the author of more than 30 books. More than half of his books concerned Dwight D. Eisenhower, a U.S. Army general and the 34th U.S. president. Ambrose told journalists that his life had been transformed during "hundreds and hundreds of hours" of interviewing Eisenhower over a five-year period before Eisenhower's death in 1969.

However, in 2009, Tim Rives, the deputy director of the Dwight D. Eisenhower Presidential Library and Museum in Abilene, Kansas, when searching for exhibits to accompany a panel to celebrate Ambrose's writings, discovered records (maintained by Eisenhower's executive assistant) of Eisenhower's activities, down to telephone calls, which showed that Eisenhower saw Ambrose only three times, for a total of less than five hours, always with other people present. Ambrose's first biography (*The Supreme Commander*, 1970) cited nine interview dates, of which seven could not have occurred. For instance, on October 7, 1965, when Ambrose claimed to have been interviewing Eisenhower at Gettysburg, his subject had been traveling from Abilene to Kansas City. On another two dates when Ambrose claimed to have interviewed his subject in Gettysburg, October 21 and October 27, 1967, Eisenhower had been on vacation at Augusta National Golf Club.

Information source: Rayner, 2010.

Avoiding Plagiarism

Academic norms and copyright law proscribe plagiarism. **Plagiarism** is the reuse of work without due attribution. Attribution is as simple as citing the source of your information (see Table 3.1). A **citation** is a reference to the source, which can be expressed in text (usually in parentheses after the referred text) or in a footnote or endnote, depending on the chosen style (see Table 3.2).

Table 3.1 When should you cite?

Do Cite	Don't Cite
Quotes or paraphrases	Common knowledge
Summaries or reviews	A fact that is easily verified
Information derived from any source other than yourself	Every sentence, if the same source contributes to several sentences
A source of further information that you lack space to include	Each subsequent time you use the same information with the same source
Intellectual property belonging to any source other than yourself	Your own observations, or opinions, unless you have published them elsewhere

Table 3.2 Different citation standards

Standard	Dominant Disciplines
University of Chicago/Turabian	Political science and similar social sciences
APA (American Psychological Association)	Psychology and similar social sciences; education
AMA (American Medical Association)	Life sciences
MLA (Modern Language Association)	Arts, humanities, linguistics

In some cases, unauthorized reproduction can be considered a form of theft, with implications in criminal law. Neither malicious intent nor commitment of the act is necessary. Yes, you would be guilty of plagiarism if you simply forgot to give due credit to the source of your information! In most cases, plagiarism is the reproduction of text without citing the original author. Data too can be plagiarized. Images can be plagiarized.

Note that you could plagiarize yourself. Usually plagiarism is understood as reproducing another person's work without attribution, but you should not reproduce your own work within two different products without at least admitting the reproduction. Most academic rules on plagiarism do not permit students to submit the same work in fulfilment of two different assignments. Copyright law also prevents an author from reproducing text in a second product unless the copyright holder is the same in both cases or the initial copyright holder has granted permission.

Research in the Real World Box 3.2

A Famous Journalist Plagiarizes

Source: ©iStockphoto.com/DNY59.

Chris Hedges was a foreign correspondent for the *New York Times* from 1990 to 2005 and part of a team that won a Pulitzer Prize for reporting on global terrorism in 2002. Although Hedges was a leading thinker on the American political left, in 2014 a liberal magazine, *The New Republic*, exposed him as a serial plagiarist.

The main issue was Hedges' story on poverty in Camden, New Jersey, for *Harper's Magazine* in 2010. The editor and fact-checker found that "sections of Hedges' draft appeared to have been lifted directly from the work of a *Philadelphia Inquirer* reporter named Matt Katz, who in 2009 had published a four-part series on social and political dysfunction in Camden." The fact-checker found "[a]t least twenty instances of sentences that were exactly the same."

Subsequently, Hedges' plagiarism was proven to extend further back into his career. The director of the Center for Journalism Ethics at the University of Wisconsin-Madison, Robert Drechsel, commented, "Trust is a journalist's and journalism's most precious commodity. Difficult to gain and virtually impossible to regain once lost. If there is even a hint of the possibility that misconduct was covered up, it's even worse" (Ketcham, 2014).

Identifying plagiarism is easier than plagiarists may expect. For one thing, the writer and reader are likely to be exposed to the same specialist literature. In addition, social networks share knowledge. The person who has been plagiarized may be alerted by a stranger who realized the plagiarism. Some strangers have competitive motivations to investigate (see Research in the Real World Box 3.2). You should assume that plagiarism will be exposed!

Software has improved the capacity to spot plagiarism. Some professors pass digital copies of student submissions through software that searches for text similarities with other documents in the database. Such software is most likely to spot text that has been copied from the Internet; since the Internet is public, both the plagiarizer and the software have equal access.

CHAPTER SUMMARY

This chapter explained:

- How to define ethics
- The researcher's ethics
- How to handle the subjects of research ethically
- How to handle data ethically
- How to handle permissions and licenses ethically
- How to handle intellectual property ethically
- How to handle supporters ethically
- How to avoid misrepresentation
- How to avoid plagiarism

KEY TERMS

Citation 50

Common Rule 44

Error of commission 49

Error of omission 49

Ethics 42

Intellectual property 48

License 48

Misrepresentation 49

Permit 48

Plagiarism 50

Research ethics 42

Stake 48

Stakeholder 48

Subjects of research 43

Utilitarianism 45

Vivisection 43

QUESTIONS AND EXERCISES

1. Return to the story of the LSE's behavior from 2003 to 2011. How should the LSE have behaved?

2. Locate your university's ethical guidelines. Summarize the guidelines for ethical research.

3. What are the three fundamental ethical principles laid out by the Belmont report?

4. Provide an example of how research could violate the Common Rule.

5. How should you protect your data?

6. Explain the arguments used to justify vivisection. Explain the counterarguments.

7. How might someone become a stakeholder in someone else's intellectual property?

8. Provide an example of how you might be accused of unethically accepting support for research.

9. Explain the difference between an error of omission and an error of commission.

Scoping, Justifying, Designing, and Planning

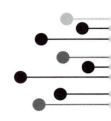

Opening Vignette: Scoping Now Saves Toil Later

Source: ©iStockphoto.com/Squaredpixels.

"One of the most important admonitions is to stop and reflect before plunging into any newly assigned task. Time spent properly framing and refining the question and scoping what is needed saves endless hours of unnecessary toil down the road" (Charles E. Allen, former United States Undersecretary for Intelligence and Analysis, Department of Homeland Security, 2005–2009, in Pherson & Pherson, 2013, p. xi).

Scoping

Scoping means defining what you intend to examine. A **scope** is a bounded view of something. You may see many other terms at the start of projects, such as:

- Specifying
- Targeting
- Refining
- Clarifying
- Narrowing
- Framing

Learning Objectives and Outcomes

At the end of this chapter, you should be able to:

1. Scope out a topic

2. Justify a topic

3. Evaluate the feasibility of a project

4. Develop a research question

5. Take the steps needed to specify, plan, and propose a research project

Source: ©iStockphoto.com/lechatnoir.

Scoping is the most comprehensive term.

Scoping tends to be intimidating. You scope your project at its start, when uncertainty is greatest. Your project can seem aimless and vast. Yet do not panic. The subsections below will explain what benefits of scoping you can expect and how to undertake the process of scoping.

The Benefits of Scoping

Many people are so eager to start that they do not scope properly. This sort of rashness will almost certainly lead to wasted effort, if not outright failure (see Practical Advice Box 4.1). You should start your project with humility and diligence regarding your scope. As the subsections below explain, scoping:

- Guides your effort

- Helps your self-discipline

- Reduces your burden

- Helps you communicate your research to others

Self-Guidance

Scoping defines what you intend to examine and helps to guide your intent. Establishing a clearer scope will help you to stay focused on whatever is within your scope and not wander outside your scope. If your scope is unclear, you may end up researching in the wrong direction, gathering too much information, not knowing what to include or exclude, and writing endlessly.

Self-Discipline

Clarity about your scope helps your self-discipline. Discipline means doing what you should be doing. Self-discipline means making yourself do what you should be doing. Self-discipline is a form of making yourself focus on whatever you should be focused on. You have probably heard people talk about someone who "lacks focus" or "needs to focus on their work."

Reduced Burden

With clearer boundaries, you are less likely to waste effort on research outside your scope. Focusing within a narrowing scope usually makes your research easier because you have less breadth to cover, although the flip side of this is that narrower scopes are expected to offer more depth. When defining your scope, you should narrow your scope enough to make it clearer and easier, without giving up so much that your research seems unambitious or valueless.

Communication

Scoping gives your research boundaries, so that you and others better understand what falls within and without your scope. A clear scope is important for your own understanding of what you intend to examine. It also helps you communicate to others what you intend to examine. In proposing your research, you will repeatedly be asked questions to the effect of, "What is your research about?" You must answer this question adequately if you expect others to understand your research, sponsor it, discuss it, or even read it.

Thus, when defining your scope, you should be mindful of your audience. A successful scope satisfies not only you; it satisfies your audience too.

Sometimes your topic is assigned by others, such as if you are employed specifically to research a client's issues. Sometimes, if you cannot come up with your own topic, one will be assigned to you. This somewhat relieves you of the burden of coming up with your own topic, but even here you should participate in the development of the topic. The people who assign the topic may not understand the topic; they may miss the real issue or misdefine it, in which case you should help them to refine it.

Often researchers refer to the *framing* of the topic. **Framing** is the context or tone of the communication. For instance, if you frame your topic as interesting to only a few people, such a frame will seem uninspiring to the rest of your audience, but if you frame your topic as a new issue or an unresolved issue, then the frame will be received as exciting or important.

Framing can introduce bias, or it can be used to mislead. A **bias** is favor toward something. A frame inherently draws attention to something, which could be described as biased. Framing that helps to impart objective understanding seems fair, but you must be aware of the ethical implications of frames that mislead (as described in Chapter 3).

How to Scope

In order to establish your scope, you should try to establish:

- The boundaries around your research
- The topic on which you plan to focus within those boundaries

Setting Boundaries

Your scope, by definition, must be bounded. A boundary demarcates where one thing ends or meets another. For instance, international borders are boundaries between countries—and these can be used to define research too. One person might research Australian cultures while another researches Mexican cultures.

Your boundaries should be established early so that they can guide the development of your project and guide others as to what to expect.

The Framing Effect

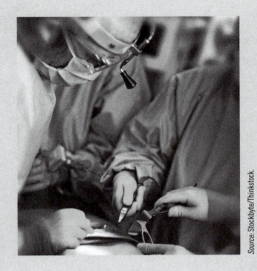

Source: Stockbyte/Thinkstock.

"The poorly defined problem is so common that it has a name: the *framing effect*. It has been described as 'the tendency to accept problems as they are presented, even when a logically equivalent reformulation would lead to diverse lines of inquiry not prompted by the original formulation.' We encounter it in many disciplines where the problem must be properly defined before it can be effectively solved. The classic example of the framing effect was a 1982 study in which U.S. doctors were presented with two different formulations for the outcome of an operation. One set of doctors was informed that the operation had a 93 percent survival rate, the other set was told that the operation had a 7 percent mortality rate. Rationally, there should have been no difference in the doctors' decisions, since both statistics have the same meaning. But the doctors showed a definite preference not to operate when they were quoted a mortality rate instead of a survival rate." (Clark, 2013, p. 20)

Table 4.1 Answer questions about your research scope

Question	Example answer	Your answer
When?	The 1920s (decade)	
Where?	New Zealand	
Who?	American artists	
What?	Art Deco	
Why?	The influence of American artists on New Zealand Art Deco remains underexplored.	

To help you find the boundaries of your own research, you should start thinking about the established academic and professional boundaries, the geographical or spatial boundaries, the human and social boundaries, and the temporal boundaries.

Academic and Professional

Some boundaries are academic or professional. The academic and professional **disciplines** are defined areas of study or work, such as biology or business. One person might research politics, while another researches economics.

One of the reasons that human beings came to talk about academic and professional disciplines is because disciplinary boundaries direct people into well-defined interests and work. Although you may choose to oppose some disciplinary boundaries or to research across disciplines, you still should choose a scope that disciplines your own interests and work.

Which is your favorite discipline or profession? To which disciplines or professions is your research relevant? Which discipline is interesting to you but perhaps more popular or employable? Some disciplines are more popular than others (see Table 1.1). Some disciplines are more employable (see Table 1.2). These data might affect your choice of where to research.

Disciplines usually can be disaggregated into commonly agreed-on units, known as **fields** and **subfields**. Each discipline is normally overseen by a society or association that defines the boundaries of the discipline and its fields and subfields, although some societies compete for authority or are in internal dispute about disciplinary structure. For instance, the American Political Science Association (APSA) claims to represent an academic discipline known as political science within a geopolitical unit defined by the borders of the United States. APSA recognizes a field called "international relations," but other American organizations as well as Canadian, British, Australian, and similar academies prefer to regard "international relations" or "international studies" as a discipline outside political science, in part because not all international relations are political and not all international studies are scientific. Some political scientists recognize a subfield called "international security," but APSA does not, although it recognizes an organizational "section" covering "international security and arms control." Some academics regard international security as self-evidently important. For instance, Richard Betts has advocated a political scientific subfield called "international politico-military" studies, which implies parity with established subfields, such as "international political economy" (Betts, 1995). However, others have ethical and practical doubts that international security can be studied without glorifying war or that academic interests can be separated from official interests. Others doubt the unscientific and partisan fields that would claim parity, such as war studies and peace studies.

Some fields may be uncontested but remain neglected by one discipline or become confused across several disciplines. For instance, the discipline of psychology has a long history of focusing on individual human psychology, leaving many readers ignorant of **social and organizational psychology**—the psychology of groups and of people within groups. Social and organizational psychology and behavior tend to be neglected because they are less tangible than individual behavior. Organizations are so pervasive that we generally filter them out (Pfeffer, 1998). Moreover, the field of "social psychology" overlaps the field of management known as "organizational behavior." Macro organization theory, of the sort that is associated with bureaucratic politics, standard operating procedures, and so forth, is best dated from 1947 (Simon, 1947). Micro organizational behavior (commonly known as simply "organizational behavior") was not recognized as a field before 1970 (Mowday & Sutton, 1993; O'Reilly, 1991).

Geographical or Spatial

Having established your academic or professional boundaries, think about the geographical or spatial boundaries. What region of the world interests you? It could be a continent, such as South America, within which you could focus on South American politics or South American trees. Your geographical scope could be an ocean, such as the Atlantic, in which case you could study fishing or pollution or transport in a particular oceanic area. Your geographical scope could be a particular country, province, or city.

However, always check whether a boundary that makes sense to you is contested by others. For instance, many people would be upset by a scope defined by the borders of Israel or Palestine, because these two political units are in dispute about many things, including their borders. This dispute is not just local; many foreign countries and supranational organizations also dispute their borders.

Be careful to choose boundaries that are least ambiguous or contentious; otherwise, you must expect to invest extra effort in justifying your boundaries to your audience or in responding to questions about your boundaries. For instance, many people have claimed to study the "Islamic world" or "the West," but where do their boundaries lie? Is Bali part of the Islamic world because it falls within the largely Muslim sovereign state of Indonesia, or should it fall without because of its largely non-Muslim population? Is

Australia Western because of its historical, cultural, economic, and political ties with Britain and the United States, or is it Asian because of its regional location? How large must the majority religion be before a country is coded as belonging to one religion over another? How do we bound a culture? Which part of geography, organization, religion, and culture is most important to a country's identity? You could not answer any of these questions to the informed reader's satisfaction without considerable research into the disputes and conventions. Make sure you do this before deciding what your boundaries should be.

Human and Social Subjects

The subjects of your research help you to find boundaries. Perhaps you are interested in a particular person, demographic group, ethnicity, religion, idea, ideology, culture, group, organization, or institution.

Organization implies a formal group with members; **institutions** include organizations, but sometimes also include informal groupings or cultures. **Cultures** are collectively held norms, beliefs, or values. **Norms** are normal values, expectations, or behaviors. **Beliefs** are things held to be true without necessarily having evidence. **Values** are things held as worthy.

Any of these things can be used to define your scope. For instance, you might be interested in studying the success of a particular union of oil-producing countries, employees, or students. You might be interested in which of two commercial organizations offers better employment. You might be interested in how a particular culture affects a behavior.

Time

Your research might be defined in time, in which case you should set **temporal** boundaries. Perhaps you are interested only in events within the 19th century, the last year, the last decade, or the last millennium, or during the lifetime of a particular historical personality, the lifetime of a policy, or the lifetime of a government. You will not need to set temporal boundaries if your research is not specific to any time period.

Focusing Within the Boundaries

Your boundaries give you a scope, but you should think about focusing even further. Focus implies a closer or clearer look at something. Disciplinary boundaries may seem narrow at first but are actually too broad for one researcher to fill. If your boundaries do not narrow your scope sufficiently, you should aim to focus on something in particular within those boundaries. In most cases, you should strive to focus even when you think you have found your scope.

You should realize that people tend to insufficiently focus—in most things, not just research. People like to follow whatever catches their interest, because distractions feel natural and effortless. Telling people to focus implies effort, and people naturally tend to avoid effort.

People also naturally resist the limitations implied by focusing, because focus implies specialization and neglect of things outside the scope. You may be ambitious and want to explain a lot of things and thus resist any curb on your ambition, but be humble (see Practical Advice Box 4.3): Your ambition may be impractical; focus can make your project easier.

These dilemmas are worth remembering, particularly when you must consider the trade-off between parsimony and depth or between wide appeal and narrow appeal. We will consider this trade-off more in Chapter 8, but for now realize that the ideal theory has both parsimony or breadth (it explains many things) and explanatory depth (it explains each thing accurately). This combination is ideal but impossible, because parsimonious theories tend to be shallow (they explain lots of things imperfectly), while deep theories tend to be narrow (they explain few things well).

Narrowing your focus is a good way to establish your scope. Start with something that interests you, then make it more specific. Drill down to as narrow and specific a topic as possible. Do not be afraid to make it narrower than you had intended—remember that most people start with a broader scope than is practical. You are unlikely to narrow it too much, but if you were to do so, you could expand your scope easily.

The Value of Your Research

Your scope will help you communicate your research to others, but communicating is not the same as justifying its value. *Value* is the worth of something from one perspective, and is thus inherently subjective—you must persuade others that your research is valuable to them. You should try to appeal to as wide an audience as possible and to appear as valuable as possible to each audience. You must justify your research to others—a **justification** is the quality of being agreeable to others.

You can justify your topic by claiming that it is one or more of the following five things:

1. Interesting

2. Important

3. Improving

4. Challenging

5. Resolving a gap in our knowledge

Ideally, your research is all of these things. It must be some of these things. For instance, most researchers would agree that research should attempt to resolve some gap in our knowledge; otherwise, the research will seem pointless by definition.

Interesting

You should be interested in your research, if only because an interest should be self-motivating, but what interests you may not interest others.

At least some of your interests are likely to be ill-disciplined and personal, so likely you should discipline and generalize your interests.

Discipline Your Interests

Your interests are likely to be dynamic, moody, overlapping, and ill defined, but a scope must be a single thing with a clear boundary. Focusing on your interests may lead you away from the self-discipline and boundaries you need to define your scope. Worse, your interests could lead you away from other justifications for your research (e.g., practical, policy-relevant, important, improving, challenging, and novel).

If you cannot pin down your interests, go back to the scope (as described above) and think about the established boundaries around things that interest you, drill down to find your focus, discipline yourself to accept this focus, use the scope to guide your research, and communicate your scope before communicating your interests.

Generalize Your Interests

Your interests are likely to be somewhat personal, which means that some people will not share your interests. If you obsess about an unpopular singer from a forgotten decade, you will struggle to persuade anyone else that he or she should be as interested. If you are obsessed with a current popular singer, you will struggle to offer anything novel to a mass of fans.

Your research must be interesting to others if it is to have any wider appeal or impact. Your experience of a crime may be very interesting to you, but less so to others unless you offer some lesson for them from your experience of crime.

The solution to personal interests is to think about how you could generalize them to a wider audience. What part of your interests is more general than personal? For instance, many people are interested in watching a sport, but are less interested in learning the intensive, slow process of developing better-performing competitors. Yet they become more interested when told that their learning could be applied to their own performance as a competitor, businessperson, or parent.

Important

You should be interested in your research, but your research should be important too. You need to persuade your consumer that your research is important, which means explicitly justifying its importance at the start of any proposal or product. Importance is easier to justify if you can claim that your research is:

- Consequential

- Salient

- Fashionable

- Employable or applicable

- Policy-relevant

Consequential

One way in which something could be important is if its consequences would affect a lot of other things or would dramatically affect just one important thing—such a thing could be described as **consequential**.

Finding something consequential will help you to argue that something is interesting. Many interests are more entertaining than consequential. For instance, sports are interesting because they are entertaining, but sports and other entertainments do not matter to most other domains—the outcome of a game does not affect climates, for instance. In fact, although most people are interested in sports, few people study or work in sports. If you can find an important relationship, such as the relationship between sports and foreign policy, the topic becomes more important.

Some things, like war, climate, health, and safety, are both interesting and important because they are consequential—they can harm people, cost money, damage economies, or cause political changes. Consequential things can be interesting just because they are consequential. Generally, you can expect people to be interested in things that could affect them. You should try to find ways to justify a subject as consequential to as wide a population as possible (see Research in the Real World Box 4.2), although you should not overreach.

However, some people are distrustful of anyone who researches harmful things. Still, you could appeal to wider sets of people by reminding them of the consequences of your work—you might study war, not because you mean to glorify war, but because you want to reduce the risks associated with war. If you were to offer another study of terrorism, you should scope your topic so that you can justifiably claim that your research will be consequential: It could reduce terrorism; reduce other crimes, such as trafficking and theft, that fund terrorists; reduce the chance of wars waged in the name of counterterrorists; or help people to understand terrorism.

Salient

Something is **salient** if it seems particularly pronounced or important.

Some topics are salient at different times. For instance, terrorism has always existed, but most of the time terrorism is a much lower risk than war or cancer. Yet terrorism became much more important after September 11, 2001 (9/11), when terrorists caused the greatest loss of life ever in any single terrorist attack. Terrorism is still rare next to other forms of violence, but 9/11 demonstrated that the risk had changed. Previously, the study of terrorism had been an ill-advised niche for academics or officials. After 9/11, demand grew for research that would help us to understand terrorism in general, how the event happened, why the event happened, how terrorism could be researched better, what counterterrorist policies of countries should adopt, and how counterterrorism could be more effective.

Beware of changing salience. Priorities today may fade quickly. For instance, the salience of terrorism studies has receded as the real risks of terrorism have been realized (the risks have not fallen; they are just less overstated than they used to be). Meanwhile, other risks have been realized as more salient. For instance, insurgency is much riskier than terrorism and has become riskier since 2001. Some of the knowledge gained from studying terrorism is useful to the study of insurgency, but the sudden claimants to expertise on terrorism after 9/11 now look less worthy, having overestimated the risks of terrorism and underestimated the risks of insurgency.

Fashionable

When selecting your research, you should ask what is most important or salient at the current time. Salience overlaps fashionability, but it is not the same.

Research in the Real World Box 4.2

The Beef Industry Is Consequential to Us All

Source: Stockbyte/Thinkstock.

"In recent decades, the beef industry has undergone a radical transformation—the small cattle farmer has been all but replaced by beef-processing companies that own huge feedlots and industrial meatpacking plants. One result of this concentration has been inexpensive and readily available meat; beef now costs half of what it did in 1970. Critics have charged, however, that the new system is inhumane to the animals and may have created new health risks." (Public Broadcasting Service, Frontline, 2014)

Something is **fashionable** when it is more popular than normal. Unfortunately, something can be salient when it is unfashionable, or it can be fashionable when it is not salient. For instance, in 2000, you might have been one of the terrorism experts who realized that terrorism was becoming riskier, and thus should have been salient, but at the time the study of terrorism was not fashionable. After 9/11, terrorism was more salient and fashionable. Unfortunately, the fashionability of terrorism was so great and enduring that it swamped greater risks, such as insurgency, hurricanes, and cyberattacks.

Fashionability is distorted by politics and psychological cycles of novelty and fatigue (see Research in the Real World Box 4.3). This puts pressure on the researcher to choose whether to challenge or accept the unfashionability of a subject. To rediscover an important subject can be great for your career, but pushing a subject that is politically incorrect or socially censured can be terrible for your career, even if objectively it really is more important than fashion would suggest.

Research in the Real World Box 4.3

The Fashionability of Neurocriminology

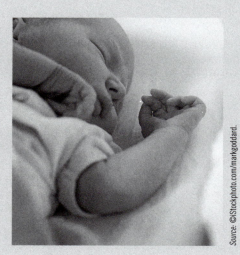

Source: ©iStockphoto.com/markgoddard.

In the nineteenth century, Cesare Lombroso was a professor of psychiatry and criminal anthropology at the University of Turin, Italy. He helped to found the discipline of criminology, but some of his theories came to be derided as something between phrenology and social Darwinism.

The two main parts of Lombroso's theory were that crime originates in the brain and that criminals are evolutionary throwbacks to a more primitive species. He thought criminals could be predicted with anatomical markers such as a large jaw and sloping forehead. He placed Jews and Northern Italians at the top of his evolutionary hierarchy (Lombroso was both Jewish and Northern Italian) and placed Southern Italians, Bolivians, and Peruvians at the bottom. In the first half of the 20th century, new political ideologies, such as Nazism in Germany, developed Lombroso's theories to justify persecution of Jews, Gypsies, and others.

Adrian Raine, since 2007 the Richard Perry University Professor of Criminology, Psychiatry, and Psychology at the University of Pennsylvania, has published rigorous scientific support for the theory that criminal behavior does have neurological causes, in books with titles including *The Psychopathology of Crime, Violence and Psychopathology, Crime and Schizophrenia*, and *The Anatomy of Violence.* Raine says that "the seeds of sinful violence are sown early . . . and not just at the time of conception" (Hughes, 2013, p. 34). They "are cultivated in utero, at the time of birth, and also in the early postnatal period to give rise to the framework for violence" (p. 34). The causes are birthing problems—such as infection and hypoxia, maternal rejection, malnutrition, and toxicity.

Raine complains that his research is unfashionable.

> One of the continuing problems is that this research field borders on the politically incorrect. Liberals and center-left parties fear that the research will be used to stigmatize individuals and take attention away from social problems, the true causes of crime. Conservatives and the center-right are concerned that it will be used to let offenders off the hook and take away responsibility and retribution. . . . The Holocaust, the experiments that were done in Nazi Germany—that certainly made it so that biology and crime is not on anyone's radar screen. It's a no-go area, or traditionally it's been viewed in that fashion. (Hughes, 2013, p. 30)

Information source: Hughes, 2013.

Practically Employable or Applicable

Something is practically employable or applicable if it can be used in the real world. For instance, applied economics is useful for managing economies, while basic economics is used to explain economies.

The word **employable** in reference to a given endeavor implies that you could get paid for doing it. Research on a cleaner-burning or more powerful version of a currently popular engine would be highly employable.

The word **applicable** implies that something is useful in practice. For instance, the management sciences produce research that is applicable to the practice of managing things.

Just because something is interesting does not make it employable or applicable. For instance, I remember attending a conference on counterterrorism just after the terrorist attacks of September 11, 2001, where one attendee claimed to explain how parasites could help us understand terrorism. He succeeded in describing lots of interesting parasitic life cycles and behaviors, but avoided questions about how any of this knowledge could be applied to counterterrorism. His research was interesting, but not applied.

Applicable research is normally employable. Probably you are thinking about your own employability when you consider your research. Stereotypically, parents and employers often complain about students who choose to study basket-weaving abroad rather than learn some skill or knowledge that will be employable at home. You may still love basket-weaving abroad and choose to study it, but do not be naive about the consequences of the choice you are making. Perhaps you should revise your scope so that it is more employable (see Table 1.2).

Your true interests may not be employable, in which case you may need to separate your interests from your employment. For instance, if your obsession is researching a particular entertainer, but you know that you would never make a career by sharing your obsession with other people, then (on economic grounds alone) you should accept your obsession as a hobby, not a career and not any basis for research within your career.

Almost everybody has multiple interests outside whatever they get paid to do. For instance, many people get paid to work in offices while they obsess about what is happening outside, in sports or entertainment, say. The trick is to have healthy interests that do not interfere with paid work.

Some people can be so obsessed with work or study that they need to be advised to get a hobby. Industrial psychologists and sports psychologists often advise intense professionals to keep a positive hobby that can distract them from obsessive study or work.

If your interests are not obviously employable, think about what interests you, then ask yourself, "How could what interests me become useful?" Many interests are unimportant in the grand scheme, although they may be very important to particular people. For instance, sports employ few people directly—players, coaches, owners, betters, advertisers, ticket sellers, and sellers of merchandise. If you can apply your interest in sports in a way that is important to any of these people, then you will have employable research. Relevant topics might include the improvement of player performance, gambling, sports advertising, ticket sales, or merchandise sales.

Think about how you combine two interests in order to produce research that is employable or applicable. The link may be tangential or indirect, but it is a good way to use your interests to bridge the gap between the useless and the useful. Perhaps you are interested in both sports and medical care, in which case you could perhaps research the medical care of a sports injury.

Policy-Relevant

Policy is guidance for behavior. Policy can be **intentional**, as in stating how the author intends to behave. Policy can be **prescriptive**, as in stating how specified actors are supposed to behave. Governments issue documents that describe how they intend to behave in domains such as foreign policy, economic policy, law enforcement policy, and so forth. The smallest commercial organizations may issue documents describing what markets they intend to serve or how they will treat their customers or their shareholders. Not all policies are described explicitly in documents—many policies emerge haphazardly as a collection of precedents and ad hoc reactions.

Your research would be policy-relevant if it does one of the following:

- Improves our understanding of policies

- Offers improvements to policies

- Improves our understanding of policy-making

- Improves our understanding of policy-makers

Be aware that some authorities (primarily public authorities) value policy-relevant research more than they value purely theoretical or historical work, while academic authorities can be dismissive of policy-relevant research, so you need to be mindful of which of these types of actors you want to please most. For instance, in the United States, the National Research Council (NRC) ranks academic programs using a method that, according to its critics, "discourages real-world relevance among scholars." The NRC's method measures an academic program's value by the number of articles published by the program's faculty in peer-reviewed journals, but policy-relevant research tends to be published in books, reports, and non-peer-reviewed journals. The NRC examines only graduate programs, neglecting the more practical and professional programs, which tend to be undergraduate and non-degree programs. Finally, the NRC's ranking of disciplinary departments ignores interdisciplinary programs (except to give credit for interdisciplinary faculty), even though policy research is more likely to be interdisciplinary (Campbell & Desch, 2013).

Improving

A useful claim is that your research will improve something. You could slow global warming or stabilize the global climate; you could terminate a disease or reduce the harm caused by an injury; you could improve safety in a particular workplace.

All of these things fulfill a general claim to improve well-being. Research that can claim to improve well-being, whether human, environmental, or global, is easier for your audience to accept as important.

Improving well-being is a claim that is easier to make in some disciplines than in others. For instance, pharmaceuticals generally claim to improve health or comfort. In other domains, such as history, a claim to improve well-being is difficult to make, but you can still claim to improve the discipline.

In whatever discipline you work, improvements can always be made in the following things:

- History (a description of what happened)

- Theory (an explanation for what happens)

- Methodology (the ways by which theories are tested)

- Policy (guidance for behavior)

- Practices (activities)

- Well-being

Challenging

Your research can be appealing if it challenges something. You could challenge a false theory or an incorrect history. You could challenge conventional wisdom. For instance, many people used to think that women were incapable of things that men were capable of, such as piloting aircraft through turns that produce forces greater than gravity, but women have proved equally capable. In turn, some societies have developed from misogynist to misanthropic, in which men are assumed to be inferior at certain skills, such as communication and parenting. Societies are large and inattentive groups, so societies are rife with myths and injustices that are worth challenging.

In order to improve knowledge, we must inherently challenge the current state of our knowledge (see Practical Advice Box 4.2). Perhaps a theory needs more depth or breadth. Perhaps a theory needs to be revised and given new facts. Perhaps the evidence needs to be improved.

Some of the things that researchers routinely challenge whenever they start new research include:

- Theories

- Methods

- Policies

- Practices

- Evidence

Less obvious things that you could challenge include:

- Assumptions

- Conventional wisdom

- Expectations

- Perceptions or conceptions

- Depictions

- Fashions or the focus of attention

While you should be looking to improve knowledge, you should not simply look to *revise* knowledge—just to offer a difference of interpretation. Good researchers are looking for new knowledge, but inferior researchers start out by alleging an "orthodoxy" that they promise to "revise." In turn, eventually others will declare the revision as orthodox, then offer a new revision, often actually a return to the first interpretation. This vicious circle of revision and counter-revision is necessarily interpretive but not necessarily creative; it is destructive of knowledge but not necessarily constructive. The worst revisionist starts out looking for something to challenge as "orthodox," then offers a slight change of emphasis or interpretation that is in turn difficult to falsify, such as a claim that one historian did not give enough credit to one historical figure over another or that one government was more righteous than previously portrayed. Since the result of this would be a vague reassessment, the revisionist avoids developing theories, testing theories, or offering new evidence. Historically, this cycle of revisionism has been strong within religions, cults, political ideologies (especially Marxism), legal discourse, and history (see Table 6.1).

Many academics unfortunately tell their students to find a topic by finding some orthodoxy ripe for revision. Researchers can be successful on the back of grand claims of "counter-orthodoxy," but their credibility is fragile. For instance, Trevor Hugh-Roper (1914–2003, Lord Dacre from 1979) feuded with many historians about the proper interpretation of Germany history, before in 1983 declaring as genuine the forged diaries of Adolf Hitler (dictator of Germany from 1933 to 1945). David Irving (1938–) was instrumental in exposing Roper's mistake, but became better known for denying Nazi atrocities against Jews.

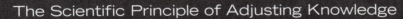

Practical Advice Box 4.2
The Scientific Principle of Adjusting Knowledge

"Science thrives on its inability—so far—to explain everything, and uses that as the spur to go on asking questions, creating possible models and testing them, so that we make our way, inch by inch, closer to the truth. If something were to happen that went against our current understanding of reality, scientists would see that as a challenge to our present model, requiring us to abandon or at least change it. It is through such adjustments and subsequent testing that we approach closer and closer to what is true." (Dawkins, 2011, p. 22)

Resolving Gaps in Knowledge

Research is inherently more interesting or important if it fills a gap in our knowledge.

To find a gap in knowledge, look within your area of interest and ask the following questions.

What Is Least Understood?

Within your area, which phenomenon, behavior, or concept is least understood or explained? Has something been ignored? Does a question remain to be asked? For instance, male-on-female rape has been the topic of much research, from anthropological to legal, but other forms of rape, in which a male is the victim, are poorly understood, even though they could have implications for all forms of rape.

Do Two Theories Contradict Each Other?

If you can find an unresolved contradiction between two theories, such as when one theory would expect the opposite of what the other expects in the same situation, and nobody has satisfactorily resolved which theory is correct, you could set out to do so. For instance, a long political philosophical tradition (known usually as **liberalism**) expects trading states to avoid war lest war interrupt the economic benefits of trade. The founders of classic liberal philosophy are Baron de Montesquieu (1689–1689), David Hume (1711–1776), and Adam Smith (1723–1790). **Realism** is a paradigm of international relations whose central argument is that states naturally struggle for power in an anarchical world without recourse to a higher authority. Realists expect economic dependence to encourage states to war in order to secure access to their material needs (Waltz, 1979).

Can Theories Be Combined?

Two theories might contradict each other but could be combined to explain something better. For instance, Dale Copeland (1996) combined the liberal and realist theories of trade and war. He argued that economic interdependence encourages peace so long as the more dependent state expects a stable relationship. If the state expects that the other state will threaten its supply, then it will consider war to secure its supply.

Is a Theory Underspecified?

Many theories contradict each other but are difficult to resolve because they are vague. For instance, some theories expect states to be more belligerent during times of economic growth, when states feel empowered. Other theories expect leaders to use war to divert the populace from economic troubles. Philip Arena (2010) found, by formal modeling, that economic difficulties incentivize political leaders in both directions—to avoid and pursue conflict, with no clear dominant expectation, so he urged theorists to better specify their theories.

Is a Theory Untested?

Many theories exist in popular culture or casual discourse without having been subjected to formal testing. For instance, popular culture routinely depicts people rationally avoiding things that could harm them, such as disastrous asteroid impacts or alien invasions. Often these depictions characterize human responses as predictable universal responses, such as mass screaming panic or defiant self-defense. Individual persons who see such depictions are probably reassured that people would respond in predictable ways. These depictions and predictions are effectively theories about how people behave (see Chapter 8) but are largely untested. If you dig deeper into real behaviors rather than popular depictions, you will find all sorts of cases where people do not behave rationally or in mass, such as when people acclimate to harm, become passive and incapable, or disrupt each other rather than unite. You could set out to test these theories, while justifying your research as a test of theories that people commonly hold but do not test.

Could You Test the Theory Better Than It Has Been Tested Before?

Just because a theory has been tested once does not mean that a gap in knowledge has been filled. The theory might be flawed, the test might be flawed, or the evidence might be provisional—that is, not conclusive. Even if the theory, test, and evidence are robust, you can still test in a different way. For instance, much research on terrorism is historical, describing how terrorists or counterterrorists behaved in the past and inducing theories about how they would behave in the future. This historical research lacks control and is vulnerable to all sorts of biases due to the unavailability of data and personal interpretation. Preferable would be a controlled experiment, which is difficult but not impossible to achieve (Newsome, 2006).

Are the Assumptions Untested?

Many things that are held as facts are actually assumptions or are deduced from assumptions. For instance, many theories assume that state leaders are rational when they go to war, but critics have separated that assumption as a theory that should be tested. Similarly, many historians and commentators have assumed that people who engage in combat must have been intrinsically motivated since they joined the military, but the motivations to join the military and the motivations to fight in combat are usually not the same or transitive; combat motivations are provided largely extrinsically, such as in the form of interpersonal bonds, after the soldier has joined the military (Newsome, 2003).

Feasibility

You may have developed the most interesting and important topic, but you must still consider whether it is feasible. Feasibility is the quality of being achievable or possible.

Usually, you face a trade-off between the feasibility of your research and your ambition. The more interesting and important your topic, the less likely it is to be feasible. For instance, if you promised to research the health of every individual person on the planet, your research would be universally interesting and important, but certainly not feasible. The more you promise from your research, the more skeptical your audience is likely to be. Conversely, if your research appears unambitious, your audience might assume that you were too lazy or unskilled to attempt something riskier.

One implication of feasibility is that the project is not certain to deliver on its promise. If your project is judged as feasible, its fulfillment is being judged as possible, but not necessarily certain. By definition, a feasible project is one that could be achieved but might not be. The possibility of failure is inherent in most projects. For instance, academic coursework normally faces an external judgment—by a professor, say—about whether it should pass for credit toward a degree or other academic qualification; if the professor decides that your submission should not pass, then your project has failed.

If someone commits to funding your research, they usually want to judge that your project would probably—not just possibly—deliver on its promise. For instance, if a potential sponsor is offering funds to help researchers to travel abroad to gather data, the potential sponsor will likely ask any petitioner to prove that the project is likely to succeed, given the data; the sponsor might interview the petitioner to assess his or her character, and the sponsor might ask the petitioner's colleagues to testify as to his or her capacity.

On the other hand, unfeasible projects can be sponsored or authorized on the grounds of importance or interest. For instance, lots of projects for research into unlikely cures for cancer are sponsored because cancer is very risky and a cure for cancer would be very valuable. Conversely, someone is unlikely to sponsor a project that is unfeasible if it does not interest them or does not seem important—they might blame the unfeasibility, but really they are just not interested. The lesson here is that you may get away with less feasible projects if the research is very important or interesting, but when your research is less important or less interesting, your stakeholders tend to demand a higher probability of delivery.

Feasibility cannot be measured perfectly, so it is usually a judgment call, by you and/or the people who would authorize or sponsor your project. Unfortunately, some judgments are unmeritorious and opaque. What you need is a match between the right project and the right sponsor—someone who will evaluate your proposal fairly by tangible dimensions of feasibility.

You can help your case by claiming each of these things:

- Your capacity, such as your skills

- Social resources, such as your mentors

- Institutional resources, such as your institutional resources and sponsors

- Available time

Your Capacity

Your project is feasible if it is within your capacity. **Capacity** is the potential for something, usually the potential to achieve something, deliver resources, acquire capabilities, or perform. Many people have the capacity to achieve something but never acquire the skills, motivations, or opportunities to actually deliver that something. They retain the capacity, but their potential is not the same as their actual performance.

You need to assess the practical limits of your capacity in order to assess how ambitious your project should be. You may also face stakeholders, such as the people who authorize or sponsor your work, who want to assess your capacity before agreeing to your ambition.

Could you activate your capacity to deliver? Can you sustain yourself financially during the project? Do you have the skills for this particular project? Are you motivated sufficiently to finish it?

Discover your capacity to determine what you might need to improve in order to deliver on your ambition. At the same time, retain some humility about what is possible within your capacity (see Practical Advice Box 4.3).

"I challenge all of you to respond the next time someone asks you what you think about genocide in Darfur, or drone attacks in Somalia, or civilian casualties in Afghanistan to say:

> 'I have no opinion. I am not an expert in everything, I have never been there. I do, however, suspect it is a highly complicated and sensitive issue and filled with more hyperbole than needed. Frankly, I do not know enough about the situation to comment on it.'

"At what point did every 21-year-old college student become an expert in human trafficking in North Africa or information operations in central Asia? The answer is never. So, be humble and stave off the need to speak about things you probably do not know much about. Most controversial global issues are complicated and have multiple layers of truth. The more you study them in academia and in the field, the more you will realize that there is no 'true' or 'right and wrong.' There are just shades of grey and a lot of players who have agendas for better or worse." (Brandon, 2013)

Social Resources

Sometimes you have the opportunity to work with or to take advice from other people. The help could come from a friend, teacher, or contractor. Increasingly, researchers are seeking help in more creative ways, such as by advertising their work online and inviting strangers to contribute.

Some people prefer to work socially, some alone. You probably know someone who just likes to be around people, listen to the radio in the background, check email for news from friends, watch other people working, or have people around who can share the joys and pains of work. Such a person is probably wasting a lot of time in distractions and multitasking. Such a person should be working alone, even though he or she prefers to work socially.

Conversely, some people prefer to work alone but could benefit from social accountability. People who like to declare loudly that they will be working now, before they shut themselves into an empty room, might then have the opportunity to do anything but work, but still have the social rewards of pretending they spend all their free time working. Such people should be working with someone who will hold them accountable, even though they prefer to work alone. In such a case, the person should seek social help. A student should seek a member of faculty who could advise on the process of research or on knowledge within the scope. A professional researcher should have a line manager or associate with more experience in research or more knowledge within the scope.

This choice is often not as obvious as you might at first think, because other people may face ethical or practical constraints, they may be destructive rather than constructive, or your personality may be such that you would work best alone.

As explained in the subsections below, when seeking social help, you should ideally select it according to:

- Ethical allowability

- Institutional conditions

- Availability or accessibility

- Specialization

- Constructiveness

- Freedom from costs

Ethical Allowability

One irony of a typical research career is that early on you will likely be forced to work alone when you could most use help, while later on you may work in a team when you are most qualified to work alone. At the start of your research career, you are likely to be in an educational institution that demands that you work alone so that your own performance can be evaluated separately from others'. Yet, at that stage, you are least qualified to work alone. In such a situation, you should seek trainers, mentors, and advisers who will contribute positively without violating the rules on individual work (see Chapter 3 on ethics). Ironically, once you are employed professionally, you are more likely to be employed in teams.

Institutional Conditions

Some institutions specify the sort of social help you must seek. Indeed, degree programs that demand theses often specify that the student should first pass a course of instruction in research skills, sign a commitment to the ethical rules, and find an adviser from the faculty who specializes in the thesis topic.

Available and Accessible

You may face practical constraints on social help. The best person to help may be unavailable or inaccessible—imagine a professor who is on sabbatical or visiting another institution in the same year that you must deliver your project, or imagine a specialist who is temporarily too distracted by his or her own project or a personal crisis. In these cases, you need to find someone more available and accessible, but in this search you may be settling for less specialized candidates. Someone may be eager to help, accessible, and available, but not a specialist on your topic.

Specialists

Sometimes you need a specialist from outside your expertise. You may be a psychologist seeking to cross-fertilize with philosophy, so likely you would benefit from help from someone who better knows philosophy. Sometimes you need a functional specialist who can spot your technical mistakes.

Constructive

In general, you should seek all the help you can get, within the constraints mentioned above, but seeking help is different from accepting it. You should not accept help from someone who would steal your work, who would not deliver on his or her promises, or whose help would be net negative.

You do need advisers or managers who are motivated to help constructively and offer superior skills or knowledge. However, ensure that your advisers do not have contradictory agendas, such as people who want you to produce research that complements or compliments their own or who would punish you for research that would usurp their own. In all human relationships, choose carefully.

You should not choose a helper who is unwarrantedly destructive or negative. Conversely, be careful about selecting helpers who have so much naive faith in you that they would not hold you accountable. You need a helper who will not damage your self-efficacy, but also someone who knows that constructive criticism is better in the long run than false cheer.

Freedom From Costs

The specialist you need may demand payment of some kind. More valuable help tends to be in higher demand and is more likely to demand compensation. However, first be sure that any payment for help will not violate any ethical rules. Also be sure that you can afford the payment and will not regret the payment later.

Be mindful of the more valuable help that you may be giving up when you refuse to pay for it. Also be wary of always reaching for friends or family for help; you may feel that you can trust them more, but your faith in their value may be corrupted by your personal relationship. Finally, be aware that an unhappy professional relationship could ruin a prior personal relationship.

Institutional Resources

In addition to social resources, you can draw on institutional resources, such as a university library. You probably take some institutions for granted—you may rely on a university's library but ignore a local library—yet you could discover in a local library a rare book that is not in any other library.

Researchers are often searching for institutions that will fund their research. That funding is normally cash based, because cash is **fungible**—it is easily converted into other resources. Usually the institution will restrictively specify how the money can be spent. The institution may demand that the researcher account for the spending at the end of the project.

Some resources are material but not fungible. For instance, some institutions simply offer space for the research—this offer is not fungible (the researcher cannot swap the space for something else) but is directly useful as a place to research.

The material requirements of research are actually broader than most inexperienced researchers would expect. A quiet or private place to work can make a profound difference to the stressed researcher. A ready supply of laboratory materials saves the researcher money and also the stress of acquisition. A human assistant relieves the advanced researcher of the simple but tedious tasks that otherwise could consume the majority of project time. Pay-to-access databases, journals, statistical software, and hardware are all extremely expensive to the personal consumer, but can be shared between members of an institution at less cost per capita. Resources as indirect as health insurance may be pertinent—for instance, some sponsors require evidence of your health insurance with the justification that your poor health would interrupt a project in which they have a stake.

Institutional support implies additional resources but also constraints. The institution that grants resources usually expects something in return. It may direct the research toward some objective with which you do not agree. It may extract a commitment from you to work on the institution's own project for a period of time after it has sponsored your private research. It may take a stake in the product. It may prevent your publication or dissemination or commercialization of your research without permission. Participation in the institution may expose your research to institutional theft or manipulation.

Often, researchers accept institutional resources for institutional objectives but use those resources to pursue private research. This is not necessarily ethical or good for your research. Perhaps you should perform better on the paid work and defer your private research or find another institution.

Private research is not necessarily good for your career, unless you produce something privately that is valued publicly. However, you could justify private research for personal reasons—as your hobby, say, or for personal gain. This is often the case when you work on something commercially valuable but personally uninteresting, while working privately on something interesting but commercially valueless—or you work publicly on something that has been judged feasible by sponsors, but work privately on something that they had incorrectly judged as infeasible.

Time

Good or Bad Deadlines

All projects must end at some point. A project that proceeds forever without producing anything useful should be regarded as a failure, so an infinite project is clearly wrong, but the optimal timing of a particular project is less obvious. A good deadline is one that gives you sufficient time to complete the project but does not let you procrastinate.

Since most people are procrastinators, most work benefits from a deadline. A deadline incentivizes people to finish the project by a useful date. Some projects are not useful beyond some point in time. For instance, research into a solution to climate change that languishes on for another century will probably deliver after climate change becomes irreversible.

Note that most products have a finite life span of utility. A theory can be superseded by an improved theory or can be disproven. Policy research becomes less valuable when the policy under study is abandoned or the conditions change. A test of a theory becomes obsolete when someone else introduces a better test. An analysis of articles downloaded from 2,812 academic and professional journals across the hard sciences, social sciences, and humanities found that the median time between publication and download was between 36 and 48 months in the social sciences; longer in the humanities, physics, and mathematics (49 to 60 months); and shorter in the health sciences

John Snow's Private Research on Cholera

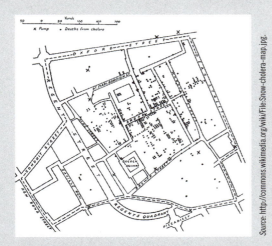

Source: http://commons.wikimedia.org/wiki/File:Snow-cholera-map.jpg.

John Snow (1813–1858) was a colliery surgeon during the London cholera epidemic of 1831–1832. He graduated as a medical doctor from the University of London in 1844. In 1849, Snow published a pamphlet ("On the Mode of Communication of Cholera") arguing that "Cholera Poison" reproduced in the human body and spread through the contamination of food or water. His theory contradicted the common theory that diseases were transmitted through inhalation of contaminated vapors. Snow had no way to prove his theory until 1854, when cholera struck England again. Snow plotted the locations of deaths related to cholera and found them most concentrated where water was delivered by a water company that drew its water from the River Thames downstream of London. At the time, London was supplied by two water companies. The other company pulled water upstream, uncontaminated by the city's waste. Additionally, Snow plotted around 500 deaths from cholera within 10 days near the intersection of Cambridge and Broad Street. Snow recommended removal of the handle of the Broad Street pump; officials complied and the epidemic was contained.

Source: Crosier, S., Center for Spatially Integrated Social Science. Retrieved fromhttp://csiss.ncgia.ucsb. edu/classics/content/8/). Copyright © 2001-2011 by Regents of University of California, Santa Barbara.

(25 to 36 months), presumably because of the short life cycle of medical treatments (Davis, 2013).

If your project's end date has been set already, at least you have the certainty of knowing the time available for completion of your project. A deadline would be bad for a project if the research were to be rushed just to meet the deadline or if the objective genuinely could not be achieved within the time allowed. Imagine that researchers have correctly estimated that they will need a decade to research a cure for some disease, just because of the long gestation of the disease, but their sponsors demand delivery within a year. When the project fails, the fault lies with the sponsors more than the researchers, even if the sponsors blame the researchers for being lazy or inattentive.

Research in the Real World Box 4.5

The Procrastination of Babbage

Source: http://commons.wikimedia.org/wiki/File:Babbage_Difference_Engine_(1).jpg.

In 1821, Charles Babbage (1791–1871) designed the Difference Engine to compile mathematical tables. Unfortunately, the machine was difficult to build using the materials of the time. The British government suspended funding in 1832 and formally terminated its involvement in 1842. In 1854, George Scheutz, a Swedish printer, successfully constructed a machine based on the designs for Babbage's Difference Engine. This machine printed mathematical, astronomical, and actuarial tables with unprecedented accuracy for the British and American governments.

In 1856, Babbage conceived the Analytical Engine, a general symbol manipulator that would perform any kind of calculation. Although he devoted most of his time and fortune to this machine, he never succeeded in manufacturing any of several designs. Babbage died in 1871. His work was continued by his son, Henry Prevost Babbage, but he achieved only a partial Analytical Engine that ran a few programs with obvious errors.

From 1985 to 1991, the Science Museum in London constructed Difference Engine Number 2 from Babbage's original designs, in time for the bicentennial of Babbage's birth. The device consists of 4,000 parts, weighs over 3 metric tons, and works as Babbage intended.

Source: University of Minnesota, n.d.

External Deadlines Versus Self-Discipline

Sometimes the researcher has some control over the end date. For instance, some degree programs allow students to choose either a thesis for honors over two academic terms or a thesis without honors over one term.

Conversely, some projects are specified with end dates that are beyond the researcher's control. For instance, a course of instruction is normally bounded by the academic term of instruction.

Sometimes the end date is negotiable. For instance, a sponsor may offer to fund all your costs if you commit to deliver within one year, but you might balk at the rush and offer to deliver within two years and to accept funds worth half the costs.

Sometimes you should refuse any deadline. This may be righteous if you are sufficiently self-disciplined and competent to deliver eventually and if all authorities or sponsors would impose an impossibly early end date. This is a risky choice and one that is open to abuse by arrogant or self-righteous researchers. Early in your career, likely you are not competent enough to disagree with experts. However, the history of creativity and industrial psychology have shown that some mavericks can prove the consensus wrong.

In practice, many professional researchers engage in both types of project—one project with an end date and another project without an end date, often at the same time. They may be researching something that is judged important or interesting enough for someone to sponsor it, with the caveat that the sponsor has imposed an end date by which the project must deliver. At the same time, they may be working on a personal project that others do not judge as important or interesting enough to justify sponsorship, so the researchers enjoy the luxury of taking their time, but they face the pitfalls of working without external deadlines and resources.

Developing a Research Question

If you have applied the advice so far in this chapter to your own research idea, you should have a much better vision of your research, but you still face a key test: Can you pose your proposed research as a question? Imagine that someone wants to study success in the workplace; a simple way to convert that topic into a question would be to ask, "Why do some people succeed in the workplace?"

Why Pose a Research Question?

Posing a question is useful because it helps to expose the justifiability and feasibility of your research. Posing a question is always more disciplined than simply posing a statement. For instance, at one university I once saw a poster advertising a talk titled "Some Thoughts on Parliament." This is an ill-disciplined offer, since the speaker is free to ramble on about any random thoughts about any Parliament and still claim to fulfill the title. Reading the poster's title, you have little idea about the talk's scope, value, or feasibility. If the talk had been reframed as a question, it would have been more disciplined and easier to justify and communicate. For instance, the title could have been posed as any of the following: "Is a Parliament the best form of legislature?" "Why do we have a Parliament?" "How popular is Parliament?"

Posing a question gives you and your consumers a better vision of what you need to do to fulfill your research. For instance, if you titled your research something like "The Problem of Disease," most people could agree that disease is a problem but remain unsure about whether you would be describing the history of the problem or proposing solutions to the problem. Your research question could be either "What is the risk of this disease?" or "How can we treat the disease?" When developed into questions, the topics are more clearly differentiated and finer: The first question is more descriptive, while the second is more prescriptive, theoretical, and applied.

When you come to write the title of your project or product, you may decide to place some of the specificity in the question and some in the following text, as in "What Causes Immigration? The Case of Malawi, 2000–2009." This question, combined with the following text, has behavioral, spatial, and temporal boundaries.

Your title may end up without any question, but must imply a question that your research will answer. For instance, your eventual title might become "Causes of Immigration in Malawi in the 2000s." Such a title is derived by first expressing the research as a question. This title essentially communicates the same scope as "What Causes Immigration? The Case of Malawi, 2000–2009."

Practical Advice Box 4.4
Two Justifications of Research Questions

"Why does it matter whether or not you have a research question? *Because you cannot do research without it.* If you try to do research without a research question, you will only end up with the Damnation of the Ten Thousand Index Cards, a lot of frustration, and—*if you are lucky*—a lousy research project. The other problem is that without a question you can't do theory, because without a question you can't explain" (Luker, 2008, p. 54, emphases in original).

"For collectors of intelligence, as for those in many other fields, the key to success is to *ask the right question.* But how do you, the analyst, know what the right question is? You don't have the knowledge that a collector has. He or she always can do things that you cannot imagine. So the collector has to understand what you really want (and therefore he or she is in the same position with respect to you that you are with respect to the customer). The solution is to share not only what you need but also why you need it." (Clark, 2013, p. 147, emphases in original)

How Should You Write Your Question?

Expressing your topic as a question is one step—you should then make sure that the question is well expressed. As explained in subsections below, a research question should be as much of the following as possible:

- Causal
- Specific
- Unambiguous
- Falsifiable

Causal

A causal question asks whether something causes something else. "Does this pathogen cause that disease?" is an example.

Look for a relationship between two things and ask whether one causes the other. Look for some behavior or attribute or quality that interest you. What causes it? What does it cause?

Imagine that someone is interested in high infant mortality within a society. This observation could be studied as a cause or an effect. What causes the infant mortality? What societal effects are caused by the infant mortality?

Imagine that you observe high immigration into that society. What causes that immigration? What effects are caused by that immigration?

Specific

The question should be as specific as possible. Something is **specific** if it is clearly defined or identified.

The question's specificity can be derived from good scoping. You should narrow your question's scope just as you have narrowed your topic. You could begin with a question such as "What causes immigration?" This is a very explicit question, but the implied scope is enormous (all immigration, anywhere, at any time). You could narrow the time and space of that question by asking, "What causes immigration in Malawi this decade?"

The most likely problem in a research question is an implied scope that is larger than intended. For instance, if you titled your project "How do we solve Africa's issues?," a reader would be left wondering whether you meant Africa's economic, political, social, medical, or other issues. The reader would doubt that you could answer a question with such enormous scope.

Practical Advice Box 4.5
Turning an Issue Into a Research Question

Think about the scope of your research project. What is the key question that your research will attempt to answer? Identify an issue, then turn it into a question (see Table 4.2).

Table 4.2   Turning an issue into a research question

Type of Issue	Types of Questions	Example Issue	Example Question
Interpretation of fact	Did it happen? What happened?	Consumers, food manufacturers, and the government blame each other for the obesity epidemic.	Which side is most responsible for obesity?
Cause	Does X cause Y? Why does it happen?	More people are becoming obese.	Are sugary or fatty diets most responsible for obesity?
Puzzle	What is the explanation for the anomaly? Why is X present in this case but not in the other?	Some professional athletes would be categorized as obese by conventional measures of body mass.	What would be a better measure of obesity?
Difference or contrast	What two things should be the same but are different? Why does one thing differ from another?	Men suffer more ill health in old age and die younger than women.	Does obesity explain the higher rate of ill health in men?
Policy	Is the policy effective? Which would be the best policy? How should the organization respond?	Obesity is becoming more prevalent despite more official warnings.	Why are official advisories on diet and exercise ineffective?
Theory	Which is the best explanation? Does the theory explain new facts?	Obesity is more prevalent in certain ethnic groups.	Does the ethnic group's culture or genetics best explain obesity?
Judgment	Is it right or wrong? Should it be done?	Some people resist official interference in their personal consumption.	Should the government tell people what to eat?

Your research question or title should ideally contain the following information about the scope:

1. Time (such as the duration of a policy war, political administration, leader's life, or treaty's period of enforcement)

2. Space (such as the geographical boundaries)

3. Level (such as national as opposed to international)

4. Behavior or activity (such as treaty-making, voting, fishing, urban development, trading, etc.)

A well-specified question contains its scope within the adjectives and nouns. For instance, the question "Does the Vietnam War affect U.S. foreign policy today?" is clear about time (the period of the Vietnam War and today), space (the United States), level (national level), behavior or activity (foreign policy), and causal relationship (the Vietnam War is a potential cause; U.S. foreign policy is a potential effect).

A research question or title cannot include all the specifications of your scope. You face a trade-off between overspecifying the first research question or title until it becomes too unwieldy and reads more like a paragraph than a sentence, and underspecifying the first research question or title so that it seems impossible to clarify or achieve. You should use the first section of your product (the introduction to your project) to specify further whatever you mean by your research question or title.

Unambiguous

The question should be unambiguous. Something is ambiguous if it could have more than one meaning or interpretation. Ambiguous research questions or titles arise when they are underspecified, as shown above. Ambiguity arises, too, if we use words or concepts with multiple meanings or contested definitions. For instance, if we were to propose to write about "Israeli society," we would literally be proposing to write about all of Israeli society, including Jews, Arabs, and every other identity within the society associated with the State of Israel. Since societal boundaries are often contested, and Israeli society is a highly contested society, we should clarify our scope by adding explanatory words to our title to produce, for instance: "Arab–Israeli society," "Jewish–Israeli society," or "Israeli society: Jewish, Arab, and other identities."

Some words may seem unambiguous on one dimension but ambiguous on another. For instance, if you titled your project "How Will Arab Society

Change?," then your reader could wonder whether your scope covers the Arabs of the Arabian Peninsula, the Arabs of Africa, or Arabs everywhere. In this case, you should lengthen the title to include the geographical boundaries of your scope, such as "How will Arab society change in the Gulf Arab states?"

Be aware, too, that some words that are common in social scientific titles unfortunately have many meanings. For instance, if you refer to a **state**, you could be referring to a sovereign state (recognized by the United Nations and most members as sovereign), or one of the constituent states within the United States of America, or the particular condition or situation that something is in at a particular time. When using such words that have multiple meanings, you need to clarify the meaning with adjectives or context.

Some words are common or acceptable within very particular fields or theories but not elsewhere, so if you were to use such words, you would appear to be aligning yourself with the particular field against others who might object. For instance, among traditionalists and instrumentalists, philosophy is a useful approach, but positivists find it too intangible to be useful and to be loaded with theoretical and methodological implications. If you use the word *philosophy* in your research question or title, you should realize that you are aligning yourself with those who find it useful and possibly alienating people who otherwise would have been interested in your research.

Unambiguous words are those with clear opposites: good and bad; effective and ineffective; right and wrong; legal and illegal; useful and useless. You should try to use such words in your research question or title—as in "Is U.S. immigration policy effective?," "Is U.S. immigration policy right?," or "Is U.S. immigration policy legal?" Each question clearly lies within the scope of U.S. immigration, but each is a different and unambiguous question. Respectively, they are questions about effectiveness, ethics, and legality.

No word can be perfectly unambiguous, so you should not become petrified trying to achieve unambiguity. For instance, if you asked whether one particular leader was a significant cause of ethnic tension, we would be left to wonder how you would define the difference between a significant and insignificant cause, but that definition could be acceptably clarified in the introduction to your project rather than in the research question or title.

Falsifiable

On scientific principles, a research question should be **falsifiable**, meaning that it can be disproven. If something is not falsifiable then you could neither prove nor disprove it. For instance, take the question "If a tree fell in the woods, but nobody was around to hear it and nothing was around to record the sound, did it make a sound?" This is an empirically unfalsifiable question because the premises preclude any measurement of the sound. It is still theoretically falsifiable, since we could prove or disprove it by argument (see Chapter 7).

Some questions are described as unfalsifiable when their concepts are intangible. For instance, many social scientists have criticized sociologists and political theorists who describe everything as the result of "power," because power is too intangible or too poorly operationalized for us to really know whether power determines anything.

Describing, Justifying, Planning, and Proposing the Research

Having settled on your topic, you are in a position to describe or prescribe it in some formal way—in order to petition for permission to proceed or for funding, say.

The medium could be a verbal proposal or a visually represented presentation, but it is usually a written document. This document could be as short as one page at the undergraduate level, but it could range to hundreds of pages at the higher commercial and official levels.

For your own purposes or others, you should proceed by:

1. Describing the scope

2. Justifying the project

3. Planning the project

4. Proposing the project for authorization or support

Describe Your Scope

In any document relating to your project, you must first describe the scope of your project. This description could be titled "Project Scope." This description is sometimes less accurately titled as the "Terms of Reference," "Statement of the Purpose," "Statement of the Problem," "Problem Definition," "Definitions and Limitations," or "Specifications."

Whatever the title, such a description should include at least:

- The research question

- The puzzle, problem, issue, or dispute from which your research question arises

- The relevant disciplines, professions, or fields within which your scope lies

- Your focus within these disciplines

- The boundaries of your scope

Justify Your Project

In addition to specifying your scope, you should justify your project by explaining:

- Why your research is interesting to a wider audience

- Why your research is important

- What your research would improve

- What your research would challenge

- What gap in knowledge your research would fill

Plan Your Project

A **plan** or **design** is a scheme for how to achieve something. The description and justification can be developed into a *research plan* or *research design*, where the added elements include:

- A review of the existing theories, practices, or policies that could solve or resolve the problem, issue, or dispute

- Your preferred theory, practice, or policy

- A review of methods available to prove your preference

- Your preferred method

- Your plan to execute this method

- A schedule for the rest of the project upon approval

Propose Your Project

A **research proposal** is a plan of research submitted as a petition for external approval or support. A good research manager or instructor will demand a formal research proposal before authorizing the research to proceed.

A research proposal should include a description of the scope, a justification of the project, and a plan for the project, before adding descriptions of:

- Its feasibility

- Your outstanding needs, demands, requests, or petitions

- What you are requesting from the recipient of your proposal

Since a research proposal or plan is usually submitted in pursuit of something, such as approval or funding, each proposal must specify what it is that you want, such as approval to proceed with your preferred theory or method, or funding to help defray the costs of traveling to a particular archive or interviewee.

CHAPTER SUMMARY

This chapter has taught you how to:

- Use a scope
  - o To guide your activities
  - o To discipline yourself
  - o To reduce your burden
  - o To communicate your research to others
- Scope your topic according to:
  - o Established academic or professional boundaries
  - o Geographical or spatial boundaries
  - o Human or social boundaries
  - o Temporal boundaries
  - o Your focus

- Explain the value of your research as:
  - o Interesting
  - o Important
    - o Consequential
    - o Salient
    - o Fashionable
    - o Practically employable or applicable
    - o Policy-relevant
  - o Improving
  - o Challenging
  - o Resolving gaps in knowledge

- Explain your project's feasibility in terms of:
  - Your capacity
  - Social resources
  - Institutional resources
  - Time available
- Develop your research question and make it as much of the following as possible:
  - Causal
  - Specific
  - Unambiguous
  - Falsifiable
- Describe your scope
- Justify your project
- Plan your project
- Propose your project

KEY TERMS

Applicable 69
Belief 62
Bias 58
Capacity 77
Consequential 65
Culture 62
Design 92
Disciplines 60
Employable 69
Falsifiable 90
Fashionable 67
Field 60

Framing 58
Fungible 81
Institution 62
Intentional 70
Justification 63
Liberalism 74
Norm 62
Organization 62
Plan 92
Policy 70
Prescriptive 70
Realism 74

Research proposal 93
Salient 66
Scope 55
Scoping 55
Social and organizational
    psychology 61
Specific 87
State 90
Subfield 60
Temporal 62
Value 62

QUESTIONS AND EXERCISES

Think of your own prospective project:

1. Write a research question. How could the research question be more causal, more specific, less ambiguous, and more falsifiable?

2. What are the boundaries?
   a. Academic and professional boundaries?
   b. Geographical or spatial boundaries?
   c. Human or social boundaries?
   d. Temporal boundaries?
   e. Disciplinary boundaries?

3. Is it important?
   a. How is it consequential?
   b. How is it salient?
   c. How is it fashionable?
   d. How is it practically employable?
   e. How is it policy-relevant?

4. What would it improve, challenge, or resolve?

Reading and Reviewing

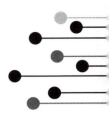

Opening Vignette: Savor Your Reading

Regan Forer

"As an undergrad, I have found it is important to view reading assignments not as a burdensome chore, but as an opportunity; as an occasion to be savored and celebrated. With assignments piling up from a slew of classes each semester, reading can sometimes feel more like a task than like the fortuity it actually is. When I begin to feel overwhelmed by the daunting load of texts allocated, I remind myself to step outside of just viewing reading as an assignment to be checked off of a list, and remember that each text, each sentence, is a gifted moment, in which I am given the chance to drink in something I didn't previously have: a bit of knowledge; an emotional response; a new intriguing word; even an 'ah-ha' moment. All of this is a reminder that reading is, in fact, not the enemy, but rather one of the greatest nonpareils life has to offer." (Regan Forer is majoring in conservation and resource studies at the University of California, Berkeley, class of 2015.)

Learning Objectives and Outcomes

At the end of this chapter, you should be able to:

1. Read efficiently

2. Analyze content

3. Select, categorize, prioritize, and record sources

4. Write a review of a source

Sources

This section will explain sources, how to prioritize sources in general, secondary sources, and primary sources.

What Are Sources?

Your **sources** are the things from which you get your information.

When we discuss sources, we commonly imagine **books** and journal **articles**. Academics tend to discuss the "literature" as if all their sources were written texts. Indeed, in academic research, most of your sources likely will be written texts. A library is the best first stop for such sources (see Practical Advice Box 5.1).

Yet sources range beyond just written texts. A text could be found on all sorts of media: paper, plastic, even stone, as well as on an Internet site or inside a computer program. Your sources can extend beyond texts. Already, you likely get information from friends and other interpersonal contacts, interviewees or respondents, social media, news media, and even your own observations. In some projects, researchers spend more time with pieces of art, architecture, living organisms, geographical features, or artifacts, although they likely spend some time reading about these things too.

Tertiary Sources

Tertiary sources are guides to other sources. For instance, an encyclopedia is useful for looking up facts or tracing other sources related to that fact, but is probably otherwise not worthy of citation—it will direct you to other sources, without serving as a direct source for anything you will write into your own

Table 5.1 Examples of primary, secondary, and tertiary sources			
Scope	**Primary**	**Secondary**	**Tertiary**
Automobiles	A specific model and make of car	A book about the supplier of the car	An encyclopedia of cars
Trees	Genetic material from an extinct tree	A journal article that tries to place the tree in a genus	A guide to research on trees
Art	A piece of pottery	A biography of the potter	A webpage with a guide to sources on pottery

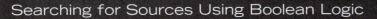

©iStockphoto.com/AmmentorpDK

Online libraries and other digital databases usually allow you to search for sources using Boolean logic, meaning that you can insert the following words or characters to define your search:

- AND: The system will search for more than one term. For instance, if you want to find sources on egg-laying mammals that live in Australia, you can type *egg AND mammal AND Australia*.

- OR: The system will search for any term in a list. For instance, if you want to find sources on something with more than one spelling, you can type *color OR colour*.

- NOT: The system will search for a term while excluding any sources that contain something else. For instance, if you want to find sources on the island of Java but are tired of finding sources on Java-type coffees, you can type *Java NOT coffee*.

- BETWEEN: The system will search for a term found between two other terms. For instance, imagine that you remember a title of a book as something like "the development of the island of Java in the nineteenth century." You could type *Java BETWEEN development AND nineteenth*.

- Parentheses or brackets: The system will report on records that fulfill instructions within the parentheses before reporting on whatever fulfills instructions outside the parentheses. For instance, imagine that you are most interested in sources about Java's economic development but realize that some sources about Java's history may refer to its economic development too. You could type *(Java AND economic) OR Java history*.

- Quotation marks: Putting a phrase within quotation marks will prompt the system to search for the exact phrase, with the words in the same order and with the same spelling. For instance, if you are interested in finding titles containing the phrase *island of Java*, then simply type that phrase within quotation marks.

- Note that you can combine any of the options above. For instance, if you want to find a source of a certain title ("the color of Java"), in either of two spellings, while excluding sources on coffee, you could type *"the color of Java" OR "the colour of Java" NOT coffee*.

product. Sometimes tertiary sources are explicit guides for further research. Others are interesting or useful in their own right, but effectively most useful to you as tertiary sources.

Secondary Sources

In most reviews, you should start by reviewing secondary sources. **Secondary sources** derive their information from primary sources or secondary sources, but are not themselves the ultimate sources of information (i.e., primary sources; see Table 5.1).

These categories sometimes overlap in the same source. For instance, a source may report mostly what primary sources have reported, in which case it is mostly a secondary source. In the process, the author could reveal some personal experience, for which it is the primary source.

The following sources are likely to be mostly secondary:

- Reviews of other sources

- Official reports

- Dissertations and theses

- Conference proceedings

In most of your reading, you should start with secondary sources that explicitly review other secondary sources before you choose which other sources to read.

Furthermore, early in your project your purposes are mostly related to exploring the topic, choosing a topic, reviewing the theories, reviewing the methods, and reviewing the potential sources of data. These purposes are served mostly by secondary sources.

Later in the project you will be looking for data to check on the secondary sources' interpretations or to test a theory. To code your own data, you would read mostly primary sources, but a secondary source that introduces the primary sources is still a good read before identifying the primary sources.

Official reports are often secondary sources, as they typically review government activities or performance and report data that have been reported to the government. Official reports are sometimes primary sources if they directly report a government's opinion, intention, or activity. Policy documents and notes on meetings and so forth are certainly primary sources.

Academic dissertations and theses are almost always wholly secondary sources. They typically review other literature and gather data from other sources. However, where the author reports a personal experience, such as a personal observation of a crime while studying how police forces counter crime, we have a primary source. Most dissertations and theses gather data from subjects, such as the victims who experienced the crime, and report these data in a summary way, in which case they are clearly secondary. If we wanted the primary sources, we would need to request them from the author. In some secondary sources, authors may include a transcript of an interview with a primary actor or report their direct observations of the interviewee; that transcript and those observations are primary, even though the rest of the document is a secondary source.

Conference proceedings are almost always entirely secondary sources, as they usually report what others reported at the conference. These proceedings are not particularly useful unless they reproduce a source that cannot be found elsewhere. The information reported is usually who attended a conference and what they said. Sometimes only a précis or summary of what they said is reported, although sometimes whole speeches or presentations are reproduced. Anything said as a personal experience would count as primary; the rest is probably secondary.

Primary Sources

Primary sources are the ultimate origins of information. They report direct observations or experiences rather than reporting information from other sources.

The following sources are likely to be mostly primary:

- Letters, emails, and other personal correspondence

- Personal diaries, schedules, journals, and sign-in records

- Memoirs

- Notes, minutes, recordings, or transcripts of interviews, conversations, meetings, and court proceedings

- Logs or records

- Orders

- Policies

- Manuals

- Photographs, moving pictures, and other images

- Advertisements and other trade material

- Artifacts

- Archaeology

Personal diaries, schedules, and journals are likely to be the purest of your primary sources, because they are likely to be written closest in time to the described events. A personal diary or schedule could record the timing, participants, and purpose of activities for the day ahead. Someone could record in a diary or journal what happened in the day past. Some sites, organizations, and persons keep signing-in books to record visitors and their purposes or hosts.

Sometimes these sources have turned out to be fake, such as diaries in which criminals record fake activities as alibis, or schedules for businesses that are fronts for ulterior organizations. Sometimes primary sources are forged for personal gain. For instance, in April 1983, a German magazine (*Stern*) followed by a British newspaper (*The Times*) published extracts from diaries supposedly written by Adolf Hitler, who had led the Nazi Party and Germany from 1933 to 1945. Two academic historians (Hugh Trevor-Roper from Britain and Gerhard Weinberg from America) declared the material to be authentic, while retained by *The Times*, but within the month others pointed out historical inaccuracies in the content and medium. In 1984, the forger (Konrad Kujau) and his accomplice (the journalist Gerd Heidemann) were convicted of forgery and embezzlement.

Letters and emails are primary sources when the author describes his or her personal experiences or feelings. Letters and emails are likely to be written very close in time to whatever the author is describing and to be uncorrupted by coauthors or intermediaries. Having said that, a letter may be written decades after the event, by someone reporting hearsay, in which case it should not be described as primary.

Memoirs are primary sources because they are personal recollections. However, memoirs may be written long after the event and be corrupted by intervening events, biases, motivations, and decaying memory (see Research in the Real World Box 5.1).

Notes, minutes, audio recordings, and transcripts are primary records of what was said at meetings, conferences, interviews, and court proceedings.

Activities may be recorded in activity logs. Policies and strategies are evidence for what an organization intended to do. Manuals and standard operating procedures are evidence for how its members are supposed to behave.

Note that some primary sources are not texts. Photographs and moving pictures are primary sources in that they record images from the camera's perspective. Cameras are persuasive instruments, because they record visual images, which human beings find more recognizable and memorable than information that they read or hear. Cameras are objective primary sources in the sense that they have no mind of their own, but their images can be misleading because of their narrow scope and the unrecorded choices made by the camera operators—unrecorded choices such as what to include within their narrow scope, what images to take, and what images to delete. Worse, image-editing software programs can be used to manipulate images.

Drawings and paintings are primary sources if the artist is depicting something seen personally, but the artist can add much imagination to the images without the imaginative parts being obvious to the viewer. Images are entirely secondary when the artist is depicting something entirely imagined. To the uninformed viewer, an entirely imagined image looks similar to an entirely honest image.

Advertisements and other trade material are primary sources in that they show the information that the actor cared to advertise—information such as what the organization was advertising, the prices that the organization was charging for something, the organization's representatives, or what the organization was developing.

Artifacts are the physical and materials things left over from some process. For instance, industrial processes lead to products, geological processes leave behind rocks and soils, biological processes leave behind waste, and almost any human activity leaves behind something physical or material. Sometimes the term *artifact* is used to mean a by-product, such as slag, which is a by-product from the smelting of metals from ores. Slag can reveal the materials with which past humans were working, their processes for smelting, and their productivity. These artifacts can be used as sources on their own merit. Pottery reveals the materials available to the potters, their technology, their art, and even the things that they cared to contain in pottery.

Archaeology is a collection of artifacts or the study of artifacts. An **archaeologist** is a person who professionally studies human history and history by examining physical artifacts. For instance, digging through the detritus of human habitation reveals what people once threw away as surplus or as worthless, what they

Research in the Real World Box 5.1

The Accuracy of Churchill's Memoirs

Source: http://commons.wikimedia.org/wiki/File:Winston_Churchill_cph.3b12010.jpg.

Winston Churchill

Winston Churchill (1874–1965) is most famous for serving as Britain's prime minister from May 1940 to May 1945. Churchill's reputation is still based largely on inspiring wartime speeches and his postwar memoir, inaccurately marketed as a history (*The Second World War*, six volumes, 1948–1953).

Churchill left the premiership with an extraordinary agreement from the cabinet secretary for all his official papers to be classified as his property and transferred to his home. His memoir (about 2 million words) reproduced some of these official documents, decades before they were available anywhere else.

Along the way Churchill criticized many of his peers, without admitting their perspective. None of the official documents were released to the public until the 1960s at the earliest, by which time his version was dominant. Since then, comparison of archival material with the material that Churchill had chosen to publish has exposed Churchill's dishonest representations (Reynolds, 2004).

consumed, their health as revealed by their feces, and the flora and fauna in their environment, including the foods that they farmed and the parasites that lived inside them.

Prioritizing Sources

In what order should you read sources? Often people describe a source as "good" or "bad" without much explanation or justification. Some subjectivity is inevitable and allowable; we should allow people to have some feeling about a source before they can articulate their reason. However, an unjustified opinion should be less persuasive than a well-reasoned argument or observation.

We should choose the source by time of completion, authoritativeness, credibility, rigor, and robustness, as described in the subsections below.

Time of Completion

The time of completion has implications for the source's authenticity and comprehensiveness. The implications for primary and secondary sources run in converse directions. Primary sources (the ultimate origins of information) produced closer in time to the events that they describe are likely to be more authentic than primary sources produced later in time. Conversely, secondary sources (which report information from primary or secondary sources) produced more recently are likely to be more comprehensive and up-to-date with the latest revelations.

Consider primary sources first. Generally, we should use the source that was produced soonest after the event. If someone experiences an event, his or her most accurate account should be the one he or she recorded immediately, not later, after memory has faded or has been corrupted by intervening events and biases. Effectively, memoirs are partially fictionalized by imperfect recall, self-censorship, social censure, and official censorship.

Sometimes an author produces more than one source of the same information. For instance, a politician could take notes during a negotiation between other politicians; later that same politician could write a memoir about the negotiation. Which source should you use? The politician's notes during the event are likely to be more accurate than his memoir after the event. In fact, his memoir may be based solely on the notes. The memoir may add some details from memory that were not in the notes, in which case we should be reading both the notes and the memoir so that we will get the most complete understanding, but where the notes and the memoir contradict each other we should trust the notes.

Now consider secondary sources. While primary sources should have been produced as close in time as possible to the thing being studied, secondary sources should be as recent as possible so that they are informed by all the literature to date. An older source had the opportunity to review only preceding sources.

For most purposes, the timing of production is indicated by the date of publication, although production precedes publication. Normally, a book is printed within a year of receipt of a text from the author. Normally the author completes that text within months of submission, although the text may have been in production for years. Thus, most sources are current to within a couple of years of publication. However, you should take some care with your dating of a text's currency. Some texts may have been written years, decades, or even centuries before publication. For instance, an author might write a memoir but forbid publication until after death. An author might keep a diary that is discovered centuries after his or her death. Some texts appear to be published recently, but are actually reprints of much older publications. Some authors may have published recently but have read only the oldest sources.

Authoritativeness

Something is **authoritative** if it is derived from a higher authority. An **authority** is an entity with the right or capacity to make decisions, judgments, or orders. For instance, organizations can authoritatively state their own policies; courts judge whether crimes were or were not committed.

Authoritativeness can be contested. Entities may claim superior expertise, jurisdiction, or rights. You must judge the authoritativeness of your sources. Where you cannot find evidence to support your own judgment either way, you will be forced to review other people's judgments, which in turn can mean reviewing their authoritativeness, so an investigation into one source can turn into a much wider and deeper investigation.

Researchers can judge authoritativeness by either formal authorization or normative acceptance.

Formal Authorization. Some authorities have clear formal, constitutional, or normative mandates. Governments pass legislation that authorizes courts to adjudicate criminal and civil cases; these courts then grant property rights, child custody, and other grants that are effectively authorizations.

Some international institutions are more authoritative than national governments. For instance, the International Committee of the Red Cross (ICRC) is the highest authority on what constitutes torture, as agreed by several international conventions dating back to the 19th century. In February 2007, the ICRC reported to the U.S. government that its treatment of some alleged terrorist suspects amounted to torture, while the U.S. government of the time denied torture. The ICRC was the highest authority, so on that basis alone many commentators accepted the ICRC's judgment. The ICRC's authoritativeness was confirmed by other investigators and a new U.S. political administration that took over in 2008, which repudiated the previous administration's treatment of terrorist suspects and described some of the treatment as torture.

Normative Acceptance. Sometimes some actors are normatively accepted as most authoritative. A *norm* is something that a majority accepts as true, or a behavior that a majority practices. A community that has always treated some actor as most authoritative has effectively established a norm that the actor is authoritative, without conferring any formal authority. The actor's authoritativeness is thus normative rather than legal or institutional. Such normative grants of authoritativeness are justified, when an expert proves his or her expertise gradually through a series of well-received—and acknowledged—demonstrations of expertise. For instance, a historian may publish a series of well-argued and well-proven books on a certain topic, on the basis of which the community of historians may treat that person as the expert on that topic.

However, the system does not work when authoritativeness is conferred without objective justification, or where it outlasts the expertise. For instance, many art historians have complained that the art community still accepts only one authority's authentication of works by a certain artist, long after new evidence comes to light debunking some of the items on the list or proving that some items are missing from the list. The difference between an item on the list or off the list can mean the difference between a priceless work of art and a worthless work of art.

Credibility

Credibility is the extent to which a source should be believed. Just because an organization is formally superior to another in hierarchical terms does not mean that it is not mistaken or biased or otherwise incredible. For instance, an account by a witness is more credible than an account by someone who was not there, because the witness's presence grants him or her direct knowledge and thus credibility regarding what happened. An organization may have authority over the individual and claim that the individual has no authority to judge, but the organization is not credible if it is not there to bear witness.

Lower personnel who report on malpractice are less authoritative in strictly hierarchical terms, but are more credible than their superiors where they are reporting on something within their direct observation, have less reason to be biased, and have more technical expertise than their superiors. Their report is more credible in the sense of their being in a better position to know or have a more objective frame of mind to judge.

Such people are granted extra credibility when they take risks to make their reports, such as the chance of punishment by their superiors. Some laws protect such people from retaliation. Such people are often known as "whistle-blowers," and thus the laws are known as "whistle-blower protections."

In general, being more directly connected with activities suggests more credibility. For these reasons, officials are often assumed to offer more authoritative reports on official activities. The government should be best placed and more capable of reporting on what it is doing.

However, just because an actor is more directly connected to its own activities does not mean that it cannot be biased. Officials have many self-interested reasons to mislead, albeit sometimes unconsciously. At worst, official reports are deliberately misleading. In fact, many governments commission reports to give a one-sided view or to forestall more critical reports. Conversely, many critics of governments are given more credibility than the governments themselves, until the biases of these critics are revealed. You must navigate carefully between these extremes (see Practical Advice Box 5.2).

Rigorous and Robust

A source is **rigorous** if it has been prepared carefully or in accordance with applicable standards. Research is **robust** if it survives challenges or new tests.

Unfortunately, both terms (rigorous and robust) have been abused, particularly in politics, so that they have lost some of their true meaning and weight. You can still use these terms in their scientific senses, but you should define them when you use them, to remind your audience of what they really mean.

Rigor implies credibility and, more importantly, quality. You can make your own judgments about another source's rigor, but such judgments can become highly technical, so you probably should review others' judgments first or educate yourself in the technical skills necessary to form your own technical judgment.

To maintain standards of quality, a common practice is **peer review**—this means subjecting the product to review by the author's peers before passing the product for release. The author's **peers** are people of similar rank, training, or expertise. Academic journals commonly send submissions for review by peers before deciding whether to publish an article. Publishers of more academically oriented books also usually send submissions for peer review before publication (see Research in the Real World Box 5.2). The expectation of peer review motivates the author to be more rigorous; the peers could make suggestions that improve the product's rigor.

Generally, you should have more confidence in sources that were sent for peer review before publication, and less confidence in sources that were prepared by an author who never consulted anyone before publication.

However, some publishers are incestuous, with all the reviewers coming from a very narrow circle that tends to approve friends, political supporters, or advocates of narrow theoretical or methodological interests. Their publications, although peer-reviewed, are likely to be of narrower interest or lower quality than publications with more credible reviewers. The difference

Practical Advice Box 5.2
Evaluating Human Sources

Source: Medioimages/Photodisc/Thinkstock.

"Accept nothing at face value. Evaluate the source of evidence

carefully and beware of the source's motives for providing the information. Evaluating the source involves answering three questions:

1. Is the source competent (knowledgeable about the information being given)?

2. Did the source have the access needed to get the information?

3. Does the source have a vested interest or bias?" (Clark, 2013, pp. 128–129)

between a credible publisher and an incestuous publisher is difficult to determine without good advice or experience, so this is one dilemma for which most of us need to develop our own awareness. Watch out for publishers whose products seem to share a political bias or whose authors mostly work together or are graduates of the same school. Watch out for newspapers whose editors or owners use the content to support a particular political party or ideology.

Anyone can engage in peer review. You may be an undergraduate student with no intention of submitting your product for publication, but if you want to improve its rigor, you should ask your peers to review it. Better still, you should ask people of greater expertise to review it, if they are willing.

How to Read Efficiently

In this section, you will learn the most basic of skills associated with **reading**, which is the process of interpreting writing. Writing is the visual representation of information. Literally, reading means using one's eyes to interpret writing, but

RAND's Statement on Its Peer Review Process

Source: https://www.flickr.com/photos/ajc1/673592
9719.

"Peer review is an integral part of all RAND research projects. Prior to publication, this document, as with all documents in the RAND monograph series, was subject to a quality assurance process to ensure that the research meets several standards, including the following: The problem is well formulated; the research approach is well designed and well executed; the data and assumptions are sound; the findings are useful and advance knowledge; the implications and recommendations follow logically from the findings and are explained thoroughly; the documentation is accurate, understandable, cogent, and temperate in tone; the research demonstrated understanding of related previous studies; and the research is relevant, independent, and balanced. Peer review is conducted by research professionals who were not members of the project team." (Hollywood, Snyder, McKay, & Boon, 2004, p. v)

The RAND Corporation is a private, not-for-profit corporation founded in 1948 with major funding from the United States Air Force. It is now home to several federally funded research and development centers. It publishes some of its products in the public domain. These are freely downloadable through its website: www.rand.org.

some writing can be read out loud or converted into spoken words by a machine so that the "reader" will receive the information via his or her ears, not his or her eyes. Some people prefer to read with their eyes and speak the words out loud to help their comprehension or retention.

The **literature** is a collection of discrete writings. Different collections of writings can be associated with different disciplines, domains, or subjects. For instance, we could talk about the literature on politics, the literature on American politics (a recognized field of political science), the literature on American presidents in general, or the literature on a particular American president.

Research would be difficult to imagine without some reading. Researchers typically read theories, opinions, studies, evidence, and methodological options.

Even when a researcher is writing, he or she must read in order to edit. Since most writing is intended for reading, good writing is difficult to imagine without thoughtful attention to reading.

Many students are intimidated by reading. This is unavoidable in quantitative terms; typically you must read volumes of material that few others would read for fun in order to truly master your scope. In the quantitative sense, reading is one task that you can excel at simply by being dedicated. Some experts are simply "well read."

Although you must dedicate yourself to reading for your research, reading does not need to be a hard slog through everything ever written on your topic. You can learn to be an efficient **reader**, not just a dedicated reader, although you cannot get away without dedication too.

In practice, perfect efficiency is impossible, so you should not kick yourself for reading something that turns out to be useless if it has claimed otherwise.

Practicalities aside, ideally speaking, an efficient reader:

1. Prioritizes the most useful and necessary readings

2. Gets what is needed from a single read-through

3. Understands the relationships between readings

4. Reads without bias

5. Records what might be useful for the rest of the research

Prioritize the Most Useful and Necessary Readings

You should not read only what you expected to find or agree with. *Bias* is favor toward something. **Selection bias** is an agent's biased selection of one thing over another. Selection bias can arise if you read only what is available, what you agree with, or what your friends have written. For instance, you would be wrong to claim to have reviewed the literature on capital punishment if you have presented the literature provided by either only advocates or only opponents of capital punishment, not both. Similarly, you would be wrong to claim to have reviewed the literature on socioeconomics if you have presented only the literature written by sociologists or only the literature written by economists.

You do not need to read everything (see Practical Advice Box 5.4). You do not need to read as if each source is equally necessary. You will be most efficient if you prioritize the readings in order of utility or necessity. You can identify the most useful and necessary readings by these two criteria:

1. The most pertinent readings for the moment of your project life cycle

2. The most directional readings for the moment

The most pertinent readings are those that are most relevant to the moment or stage you have reached in your particular project's life cycle. At the start of the project, you should be reading to identify your research scope. When trying to work out your own theory, you should be reading other people's theories. Later still, you should be reading about methods as you start to think about how you would test a theory. At another point you might be reading more descriptive readings in order to gather data from them.

Directional readings guide you to other readings that you should be reading next. At the start of the project, you will find most helpful any readings that introduce you to the literature and help you to choose the main readings within your scope. Some books are written explicitly to introduce the literature to the starting researcher. In reading one book, you should see references to other writings, perhaps with some description that will help you to decide whether you should read those other writings.

The order in which you read books affects your efficiency. Ideally, you will read from the general to the specific, each source gradually introducing you to more specialized knowledge and sources. If you were to start with something narrower than your scope and follow sources to more specialized books, you would not learn about the wider context.

Get What You Need the First Time

Choosing the most pertinent and directional readings will help you to get what you most need at any given moment. However, even given the right reading, you will still need to read it. At your most efficient, you would read only what you needed, read it once, understand it all, and not need to return to it. At worst, you would read the book aimlessly or distractedly, without understanding anything, despite returning to it repeatedly. The efficiency of your process of reading varies with your skills, intents, attentiveness, distractions, and so forth.

Fortunately, you can consciously improve the efficiency of your reading. For a start, do not automatically read anything from start to finish until you have

Source: ©iStockphoto.com/pixdeluxe.

1. Search for sources that could contribute to your research.

2. For each source, assign a separate piece of paper. On each piece of paper:

   a. Write the full citation

   b. Evaluate its time of completion, authoritativeness, credibility, rigor, and robustness, and code it as tertiary, secondary, or primary

   c. Summarize the content of the source

   d. Justify the value of the content to your research

   e. Estimate which part of your research product the source will contribute to

   f. List any sources that you have not accessed yet and should access before completing your search

3. Collect the sources that seem more introductory, such as general reviews of the history or issues of the subject. These sources are useful for the first or introductory part of your product. Stack them in a column on the left-hand edge of a table. Label this column "Introduction."

4. Distribute the other sources across other likely parts of your product. For each part, place a label on the table and arrange a column of sources below that label. Arrange the columns from left to right in the order that you would likely write them into your product. If you are unsure about what the parts should be, separate sources by approach (perhaps some are mostly theoretical, while others are mostly tests) or subject. Consider whether some of these subjects are subordinate to or narrower than other subjects (suggesting subordinate parts of your product).

5. Within each column, evaluate the sources in comparison to each other. Priorities should be placed toward the top of the column.

6. Which columns have more sources than others? What does this distribution reveal about your own search biases? Which columns need more sources?

identified what would be most useful to you. Imagine a thick book that describes the history of South America over two millennia. If your project covered South America in just the 16th century, you would not need to read across two millennia, although you might do it anyway just for fun or for contextual knowledge.

Sometimes we do read outside our scope in order to better place a narrow scope within a wider context. Sometimes our scope is actually wider than a superficial reading would suggest. For instance, if our project intends to explain the effects of events in the 16th century on South America's subsequent development, then our scope actually extends beyond the 16th century. Perhaps an event during the 16th century was heavily influenced by memories of events during the 15th century.

Whatever your scope, you will read most efficiently if you pick up a reading and search through it for the most pertinent or directional part. You may choose to read the whole from start to finish only if you trust that the writer has structured the whole in a way that is necessary to your understanding of the part. For instance, imagine that the author has focused narrowly on the effect of some obscure event on some country's development and has begun with a description of the context, the background of the event, and the event itself. Given such a sensible structure, probably you should read the whole. Ideally, all authors would properly structure their writings and write usefully and efficiently, in which case you should trust that you should read from start to finish. Unfortunately, some writing is inefficiently written and would be inefficient to read from start to finish. You are fairly self-interested and righteous when you fairly choose what to read.

Understand the Relationships Between Readings

One trick to understanding a reading is to understand how it relates to other readings. One reading might be a source for another; one might be the theoretical source, while another is the source of data; yet another might be the inspiration for the topic.

Sometimes readings are related to each other in a chronological chain. Imagine that one author writes a memoir, while another author uses that memoir and other memoirs as sources for a history of some group of people; a third author criticizes the second author for misinterpreting the memoir; a fourth author reviews the different interpretations of the group; and so on. Understanding the relationships between these writings helps us to describe them relative to each other. We could fairly describe the first writing as a

memoir, the second as a history, the third as a critical review, and the fourth as a wider review.

Understanding the relationships also helps us to decide what we should read next. If we read a memoir but are unsure how to interpret it, we can fairly look for a review of the memoir. When we read one interpretation of a group of people, we should look for different interpretations.

Understanding the relationships will help you to understand how to describe your own work: Is your current work describing, criticizing, reviewing, interpreting, testing, or something else?

Read Without Bias

Selection bias applies to your choices of readings and to the care with which you read within a reading. Selection bias is unfair to your sources because you end up reading a partial view or a biased view. You may be tempted to skip some text to speed up your reading, but you could miss important details of an argument or a case. Similarly, you might skip over some text with which you disagree, but you might also miss something that could change your mind.

Try to be aware of how you feel about what you are reading and of how your feelings might introduce bias. Be particularly mindful when reading arguments, nuances, and qualifiers that contradict your prior assumptions and biases; otherwise you might be unfairly dismissive or inattentive.

You should be mindful of your own disciplinary assumptions and biases. Your training in one particular discipline inevitably exposes you to that discipline's theories and methods and neglects those of other disciplines.

Your personal experiences, your politics, the views of your friends and family, and even your mood at the time of reading affect how you read.

Record What You Read That You Might Make Use Of

To be efficient, ideally you will not read anything more than you need. To be effective, ideally you will read everything that you need.

You can help yourself toward these ideals by recording as you read so that you can be informed about what to use:

- At the least, you should record sufficient information for you to find the source again (information such as the library's call number or a website) or to cite the source (information such as authorship, title, publisher, and place and year of publication).

- You could write your own summary or abstract of the source so that you can remind yourself of the content later.

- You could also record the value of the source to your research.

- During a literature review, particularly, you should record the source's sources so that you can decide what to read next (see Exercise Box 5.1 for suggestions about what to record about a source).

While you read, if you have ideas about how to utilize the source in your current research, you should record those ideas and the associated content. In practice, this usually involves taking notes about what you are reading. You should record the content with the chapter number or page numbers so that later you can find the information again and cite it accurately.

Some researchers record such information by:

- Marking the source pages and keeping the source as hand, although this is not ethical unless you own the source

- Photocopying the pages or scanning the pages into digital records

- Writing notes on paper or typing notes into a digital document

- Entering information into a spreadsheet or specialized software for managing citations or sources

- Entering the information directly into a draft of the project's final product, although the information may need to be edited or moved later

Content Analysis

Purpose

Content analysis is a systematic examination of the content of a source. The content is the ingredients, information, or message within the source. Content can be found in documents, speech, radio broadcasts, images, moving pictures (films and videos), games, and art. Each of these things is a **medium**—meaning a vehicle for the content.

Although all these things have content, that content varies in quantity and quality. The content may be unclear—it may be open to interpretation, so we should focus on tangible content. For instance, you might observe a piece of art that seems like a mass of colors—these colors and their materials are tangible content and are unlikely to be contested. **Art** is the expression or application of creative skill and imagination, especially through a visual medium such as painting or sculpture, or an activity with an aesthetic component requiring knowledge and skill (FrameNet, https://framenet.icsi.berkeley.edu).

The message is different from the content. The **message** is whatever the content is communicating. The message may be less clear than the content—in practice, the message is almost always interpretative. For instance, one person may interpret a photograph of civilian refugees escaping a natural disaster as a human tragedy while another interprets it as a human triumph. The message is in the eye of the beholder, as long as the creator of the source refuses to reveal the intended message. Even when the creator reveals his or her intent, others may claim to know better the creator's real intent or subconscious message. Some content may have been created without any intended message.

Method

Content analysis has two main approaches: conceptual analysis and relational analysis.

In **conceptual analysis**, we measure how many times particular concepts and related things appear in the content. Normally we are counting the frequency with which something appears within a bounded piece of content. You could be counting:

- Words

- Concepts

- Themes

You could also count the amount of text dedicated to a certain subject. Depending on your desired sensitivity, you could measure the amount in terms of:

- Words

- Sentences

- Paragraphs

- Pages

- Sections

- Chapters

Relational analysis is a little more involved. **Relational analysis** measures the relationships between concepts. Each relationship could be measured in terms of:

- The direction in which one item influences the other (for instance, "tree" and "lumber" has a direction from tree to lumber, not the other way around, because a tree can be turned into lumber—the tree comes first)

- The **sign**, that is, whether the items are positive or negative toward each other (for instance, if a text described both a critic and an advocate of a policy, you could code a negative relationship between the critic and the policy and a positive relationship between the advocate and the policy)

- The strength of the relationship (for instance, if a text described someone as generally positive toward a policy but critical of a part, then you could code the critic as mildly critical compared to another critic who hates the whole policy)

All content analysis must follow a process. A minimal process has the following six steps:

1. Identify what you want to find

2. Define the content in which you will be looking (the **sample content**)

3. Decide the type of analysis (usually a choice between conceptual and relational analysis)

4. Search for what you are looking

5. Code what you find (which means attaching some value to your observation, such as "small," "normal," "big")

6. Statistically summarize and analyze the data

Software is available to help with content analysis. You could use a simple spreadsheet with a term or word in each of the columns and a source in each of the rows. Where the columns and rows intersect, you would enter the number of times that the word or term appears in that source. Some software is especially designed for analyzing content—it can accept a sample content and produce various reports based on user-defined criteria.

You may be counting words or terms manually, which is overly burdensome with a lot of content. If you can get hold of some digital form of content, you should be able to use word-processing software to search for a word or term in the content. Some data on content are readily available. For instance, since 2010, Google has offered an online tool known as Ngram Viewer (https://books.google.com/ngrams) that allows the user to query the frequency with which a word or term is used in the books scanned by Google (Google claims to have scanned more than 5 million books, with years of publication from 1500 to 2008).

Official analysis of foreign news media became routine in the mid 20th century, and much of the resulting data is in the public domain, particularly from World War II and the Cold War, so the researcher is well provided with data on public news media content from these periods.

Analysis of advertising and marketing content has been routine for more than 70 years now. Although the resulting data tends to be most useful to marketers, some of the data can be used creatively by other researchers. For instance, sociologists and historians often study data on marketing content in order to track changing representations of different human groups and use the data as correlates of attitudes toward these different groups.

Content analysis is useful in research to measure:

- An author's or creator's foci or biases

- An author's or creator's influences

- An author's or creator's personality, attitudes, feelings, and so forth

- The authenticity of a source

- The audience's exposure to something

The subsections below explore these uses.

Foci and Biases

Content analysis can be used to measure bias or focus. Imagine that someone offers a new history of global politics. We could measure the number of times that the author mentions one region (such as Africa) versus another region (such as Asia) as evidence for the author's greater focus on African than Asian history.

Analysts could measure the content of all the newspapers in a country in order to measure a national newspaper bias, cultural bias, or official censorship.

Analysts sometimes measure the number of times that a news item is mentioned in one newspaper versus another as a correlate of each newspaper's bias or focus. Content analysis might reveal that one newspaper uses most of its content to report on domestic news, while another newspaper reports more on foreign news.

Analysts can look for the words used in association with a certain subject in order to measure how that subject is being represented. For instance, perhaps one newspaper uses more negative words when discussing Political Party A than when discussing Political Party B. This is evidence for the newspaper's favor toward B over A. If we found that all newspapers used more negative words toward A than B, then we would conclude that newspapers had reached consensus on the inferiority of A. Perhaps this consensus is due to general bias against A or to something objectively wrong with A.

Influences

Content analysis can be used to measure the influences on an author or creator. Imagine a theoretical text. We could measure the number of times that the author mentions one theorist's name versus another as evidence for the relative influence of the first theorist versus the second theorist. We could measure the number of times that the author mentions different observations so that we know which observations were most influential on the author's theory.

Personality

Content analysis can be used to measure the author's personality, attitudes, and feelings. Imagine an autobiographical text. We could measure the number of times that *anger*, *hate*, or similar words appear in the text, versus the number of times that *happiness*, *love*, or similar words appear. Such measurement provides evidence for the author's feelings and temperament. Perhaps we could analyze the words used by the author to describe an earlier part of his or her life versus the words used to describe a later part, in order to show the author's happier memories of one part versus the other. Perhaps we could compare two autobiographies written by the same person at different stages of his or her life as evidence for a change in the author's personality. Perhaps we could compare autobiographies by two different people to give evidence of their different personalities.

Authorship

Content analysis is sometimes used to prove authorship. For instance, from other evidence we might know that a certain writer wrote 10 books. Content analysis might reveal that the author used a peculiar set of words at a peculiar frequency in each of these books. Then someone might claim to have discovered an 11th book by the same author, but the authorship is contested. We could look for the same peculiar set of words and frequency as evidence that this book is by the same author.

Audience Exposure

Analysis of different media is useful for measuring an audience's exposure to different content. A simple research strategy is to analyze the content of official propaganda, official textbooks issued to students in public schools, or official statements. For instance, analysts have shown that people who live in Middle Eastern countries are exposed to much more religious content and much less sexual content than people living in the United States (Pew Research Center, 2013).

Reviews

This section explains how to understand and perform a review.

What Is a Review?

A **review** can be interpreted in two ways:

1. The process of examination

2. A report on something examined

In casual language, a review can mean a second look, a closer look, or a retelling. For instance, you might review a textbook or your notes when studying for an exam. You might return to a piece of art that you like. You might retell something that happened to you.

In commercial and consumerist situations, a review usually means an assessment of something's value or utility. For instance, probably you have told friends about a restaurant or television program that you liked or hated.

In academic discourse, normally a review is a review of sources, in which case the term *literature review* is often used, although this is an inaccurate term, because sources range further than just the written texts implied by the term *literature*. The term *literature review* is misleading, as it tells nothing about the purpose of the review. Simply reviewing literature would be purposeless, unless you were reading for fun or to stimulate identification of your purpose. Rather than thinking about reviewing literature in general, think about reviewing particular literature with a purpose in mind. A "literature review" should not be random, but should be a review of theory, knowledge, methods, or data.

In social science projects, you would conduct at least the following four reviews:

- At the start of the project, you should review potential topics, before choosing the topic of your project

- Having chosen your topic, you should review knowledge about the topic in order to identify the gap, dispute, or puzzle that justifies your project

- Before developing your own theory or choosing a theory, you should review the relevant theories

- Before choosing a method to test a theory, you should review methods

- In testing your theory, you should be reviewing data

Tone

The correct attitude to have toward your readings is objective and impersonal. Interrogate the content and be prepared to be fairly respectful or critical of the content on the basis of the content alone, not your preconceptions or feelings. This is what educators used to mean by **critical thinking** or **critical analysis**: fair engagement without any predetermined favor or disfavor ("clinical"). They did not mean that you should presume to be critical. You should respect the source's intended meaning, even if you disagree with it or it makes you uncomfortable.

When reporting your view, your tone should be objective and impersonal. You should not be deferential to the source out of misplaced respect for the source. You can report your disagreement—perhaps on the grounds of its lack of timeliness of completion or authoritativeness, but in any case you must justify your assessment. Do not report on only the literature with which you agree or disagree—you should be fair to both.

A related sort of bias is to report or quote something out of context, meaning to misrepresent something without providing the other information necessary to properly represent the intended meaning. For instance, a politician may have told an audience that he or she disagrees with capital punishment, but agree

that other states have the right to set their own laws on capital punishment. A journalist would be misleading if he or she reported that the politician agrees with capital punishment in those states.

Approach

Your approach when writing your review should be:

- Descriptive

- Analytical

- Evaluative

You should be descriptive because you need to describe to your audience what you actually are reviewing. What was your source? Who wrote it? What does it say? What is its value? Why is it relevant? How does it differ from other sources?

You should be analytical (see Chapter 6) so that you can fully identify the source, disaggregate its content, categorize it separately from other types of sources, compare it with other sources, and relate the sources to each other.

You should be evaluative, meaning that you evaluate the sources in relation to your project. Is the source timely, authoritative, credible, rigorous, or robust? Does the source contribute to theory or evidence?

As you write, make sure that you are staying within your scope and not describing, analyzing, or evaluating things that are not relevant.

Key questions to answer in most literature reviews are:

- What is the literature about?

- What are the key concepts?

- What are the definitions of the key concepts?

- What are the assumptions?

- What are the competing theories, or what remains theoretically unresolved?

- What methodological approaches were used to test the different theories?

Do not be afraid to start writing your review before you have completed your readings. You could start by writing down observations about a single source before updating your review with observations about new sources. In practice, you are likely to be returning to your review even after you have focused on other parts of your project.

CHAPTER SUMMARY

This chapter has taught you how to:

- Read efficiently, by:

  o Selecting the most useful and necessary readings

  o Getting what you need during the first read through

  o Understanding the relationship between readings

  o Avoiding bias

  o Recording what you might make use of

- Analyze content, in order to measure:

  o An author's or creator's foci or biases

  o An author's or creator's influences

- An author's or creator's personality, attitudes, feelings, and so forth
- The authenticity of authorship
- The audience's exposure to something

- Define sources
- Prioritize sources, by time of completion, authoritativeness, credibility, rigor, and robustness

- Understand the difference between secondary and primary sources
- Understand the purposes of any literature review
- Write a literature review

KEY TERMS

Archaeologist 103
Archaeology 103
Art 117
Article 98
Artifacts 103
Authoritative 106
Authority 106
Book 98
Conceptual analysis 118
Content analysis 117
Credibility 107

Critical analysis 123
Critical thinking 123
Literature 110
Medium 117
Message 118
Peer 108
Peer review 108
Primary source 101
Reader 111
Reading 109
Relational analysis 118

Review 122
Rigorous 108
Robust 108
Sample content 119
Secondary source 100
Selection bias 111
Sign 119
Source 98
Tertiary sources 98

QUESTIONS AND EXERCISES

1. For each of the following notional sources, decide whether the source is best described as secondary, primary, or both:

   a. A verbal interview taped for a documentary about a sit-in on a campus in 1964. The interviewee was present for the sit-in. The interviewee recounts the speech that she made during the sit-in.

   b. A document titled "The Impact of Social Movement Organizations on Public Policy."

   c. A letter from the Narcotic Officers' Association to a federal judge.

   d. A policy paper suggesting the legalization of new medicine.

   e. A paper about the importance of hieroglyphics in recording aspects of ancient Egyptian life.

   f. Pottery fragments found at the site of Pompeii, which was buried by ash during the eruption of Mount Vesuvius in 79 A.D.

g. A book written by a historian recounting the events surrounding the imprisonment of a human rights campaigner in 1958.

h. Video footage of a speech taken by a U.S. news agency.

i. Statistics provided by the World Bank on the amount of carbon dioxide emitted by year by country.

j. A news article about a disaster that includes personal interviews from survivors.

2. Select two real sources of relevance to your research:

a. Identify how one is more useful or necessary than the other.

b. Identify how one is more directional than the other.

c. Identify your biases toward one over the other.

d. Select a source.

e. Identify examples of content, medium, and message.

f. In the content, identify a relationship.

g. Identify the relationship's sign.

h. Identify the relationship's direction.

i. Identify the relationship's strength.

6

Analysis

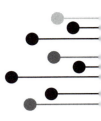

Opening Vignette: Analyzing Sub-Saharan Development

Source: ©iStockphoto.com/stevenallan.

Imagine that you work for an organization promoting economic development in poor countries. You have just been asked to report on the past development of various Sub-Saharan African countries. In conducting your research, you build a narrative of each country's economic history while you analyze the causes and effects. You compare and contrast former colonies with countries that were never colonized. Diving deeper, you compare and contrast demographic attributes. You notice that some economic woes reflect ethnic hierarchies, corrupt leaders, geographical barriers, and debts to international institutions. Your analysis has identified issues that your organization could address individually to help those in need.

What Is Analysis?

Analysis is the examination of something in order to better understand it.

The terms *analysis* and *research* are often used interchangeably, but analysis is not literally the same as research. *Research* is the process or product of acquiring knowledge. In practice, analysis is important to most forms of research and is inherent to most activities during research. For instance, we analyze our scope, we analyze theories when we review theories, and we analyze data during our tests.

Learning Objectives and Outcomes

At the end of this chapter, you should be able to:

1. Decide when to analyze

2. Identify what to analyze

3. Disaggregate information

4. Categorize and classify information

5. Compare and contrast information

6. Relate things to each other

The term *analysis* is commonly used interchangeably with assessment or estimation, but whereas analysis is about looking inside something or at one thing among many, assessments and estimations are imperfect measurements of something. The term **assessment** implies a more objective measurement, while the term **estimation** implies a more judgmental measurement, but these terms are also used interchangeably.

Why Do We Analyze?

Whether you realize it or not, analysis is natural and routine. All conscious beings analyze the world around them, their own activities, and their stimuli. They may not be conscious of their analyses, but no being could be strategic or adaptive without being analytical first.

Human beings have the most biological capacity for analysis. They routinely analyze their environments, intents, motivations, hopes, fears, relationships, spending, voting, and most of the things they feel or do. Most people are probably not conscious of most of their analyses, but that does not mean they are not being analytical. Just crossing a street involves analysis before you determine where and when you cross. If people lost the capacity to analyze, they would not survive.

Having said that, just because we have the capacity for analysis does not mean that our analysis is good. Analysis takes effort; people naturally take inferior shortcuts, such as generalizations, simplifications, conventional wisdom, popular opinion, and narratives (see Research in the Real World Box 6.1).

Analysis is central to science because we must analyze current knowledge, theory, methods, data, and so forth if we are to improve on any of these things. Analysis can be as simple as organizing our knowledge. The German philosopher Immanuel Kant once wrote, in his seminal *Critique of Pure Reason* (1781), "Science is organized knowledge."

Analysis is central to commercial and official activities and useful to any endeavor.

How Are We Told to Analyze?

Despite routine demand for analysis, analysis is rarely described as a skill set. When analysis is separated from other forms of research, it is often taught in the same way as general research or general science. Analysis is so inherent to research that most social scientists either ignore analysis when explaining research or provide prescriptions that look like descriptions of research.

Research in the Real World Box 6.1

Past Under-attention to Basic Analytical Skills

Source: ©iStockphoto.com/kemalbas.

"When we look back at past responses to intelligence surprises or shortcomings, recommendations for improvements are uncannily similar. Almost every postmortem of past intelligence failures concludes that analysts were working from outdated or flawed mental mindsets and had failed to consider alternative explanations. Most recently, the Iraq WMD Commission's indictment of 'poor tradecraft' and the 9/11 Commission's judgment that analysis suffered from 'a failure of imagination'

signaled the need to incorporate more rigor and creativity into the analytic process.

"In response, the government has commissioned major research and development (R&D) efforts to create new models, new algorithms, and new computer tools to address our analytic weaknesses. Unfortunately, most of this investment has gone to collection, data mining, and other IT infrastructure improvements and precious little to supporting the analytic process.

"Only on rare occasions have these R&D efforts produced analytic tools that analysts have integrated into their daily routines. R&D programs aspire to develop tools that will do the analysts' work for them, crunching reams of data, and extracting answers with the application of sophisticated algorithms. Practicing analysts actually use few such systems today. Far more preferable would be the development of simpler tools that can structure analysts' thinking, help them engage peers in problem solving, and, more important, save them time." (Pherson & Pherson, 2013, p. xxi)

Meanwhile, some professional analysts are trained by their employer, but their training is often protected as an official or commercial secret. Even after years of working as analysts, professional analysts can have difficulty describing their analytical skills or processes (see Research in the Real World Box 6.2).

This helps to explain how few sources are dedicated to analysis alone and why most students have difficulty differentiating between acts of analysis and other research activities.

The flip side of this is that anyone properly trained in social scientific research should develop sufficient analytical skills. In fact, many social scientists end up as professional analysts.

Some disciplines and professions have long-standing forms of analysis that are so established as to have earned the status of academic fields or professional specialties. These established forms of analysis can be very technical—so technical that few people could hope to practice them without the appropriate higher education and capacity. By their disciplines or professions, these established forms of analysis include:

- Mathematics
  - o Statistical analysis; probability analysis; actuarial science
- Economics
  - o Financial analysis; cost-benefit analysis; systems analysis
- Business
  - o Price analysis; market analysis; competitor analysis; stakeholder analysis; risk analysis
- Criminology
  - o Crime analysis; legal analysis
- Politics
  - o Policy analysis; comparative political analysis
- International relations
  - o Trade analysis; intelligence analysis
- Military, defense, and security
  - o Net assessment (comparative military capabilities); operational analysis; security analysis

Some of these specialized forms of analysis have their own specialist books, certification programs, jobs/roles, professors, and software. Perhaps the most interdisciplinary of the skills is statistical analysis, which is used across the sciences. Statistical analysis has become more accessible in recent decades thanks to cheaper and friendlier statistical software.

Some of these forms of analysis have been adopted across disciplines, although sometimes in new forms that are contested. Such cross-fertilization tends to be roughest when the transfer is from a hard science, such as mathematics, to one of the humanities or liberal arts, such as history—sometimes leading to bitter complaints about misuse or abuse of the original application.

One reason that people avoid real analysis is laziness. Another reason is a fear of betraying a lack of knowledge on the subject. Yet another reason is discomfort with the implications of finer knowledge. You likely can recall someone who spoke vaguely, avoided questions, denied the utility of further discussion, refused to define what he or she was talking about, or discussed things in contradictory ways. Such a person was probably avoiding further analysis for fear of revealing his or her own lack of knowledge or discomfort with the facts. Such fears may be entirely subconscious. Sometimes avoidance of analysis is deliberate. In political discourse, people can become expert at consciously avoiding further analysis.

Providing a superficial description of something is easier than analyzing it. You may recall having read a source that simply described something without giving you any remarkable new insight or understanding of that thing. That source was probably descriptive without being analytical.

This difference between description and analysis is best illustrated by the difference between narrative history and analytical history (see Table 6.1). Often narrative history is guilty of other problems that are related elsewhere in this book, such as reductionism (see Chapter 7) and revisionism (see Chapter 4). At best, a narrative history describes a series of past events. At worst, the author adds a causal explanation for the narrative as a whole, without admitting that some events could have had independent causes that have been lost to history or were practically random—a mistake that has been termed the **narrative fallacy** (see Practical Advice Box 6.1).

Reading a narrative history can be an entertaining and gripping experience, but the desire for narrative can get in the way of accuracy, and experience is not the same as understanding. For instance, I remember as a student being forced to read a 600-page history of early modern European relations, with a conclusion just a few pages long, which described the history as interesting and complex.

By contrast, a good analytical history examines the story to better understand it, not just retell it. It may do this by:

- Disaggregating the story into its parts, such as the actors, their activities, the situations, the geography, the economic context, the cultures, and so forth

- Categorizing the parts by type, such as economic activities versus social activities

- Comparing the parts, such as comparing the actors' capabilities

- Relating the parts, such as the personal or political relationships between actors and the causal relationships between events

Clearly, this analytical history would be more meaningful than a purely narrative history.

How Should We Analyze?

Analysis, like research, can mean both a product and a process. Any process can be described, developed, and prescribed (see Practical Advice Box 6.2).

Analysis is the process of identifying, disaggregating, categorizing, comparing, and relating something in order to better understand it. These five main skills/steps in the process above are discussed in the subsections below. Here are summaries of these steps:

Table 6.1 Achieving analytical rather than just narrative history

Don't Just	Example	Do	Example
Tell stories	What happened, when it happened	Explain	Why it happened, how it happened
Revise past narratives	Criticisms of prior emphases	Discover new knowledge	What happened at lower levels
Reduce and homogenize	Socioeconomic units and leaders	Disaggregate and associate	Multiple levels of analysis
Isolate the field	Applicatory method	Cross-fertilize with other fields	Organizational theories
Make assumptions	Perfect information	Make observations	What information was available
Platitudes and tautologies	Leadership is difficult	Tangible measures	The current speed of communications
Polarize just two alternatives	Right and wrong decisions	Acknowledge all the trade-offs	Faster but less accurate decisions
End the story	What happened at the end	Draw lessons, make recommendations	Flaws, best practices

Sources: Newsome, B. (2003); Newsome, B. (2007) Chapter 3.

Identification means determining what entity you will examine. This sounds simple, but many things are unclear or contested, in which case you must separate one thing from another by clarifying its definitions and boundaries. For instance, if you are interested in studying marriage, you need to struggle with contests about whether marriage must be legal or can be declared by people outside legal authorities, or whether marriage is purely heterosexual or can be homosexual.

Disaggregation means breaking something into its parts. The analytical purpose is to better understand it as a whole. For instance, we might disaggregate a transport system into its ways and nodes, we might disaggregate a social network into persons and relationships, or we might disaggregate a democracy into its legislative, executive, and judiciary branches.

Categorizing means placing things into distinct **categories**, in which things are different from things in other categories. Categorizing often involves identifying a higher category within which the things are the same (such as human beings),

Research in the Real World Box 6.2

Proliferation of U.S. Intelligence Analysis

Source: ©iStockphoto.com/everythingpossible.

"Studies have found that no baseline standard method exists in the U.S. intelligence community. Any large intelligence community is made up of a variety of disciplines, each with its own analytic methodology. Furthermore, intelligence analysts routinely generate ad hoc methods to solve specific analytic problems. This individualistic approach to analysis has resulted in a great variety of analytic methods, more than 160 of which have been identified as available to U.S. intelligence analysts.

"There are good reasons for this proliferation of methods. Methodologies are developed to handle very specific problems, and they are often unique to a discipline, such as economic or scientific and technical (S&T) analysis (which probably has the largest collection of problem-solving methodologies). As an example of how methodologies proliferate, after the Soviet Union collapsed [in 1991], economists who had spent their entire professional lives analyzing a command economy were suddenly confronted with free market prices and privatization. No model existed anywhere for such an economic transition, and analysts had to devise from scratch methods to, for example, gauge the size of Russia's private sector." (Clark, 2013, p. xxiii)

then subcategorizing them (males and females). Disaggregation naturally leads to subcategorization: once you have identified a part, you should categorize the part.

Comparing means examining the similarities and/or differences between things within the same category or along the same scale or dimension. For the purposes of comparison, we might declare that one thing is bigger, cheaper, closer, better, or older than another thing. For instance, transport vehicles are routinely categorized by the light, medium, or heavy loads they can carry.

Relating means describing the relationship between things. A relationship is a connection between things. The three main types of relationship are of (a) authority or responsibility; (b) some flow, exchange, communication, or

Practical Advice Box 6.2
An Anthropological Metaphor for Analysis

Source: ©iStockphoto.com/herreid14.

"One of our colleagues thinks of this process in anthropological terms. Primitive man first gathered food and materials he knew existed, then hunted for what else he needed, and finally grew or raised food he could not obtain in other ways. Applied to analysis, this translates as follows:

- Gathering—surveying current knowledge relating to the question.

- Hunting—figuring out what is needed to answer the question.

- Farming—creating knowledge relevant to answering the question." (Pherson & Pherson, 2013, p. 44)

movement; and (c) development or parentage. For instance, the trade between two countries and their diplomatic exchanges are flows. The subsection below will explain this further.

Identifying What to Analyze

The first step in the analytical process is to identify what to analyze. Analysis can be applied to anything. You could analyze politics, societies, economies, markets, behaviors, or anything else you could imagine in order to better understand them. You could analyze your private weekly shopping just as well as your government's annual expenditures.

In practice, you will be analyzing something at every stage of your project. You must analyze an academic discipline or field in order to work out your scope. You must analyze theories in the process of reviewing them or in order to develop your own. You must analyze methods in order to choose the appropriate method for your test. You must analyze data during your test. You must analyze your own writing in order to edit it.

Analysis might seem intimidating in some situations. You might feel uncertain of where to start or you might not yet realize anything meaningful about the thing you want to analyze.

Start by identifying the subject of your analysis. If you are still uncertain, look for one of the following:

- A **phenomenon**, which is anything observable, such as an event, a behavior, or entity.

- A **concept**, which is an abstract idea or symbol, such as the "economy," or an abstract collection of tangible entities, such as businesses and business activities.

- A **definition**, which is a description of meaning; the more precise the description, the easier it will be to differentiate.

- A **relationship**, which is a connection or comparison between things, such as a trade agreement or a signal.

- A **system**, which is a set of entities that interact, such as cultures within a society.

- A **structure**, which is a pattern of relationships, such as a network of friendships or a hierarchy of authority.

- A **process**, which is a sequence of actions or changes, such as international intervention in another country's economy or the development of that country's economy.

Disaggregation

The second analytical step is disaggregation, which involves identifying a thing's parts. These parts might be identified by examining conventional anatomies. For instance, the human body has organs, limbs, and vessels, while organizations usually have leaders and followers, authorities and subordinates, functional departments and administrators.

In general, you can disaggregate anything by units of analysis and levels of analysis. A **unit of analysis** is the common entity under examination. For instance, you could disaggregate a year of time into quarters or months. You could have more than one unit of analysis, such as when economists examine economic growth by both quarters and months.

A **level of analysis** is one step in a hierarchy. **Hierarchies** have levels from the lowest or most inferior to the highest or most superior. For instance, geologists and archaeologists routinely analyze earthly deposits in layers, from the topsoil to the bedrock, or from the first meter of depth through each subsequent meter. Similarly, a political system can be analyzed down through the international, national, provincial, city, and local levels. An educational system can be analyzed up through the elementary, middle, high, and higher education institutions. Such levels are often defined by authorities or established by conventional discourse.

If you are still uncertain about the parts, go through the following list of potential things:

1. A material thing, such as an industrial product, has components and materials.

2. A society, such as a labor union, has members, leaders, representatives, and activities. It probably has a structure too (below).

3. A process, such as the process of research, has activities, steps, inputs, and outputs. A *process* is a sequence of actions or changes. A process can be disaggregated into the activities and changes that lead to the ultimate outcome.

4. Time can be disaggregated into smaller units, such as years, quarters, months, weeks, days, hours, minutes, and seconds.

5. A system, such as a communications system, has nodes, relationships, and sometimes systems within systems. A *system* is a set of entities that interact. A human body is a system of organs and other things. A system could be conceived as a *system of systems*. For instance, the human body has both a nervous system and a cardiovascular system.

6. A structure, such as the U.S. government, has hierarchies, authorities, and responsibilities. A *structure* is a pattern of relationships, usually defined by authorities or responsibilities or by some other scale. Thus, levels of analysis inherently emerge when examining structures. *Authorities* are entities with rights or capacities to determine things. *Responsibilities* are duties or things that are supposed to lie within one entity's purview.

Categorization and Classification

The third step in the analytical process is **categorization** or **classification**—the separation of things into distinct categories. Sometimes categories are called **classes**.

Comparative analysis is a natural skill that you started learning at least by the time you discovered through play that a round peg goes through a round hole while a square peg goes through the square hole.

Usually, we start with some defined category (such as fruit), which is agreeably defined and bounded, then subcategorize it. For instance, apples and oranges are fruit (they occupy the same category known as fruit) but categorically different species of fruit. Vehicles could be subcategorized by the medium through or on which they travel, usually air, water, or land. Mammals are distinct from reptiles. Organic chemistry is distinct from inorganic chemistry.

Comparative Analysis

The fourth step involves comparing things within the same category or along the same dimension or scale, such as size, age, distance, or weight. For the purposes of comparison, we might declare that one thing is bigger, cheaper, closer, better, or older than another thing. For instance, if we categorize democracies into strong or weak democracies, all these democracies share the distinction of being democracies, but along this scale or dimension ("democraticness") some democracies are stronger, some weaker. Similarly, we could choose to compare societies as small, medium, and large states; we could choose to compare subpopulations as wealthy, middle income, or poor; we could choose to compare businesses as small, medium, or large businesses.

In academia, these parts of analysis are tested directly by questions asking you to compare or contrast things. Essentially the skill set being tested is "comparative analysis." Within disciplines and professions, comparative analysis can become extremely narrow and technical, such as the comparative analysis of one state's capabilities against another's (usually known as **net assessment** in American English) or of one business' capabilities against another's (usually known as **competitive intelligence** or **benchmarking** in American English). Some fields and disciplines are defined as comparatives. For instance, American political science recognizes a field called "comparative politics," which mostly compares national political systems, while the United States Defense Intelligence Agency specializes in the comparison of national military capabilities ("net assessment").

Chances are that you were performing comparative analysis in secondary school, when you were asked to compare or contrast two things, such as two readings, two historically important persons, two theories, two countries, two samples of soil, two toothpastes, and so on.

Comparisons engage with both similarities and differences, while contrasts highlight only the differences, although the differences may not be meaningful unless compared with the similarities.

Comparisons should begin with the similarities. Think about the categories into which both things could be placed. For instance, when asked to compare apples and oranges, you should first admit that both apples and oranges are fruit. They both also are edible, are grown agriculturally, contain seeds, have skins, and so forth.

You should be asking yourself whether some of their similarities are trivial or irrelevant to the project. You need to consider the purpose of the analysis in order to judge what sort of comparison would be trivial or irrelevant. For instance, if you were asked to compare apples and oranges as commercially viable fruit, then their susceptibility to the same pests would be relevant information, but their representation in the paintings of Vincent Van Gogh (Dutch, 1858–1890) probably would not be.

When making contrasts, think about the categories in which the things could not be placed together. For instance, when asked to contrast apples and oranges, you might remember that oranges fit into the class of fruits known as citrus, but apples do not.

You may feel that a list of similarities and differences is boring and wonder how you could write your comparison in an interesting way. To make your comparative analysis more interesting or meaningful, look for:

1. A frame of reference

2. Surprises

3. Similarities in a host of differences

4. Differences in a host of similarities

5. Meanings

First, start your comparison through some **frame of reference**. This is the context within which you place the things you plan to compare, such as the environmental, biographical, or historical context. You can derive a frame of reference from your scope (see Chapter 4). For instance, you might be tasked with comparing two Indonesian politicians—you could choose to compare them as either politicians or Indonesians.

Do not assume that you should devote as much weight to the differences as the similarities. The weighting depends on the relative proportion of differences to similarities and the importance of any particular difference or similarity. The frame of reference also should guide your weight. For instance, if you were tasked with comparing two theorists' opposing explanations for a new empirical finding, you should briefly review their theoretical similarities before devoting the bulk of the text to the contrast between their theoretical positions.

Second, identify something on the list that surprises you. You could write your report around this surprise. Comparisons can be surprising when you start out with things that seem similar, but discover profound differences. For instance, you might be researching how different insects harm the fruit crop. You could start with the assumption that all the insects under review must harm the fruit crop in some way, only to discover that one of the insects does no harm to the fruit but harms only pests.

Comparisons can be surprising too when you start out with things that initially appear to be different but turn out to have something in common. For instance, you might be asked to contrast the policies of two politicians from opposing parties, only to discover that each politician has proposed similar policies. A surprising or interesting comparison is indicated by sentences beginning with the phrases "Even though" or "Despite."

Third, identify the similarities in a host of differences. You might report a similarity as simply surprising, but you might go further by explaining why the similarity is possible despite the differences. For instance, many researchers have been interested in the surprising frequency of cooperation between two sides of a conflict. People on opposing sides might routinely try to kill each other; they might be very different in ethnic, religious, or cultural terms; and they might even frame their activities against the other side as hateful or righteous, but they typically will not try to kill each other's medical personnel, they will eschew certain weapons, and they may give up fighting on the same holidays (Axelrod, 1984). How are these commonalities possible despite the opposition?

Fourth, identify the few differences in a host of similarities. The differences could be reported as simply surprising, but try to analyze why the differences are possible despite the similarities. For instance, most cats are carnivores that eat other mammals and dislike water, but a few cats eat mostly fish and routinely swim. Why are those few cats able to live that way? If you analyzed further in pursuit of an answer to this question, you would discover that the fishing cats have evolved with advantages for swimming, such as slightly webbed feet.

Fifth, look for meanings in the similarities or differences. You might report a similarity despite the differences as simply surprising, but you could also look for the meaning. Imagine two politicians who seem to oppose each other on every policy, but somehow agree on something. What does this mean for how much they really oppose each other fundamentally versus for partisan reasons? What does this mean for how they might cooperate in the future? Answering these questions would lead you to a more useful analysis than simply listing their similarities and differences.

When discussing the similarities and differences, you face two main choices about structure:

1. In text-by-text structure, you discuss one thing before discussing the other thing. For instance, in comparing apples and oranges, a text-by-text structure would discuss apples before oranges.

2. In point-by-point structure, you compare the two things on one dimension, then compare both things on another dimension, and so forth, through all the dimensions. For instance, you could compare the color of apples and oranges, the water content of apples and oranges, the different markets for apples and oranges, and so on.

If you are asked or choose to analyze one thing (the "focus") through the "lens" of something else, then here also you should choose a text-by-text structure, starting with the lens, then devoting the bulk of the analysis to the focus. The lens is merely a vehicle for discovering whether the focus is appropriate to the lens. For instance, imagine that you have been led to believe that a new theory is another example of a certain class of theories. Your analysis would begin with a review of the class of theories (the lens), then compare the new theory with the class to reveal the similarities and differences. You might discover that the new theory is not different enough to be considered new, you might clarify the differences, or you might discover that the new theory is so different that it should not be placed in the same class at all.

If you sense that the two things are the same, except that the second thing is somehow a bigger, more interesting, or more developed version of the first thing, you should use the text-by-text structure, starting with the first thing, followed by the second thing.

If you sense that the things are opposing or in conflict, a point-by-point structure highlights the opposing things.

However, the point-by-point structure can feel like an exhausting and repetitive swing back and forth between each thing. You can mitigate this effect by grouping a few points together, thereby cutting down on the number of times you swing from one to the other.

Relational Analysis

Relating describes the connection between two things. For instance, you might describe the trade or diplomatic exchanges between two countries. A relationship can be the basis for describing the things themselves. For instance, you could describe two countries as allies, trading partners, or members of the same international organization.

A *relationship* is the connection between two things. You should look for any of four types of relationship:

1. A **flow** is some exchange, movement, or communication, such as trade, migration, and diplomatic communications between two regions. A change of state is also a flow, such as enrollment, graduation, death, and decay. A specialized form of flows analysis is **communications analysis**. The nodes are the origins and terminals of communications flows; the flows between nodes are the relations.

2. A **relationship of authority or responsibility** is a relationship based on the authority and/or responsibility of one of the parties in regard to the other. *Authorities* are entities with rights or capacities to determine things. *Responsibilities* are duties or things that are supposed to lie within one entity's purview. For instance, an organization probably has constituted authorities from the directors to the subordinates. Members of the organization probably have separate responsibilities, such as accounting or selling. Be aware that simple membership is a relationship of authority or responsibility between the member and whatever the member has joined. Be aware too that relationships of authority or responsibility are inherently structural relationships.

Research in the Real World Box 6.3

Social Network Analysis in the Hunt for Usama (Osama) bin Laden

Source: ©iStockphoto.com/ollo.

Usama (Osama) bin Laden (Saudi Arabian, 1957–2011) was one of the founders of al-Qa'ida (Arabic: "the base"), a group of radical Islamists dedicated to terrorism and insurgency against whomever and whatever they regarded as apostates. The hunt for bin Laden intensified after he took the main credit for the terrorist attacks that killed almost 3,000 people on September 11, 2001, in America.

In January 2004, one of bin Laden's emissaries (Hassan Ghul) was captured in Kurdistan and thence turned over to American authorities. Ghul revealed that bin Laden relied on a single courier (Abu Ahmed al-Kuwaiti) for all his communications. The Central Intelligence Agency analyzed al-Kuwaiti's social network. Using this analysis, the National Security Agency tapped all his relatives' telephones. He was heard calling his family in Kuwait in 2009. From this call, his telephone was identified and traced to Pakistan, where he was followed to a residential compound, which was later confirmed as bin Laden's then home. There, on May 2, 2011, U.S. special operations forces killed bin Laden and four companions.

3. A **developmental relation** or **parental relation** is something derived from another thing, such as a derivative of a product or a child of a parent. (A **relation** is the connection between two things or the thing that has a connection with another thing.)

4. A **causal relationship** has a cause, an effect, and a causal direction from the cause to the effect (see Chapter 8 for more on causal relationships).

Any system could be analyzed by any of these types of relations. In the past, **relational analysis** was known as **link analysis**.

A form of relational analysis that analyzes all the types of relationship above is **social network analysis**, which analyzes entities and their social relations.

This is mostly understood in the context of human societies, but can be applied to any species. Social network analysis can be as simple as identifying people as nodes in the network and drawing relationships between people who know each other (see Research in the Real World Box 6.3). The nodes in a human network could be persons or organizations. In deeper analysis, the qualities of each relationship and the frequency of communications could be recorded. Some software is dedicated to such analysis.

Another form of relational analysis is **spatial analysis**, which relates things such as events and actors to their locations. For instance, crimes, wars, accidents, and other bad things are often mapped so that analysts can see spatial patterns and thence look for meanings or act to control the risks where they are most acute in space.

CHAPTER SUMMARY

This chapter has taught you:

- What analysis is, and how it differs from other forms of research

- Why we analyze

- The ways analysis is used every day

- The many disciplines that demand analysis

- The steps to be employed in successful analysis:
  - Identifying what to analyze
  - Disaggregating something into its parts
  - Categorizing and classifying things
  - Comparing things
  - Relating things

KEY TERMS

QUESTIONS AND EXERCISES _____

1. Give examples of when use of the terms *research*, *analysis*, *assessment*, and *estimation* would be appropriate.

2. Take the concept of "business":

   a. First, attempt to identify the concept by giving it a definition with tangible boundaries.

   b. Categorize various types of business.

   c. Disaggregate one of these types into its fundamental parts or aspects.

   d. Compare/contrast your chosen type with another type from your categories.

   e. How are the two types relatable?

3. Read the following description:

   On August 4, 2014, Guinea's Ministry of Health reported a total of 495 suspected and confirmed cases of Ebola virus disease, of whom 395 had died. Ebola is a virus that causes hemorrhagic fever. The virus is most often transmitted to people from wild animals, such as fruit bats from the Pteropodidae family. It spreads in the human population through human-to-human transmission. Fatality rates in humans run as high as 90%. Officials struggled to contain the disease from spreading out of the West African region. They looked at containment strategies employed during previous epidemics, such as those of yellow fever and smallpox.

   After reading the description, identify examples of as many of the following as you can:

   a. Phenomenon

   b. Concept

   c. Definition

   d. Relationship

   e. System

   f. Structure

   g. Process

4. Read the following description:

   The United Nations' system is based on five principal organs: the General Assembly, the Security Council, the Economic and Social

Council, the Secretariat, and the International Court of Justice. The General Assembly is the main deliberative assembly of the United Nations. It is composed of all United Nations member states, and is led by a president elected from the member states and 21 vice presidents. The General Assembly can put forth nonbinding resolutions and make recommendations on any matter within the scope of the UN to the UN Security Council. The Security Council comprises 15 member states and 5 permanent states with veto power. The Security Council is charged with maintaining peace and security among countries and makes all final and binding decisions to be pursued by the UN. The UN Secretariat is headed by the Secretary General.

It provides studies, information, and facilities needed by the UN bodies for their meetings. It also carries out tasks as directed by the Security Council, the General Assembly, the Economic and Social Council, and other UN bodies.

After reading the description, identify examples of as many of the following as you can:

a. Phenomenon

b. Concept

c. Definition

d. Relationship

e. System

f. Structure

g. Process

6. What is the difference between social network analysis, communications analysis, and spatial analysis?

CHAPTER 7

Arguing and Explaining

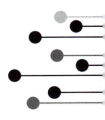

Opening Vignette: Sophists

Demosthenes

People who argue cleverly but deceptively have a derogatory name: **Sophists** (from the ancient Greek *sophistes*, meaning a "sage," from *sophos*, meaning "clever"). In ancient Greece, Sophists claimed to be able to argue any position, sold their services as lawyers or teachers, and were in demand by unscrupulous lawyers and politicians. Given less clever or attentive audiences, these clients could win legal cases and political positions using oratory that was not necessarily logical or truthful—hence the contemporaneous complaint about ancient Greek democracy: "the tyranny of the orator."

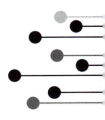

Definities
Definitions

The subsections below will define argument in general before defining hypothetical, counterfactual, prescriptive, normative, and descriptive arguments.

Argument

The term **argument** has two main meanings:

1. An exchange between parties of dissimilar views

2. The content of one party's attempt to persuade

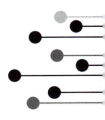

Learning Objectives and Outcomes

At the end of this chapter, you should be able to:

1. Understand an argument

2. Critique the logic of arguments

3. Deliver a logical argument

4. Deliver a true argument

5. Identify and avoid fallacious arguments

6. Identify and avoid common biases

7. Identify dialectic arguments

The first meaning should be described as a dispute, in order to avoid confusion with the second meaning.

This chapter is focused on the second meaning—the content of an attempt to persuade. The better you understand argument in the second sense, the better prepared you are to win an argument in the first sense—an exchange between parties of dissimilar views. This chapter will teach you how to analyze another's argument and how to develop your own argument.

Rhetoric (the art of persuasive communication) traditionally offers three strategies: appealing to logic, emotion, or credibility (see Table 7.1). Emotion and credibility seem to be the best bets in commerce and politics, but academic discourse is more reasonable, which is why the main section of this chapter will teach you logic.

Unlike a theory (see Chapter 8), an argument does not need to fit any facts. Thus, an argument, unlike a theory, can be purely hypothetical or counterfactual, as shown in the next sections. A theory must explain at least some of the facts. For instance, I could argue prescriptively about how a researcher should behave ethically—this argument does not need to fit any facts about how researchers really behave. A theory about how people behave must fit some of the facts about how people behave.

Unfortunately, arguments are often more about misleading audiences, such as juries in courts of law, potential consumers, and potential voters. If we do not understand what makes a good argument, we can never know what is really justifiable or true. Later sections of this chapter will teach you to identify illogical arguments, false arguments, fallacious arguments, biases, and dialectic arguments.

Table 7.1 The main types of rhetoric			
Type of Rhetoric	**Main Appeal**	**Other Appeals**	**Example**
Logos	Logic	Reason, fact, objectivity	"Given that this has always occurred before, we can expect that . . ."
Pathos	Emotion	Passion, belief, subjective sense	"I would be happy if you . . ."
Ethos	The author's character or credibility	Reputation, trustworthiness, authoritativeness	"You can trust me that . . ."

Hypotheticals

A **hypothetical** is anything imagined without being asserted as true. For instance, we could argue about how aliens would behave if they landed on earth as a way to develop a protocol for how humans should respond to alien landings. This would be a **hypothetical argument**.

Hypothetical arguments are routine in the more prescriptive or ethical fields, such as medicine and business management, which are often concerned with prescribed practices and professional ethics. A **prescription** is a declaration of what should be done, whereas a **description** is a declaration of what something is. **Ethics** is the consideration of what is right or wrong.

Hypothetical arguments are routine wherever prescriptive questions arise, such as risk management. For instance, if you were asked how we should behave if a risk were to change, your answer would be both hypothetical and prescriptive.

Hypothetical arguments are routine also wherever ethical questions arise, such as medical ethics. If you were asked how we should behave if a patient were to ask for help to end his or her life, your answer would be hypothetical, prescriptive, and of ethical relevance.

Hypotheticals are used to argue about what should be done. For instance, we might be asked to write a prescription for how medical doctors should manage patients waiting for medical attention. We could argue hypothetically about what types of symptoms would justify a doctor's prioritization of one patient over another.

While hypotheticals are useful in prescriptive and ethical arguments, they become less useful in descriptive theories, unless they are used to develop counterfactuals, as described below.

Counterfactuals

Counterfactuals are imagined alternatives to the facts. Counterfactuals are used in legal arguments and historical arguments for comparing what actually happened with what could have happened. This comparison can help to establish the justifiability of a choice. For instance, we might be asked to judge a medical doctor's responsibility for a patient who died while waiting for medical attention. We could argue hypothetically about what would have happened if the doctor had neglected other patients in order to attend to the new patient. If the other patients would have died in the same time period without the doctor's attention, then the doctor's neglect of the new patient seems more justifiable, but if they would have come to no additional harm within that same time period, then the doctor's actual behavior seems less justifiable.

Hypotheticals and counterfactuals are similar. Indeed, the terms are often used interchangeably. However, hypotheticals are not necessarily contrary to any facts, whereas counterfactuals must be contrary to at least one fact and are thus also more past oriented and descriptive (see Table 7.2).

In the discipline of history, counterfactuals may be known by less accurate terms, such as **hypothetical history**, **alternative history**, or **virtual history**.

Historians can imagine alternative histories, such as if a candidate for president had been elected instead of rejected, if an invention had occurred in a different century, or if a great historical personality had been born in a different time or space. For instance, historians may be asked to judge a state leader who appeased a neighboring threat (the fact). One historian might argue that a failure to appease would have provoked the threat into immediate attack with more harmful consequences. Another historian might argue that a choice to deter would have deterred the threat forever. Both historians share a counterfactual (imagine that the leader had not appeased), but argue toward different conclusions.

Users of **counterfactual arguments** point out that counterfactuals help to judge what actually happened. In fact, as you learned in Chapter 6, comparing one thing with another, such as comparing real history with counterfactual history, is a form of analysis. History needs analysis if it is to avoid mere storytelling.

Historians should use counterfactuals to avoid the *narrative fallacy*, which is the fitting of causes to events without admitting other potential causes. The narrative fallacy makes history look deterministic, but history could have taken many paths. The causes of actual events can be lost in the present, because the

	Hypothetical	Counterfactual
Facts	None necessary	Contrary to at least one fact
Time	Can imagine the future	Always imagines an alternative to the past
Imagination	Can be entirely imaginary	Partially but not entirely imaginary
Purpose	Mostly prescriptive	Mostly descriptive

Table 7.2 Hypotheticals and counterfactuals compared

present is an effect of those same events. For instance, biographers love to study the personalities of famous people and explain their success as an effect of their personalities, but perhaps their personalities are effects of their success. More profoundly, many people with the same personalities could have failed for other causes that are lost to history because they were never famous enough to be recorded.

Other historians object to counterfactuals as not real history, as diversions from the study of what actually happened, or as motivated by **wishful thinking**. Counterfactuals for academic purposes are sometimes categorized with **historical fiction**—fiction set in real historical contexts. Historians should use counterfactuals to better understand real history, whereas historical fiction writers focus on entertainment. Sometimes the subjects of counterfactuals and historical fiction overlap in thought-provoking ways, but often historical fiction becomes dominant in popular culture, to the detriment of the facts.

Prescriptive Arguments

A **prescriptive argument** prescribes how things should be. Prescriptive arguments can be used to develop practical prescriptions, such as laws, rules, operating procedures, and strategies.

Prescriptive arguments are common in philosophy. *Philosophy* is the reasoned study of fundamental issues. Philosophers argue about such prescriptive issues as ethical behavior, the best form of political system, fair economic systems, and justice.

Prescriptive arguments can be relevant to descriptive arguments too, such as when some social scientists study how people do behave (a descriptive question) in order to better work out how people should behave (a prescriptive question). For instance, we might be interested in how people make ethical choices. Our research into how people make ethical choices would be descriptive. Yet we should be interested also in the prescriptions that influence ethical choices—such as religious and professional ethical guidance.

Normative Arguments

A **normative argument** describes how things normally are or prescribes how things normally should be. Thus, a normative argument overlaps both prescriptive and descriptive arguments or covers the gap between them. Something is normal if it is in the majority or more likely than not. (In mathematics, the term *normal* also implies a specific distribution of observations, where most observations are close to the median observation; see Chapter 8.)

Many people use the terms *normative* and *prescriptive* interchangeably, but they should not. A behavior might be normative (the behavior normally happens) because it is prescribed, in which case we could describe the behavior as both prescribed and normative. However, a prescription might not lead to a norm (the behavior does not normally happen). Many norms arise without any prescriptions. For instance, many religions and philosophies have urged people not to lie or steal, but research has shown that most people routinely lie and steal, although they restrict their routine lying and stealing to things that they consider minor or justified. This leaves a disconnect between the prescription (people should behave in a certain way) and the norm (most people do not behave as prescribed). If you were to conflate prescriptive and normative arguments, you would miss the difference between what people should do and what they normally do.

Descriptive Arguments

A **descriptive argument** describes how things are.

A descriptive argument does not imply how things should be, just how things are. A descriptive argument could conclude that most people would kill someone else who was threatening to kill them, if they had no other alternative. This descriptive argument makes no claim about what is the right thing to do and does not tell people what they should do; rather, it claims to describe how most people would behave.

A descriptive argument and a prescriptive argument could reach the same conclusion. For instance, a descriptive argument could conclude that a person would kill another person in some situation, while a prescriptive argument could conclude that a person should kill the other person in that same situation. These are different arguments with the same conclusion.

Another descriptive argument could describe what most people do or are likely to do. This descriptive argument could be described as also a normative argument. It can be described also as a **probabilistic argument**, in the sense that its conclusion is likely or that something happens most of the time, but not necessarily all the time.

Probabilistic arguments are differentiated from **deterministic arguments**, whose conclusions claim something as certain. A law is true invariably. A law is normally stated as a single proposition, but sometimes a whole argument can be considered a law. For instance, *democratic peace theory* is a term used to describe a collection of competing theories trying to explain the empirical observation that democracies do not fight each other as frequently as other types of states fight. Jack Levy stated that "the absence of war between democracies comes as close to anything we have to an empirical law in international relations" (Levy, 1988, p. 661).

A descriptive argument does not need to be a normative argument or a probabilistic argument. A descriptive argument could describe what a minority of people do, contrary to the larger societal norms or prescriptions.

Logical Arguments

What Is logic?

In *rhetoric* (the art of persuasive communication), logic is an appeal to reason (see Table 7.1). In more formal discourse, **logic** or **logical argument** means an argument that fulfills certain rules and concepts, as shown in the sections below: proposition, premise, deduction, induction, syllogism, validity, avoidance of non sequiturs, and avoidance of antinomies.

Propositions

A **proposition** is a statement that declares or asserts some judgment or expectation, such as "That man is guilty"; "I propose that all men are created equal"; or "Anybody would have behaved just as I behaved."

You propose things at every stage of an argument, from start to finish. Arguments are often presented in casual, chaotic, and confusing ways that make your disaggregation of its propositions difficult, yet any argument should be declarable as a series of propositions—if not, then something is wrong with the argument.

When reviewing theories, you should be looking for the propositions in the argument. When building your own theory, you should be aware of what you are proposing.

Premises

A **premise** is a founding proposition—a proposition that founds the argument without being guaranteed by a preceding proposition. Some analysts refer to all the propositions before the conclusion as premises, but I prefer to separate premises from the propositions that are guaranteed by the premises.

A premise is usually one of the following four things:

1. A hypothetical or imaginary situation, such as "Imagine a human civilization with only two races"

2. An assumption, such as "Assume that all actors are rational"

3. An attribution, such as "All birds lay eggs"

4. An observation, such as "Sixty percent of the population smokes tobacco"

Premises are used to guarantee subsequent propositions. For instance, imagine an argument that assumes that the actors are rational, all the actors live within the kingdom, the king's coronation was known to all his subjects, and 20% of subjects opposed the king's coronation. This argument has four premises—none was guaranteed by any other proposition. The argument can then proceed to propose things guaranteed by these premises, such as the proposal that 20% of subjects would be unhappy about the coronation.

Deduction

A **deduction** is a proposition guaranteed by preceding propositions. For instance, if someone proposes that a material is lethally toxic and proposes that she has eaten the lethal dose, then I should conclude, if I were to accept both of these premises, that she will die.

Consider these two propositions:

1. The dog bites everybody who crosses its path.

2. To go home, I must cross its path.

What should I deduce from these two propositions? I should deduce that if I went home, I would be bitten.

Logical deductions can be made from categorical propositions about other members of the category. For instance, given the premise that all dogs have four legs, and another proposition that my friend has a dog, then logically I should conclude that my friend's dog must have four legs. Note that you cannot reverse the direction of a categorical proposition—from a specific member of the category to all members of the category. For instance, just because my friend's dog turns out to have only three legs does not mean that all dogs must have three legs.

Logical deductions from categorical propositions are always **deterministic**, meaning that the deduction is certain given the categorical premises. Consider these two premises: (a) No dogs of a particular breed ever bite anyone, and (b) my pet is of that same breed. A logical deduction would be that my pet would never bite me. This conclusion is a deterministic deduction—it is certain, not merely probable (likely). Be aware that the conclusion is certain only in a logical sense—logical determinism is not the same as truth; it is only true if the premises also were true (see the later section on truth).

Induction

An **induction** is a proposition suggested by an individual observation. For instance, if I observe a particular dog biting a person, I should induce that the dog can bite people.

Be careful that you do not mistake propositions for observations. For instance, if someone simply said that no dogs of a particular breed ever bite people, without making any explicit induction from any observation, you must treat this statement as a proposition, but not explicitly an induction.

Be aware that the term "inductive argument" does not mean that the argument is purely inductive. An inductive argument could contain deductions as well as inductions.

While the term *deduction* is common in everyday speech, the term *induction* is rarer and more likely to be used incorrectly. Indeed, the term *induction* is routinely but incorrectly used interchangeably with *deduction*. The best-known example of this error is as spoken by the fictional private detective Sherlock Holmes (created by Arthur Conan Doyle, first featured in 1887), who often said that he deduced from the evidence, but literally he would be inducing from his observations.

Conventionally, deductive arguments are differentiated as *deterministic arguments*, where the conclusion is regarded as certain so long as the argument is valid. An argument with any induction is differentiated as a *probabilistic argument*, where the conclusion is regarded as probable (likely). Unlike deductions, inductions cannot be deterministic. An induction from an observation is not a deduction guaranteed by preceding propositions; therefore, this induction is not guaranteed, and thus it is not deterministic. If I were to observe one dog of a certain breed never biting anyone, then I could induce that dogs of that breed do not bite people. This sounds deterministic, as stated, but it is **probabilistic**, as interpreted. It is not based on observations of all dogs of that breed across all of time, but on only one observation. If one person proves that most dogs of the breed do not bite, a cogent conclusion would be that a dog of that breed likely would not bite—this is still a probabilistic argument.

Be aware that a "probabilistic argument" is not necessarily probable in the sense of likely; it could be **feasible**, meaning that it is possible but not necessarily probable, or improbable, meaning that it is possible but not likely.

While deductions are guaranteed by preceding propositions, inductions are less certain. While deductions are deterministic, inductions are not. An induction based on observations of what most people do is mathematically probabilistic, but an induction based on one observation of what one person did cannot be described mathematically as probabilistic. Even so, inductive arguments are conventionally differentiated as probabilistic, in contrast to deductive arguments that are differentiated as deterministic.

Arguments that rely on inductions can be challenged by contradictory inductions (see Research in the Real World Box 7.1). For instance, the pet's owner could claim that he had never seen any dog of his pet's breed ever bite anyone and thence could propose that no dogs of that breed would ever bite anyone. Yet another person could observe a dog of that breed biting someone and conclude that all dogs of that breed bite. The contradictory inductions above are stark because they unjustifiably claim to be deterministic: One concluded that the breed never bites, the other that the breed always bites. However, as you know from the above, inductive arguments cannot be deterministic, so you would be wrong to use one observation of one member of a class to conclude about all members of the same class.

Stating your inductions as explicitly probabilistic makes your argument sound more realistic. Since people routinely misunderstand inductive arguments, you should make the inherent lack of certainty explicit by stating the argument in probabilistic terms, such as "Most people behave in a certain way, so the next person I meet *likely* will behave in the same way." If you observed that most people behave in a certain way, you could induce that the next person you meet would likely behave in the same way.

Building Arguments From Propositions

The structure of a logical argument begins with at least one premise and ends with at least one conclusion. The last proposition in an argument is the **conclusion**. An argument should conclude; otherwise it would not be an argument, just a statement. For the conclusion to be logical, it should follow logically from the preceding propositions.

At minimum, an argument has a premise and a conclusion. Another argument could have many premises and conclusions. In between a premise and a conclusion, it could have lots of other propositions.

One Actor, Two Contradictory Inductions

Source: ©iStockphoto.com/akpin.

"The success of the ancient city-state of Athens against the Persian Empire is often attributed to the high motivations of its democratic citizen soldiers, but democratic Athens would be defeated later by despotic Sparta." (Newsome, 2007, p. 14)

A logical argument has no limit on the number of propositions, but it must have at least two propositions (a premise and a conclusion) to be an argument rather than just a proposition. For instance, consider the logical argument below with just two propositions:

1. Every day the weather is rainy.

2. Tomorrow the weather will be rainy.

In the argument above, the conclusion is guaranteed by the premise.

Be mindful that someone might give you an argument with a conclusion that is not guaranteed by its explicit propositions, but is guaranteed by implied but unstated propositions. For instance, imagine that someone says to you that no reasonable person would behave as alleged, so she does not believe the allegation. The explicit structure of this argument is:

1. No reasonable person would behave as alleged.

2. I do not believe the allegation against my client.

As stated, the above argument is actually an invalid argument, because the first proposition does not guarantee the second. The client could be an unreasonable person, in which case the arguer's conclusion (the client would not behave as alleged) is not guaranteed by the argument as explicitly stated.

However, implicit in this argument is a proposition that the target of the allegation is a reasonable person. The whole argument, explicit and implicit, is:

1. No reasonable person would behave as alleged.

2. My client is a reasonable person.

3. My client did not behave as alleged.

The argument above is a valid argument because the first two propositions guarantee the third. This is still a dissatisfying argument because the threshold for what is reasonable remains unstated, so the whole argument seems prejudicial and unfalsifiable. Yet while we can criticize the truth and strength of this argument (see the next full sections), it still remains a valid argument, independent of whether or not any of the propositions are true.

Unfortunately, implicit propositions are common, particularly when the author of the argument is not trained in argument, is hasty, is struggling with a very complex argument, or is just a poor communicator. Worse, a poorly specified argument could be the product of an author who is deliberately trying to avoid logical challenges!

Even more unfortunately, implicit propositions are far too common in arguments published by academics who call themselves social scientists, partly because the skills of argument are not taught as well as they once were.

Just because the author of the argument is more senior or popular, do not be cowed into thinking that you must be at fault for missing something in an argument. The author of the argument might have failed to propose something that should have been explicit in order to guarantee the conclusion.

To be fair, however, do not assume that the author is at fault whenever you cannot follow the argument. You might not have read properly, or you might be able to fix the argument by making explicit any implicit propositions.

Syllogism

The valid three-proposition argument has a special name: **syllogism**, from the ancient Greek term for a conclusion. Typically a syllogism has two premises and one conclusion. A common illustration of a syllogism with two premises and a conclusion is:

1. All dogs have four legs.

2. My pet is a dog.

3. My pet has four legs.

A real example of a syllogism from biological theory, which existed before its conclusion was proven as true, is:

1. An animal inherits exclusively from its mother all its mitochondrial DNA (deoxyribonucleic acid—a molecule recording genetic information).

2. All humans are animals.

3. Therefore, all humans must share mitochondrial DNA from a single prehistoric mother (Dawkins, 2011, Chapter 2).

Your argument should be logical, but it does not need to be a syllogism. No argument need stop at three propositions. An argument can have as many propositions as are needed to reach the desired conclusion. At the same time, simpler arguments are preferable, all other things being equal.

The ancient Greeks used syllogisms as exercises and illustrations. Syllogisms came to be conventional in scholarly culture and probably have psychological appeal too, such as the appeal of a thing in three parts, so people tend to structure their arguments as syllogisms even if they have no training in logic. People commonly argue that one thing is true, the other thing is true, and so a third thing must be true. If such an argument reached the conclusion logically, then it would be a syllogism. A syllogism does not need to be true; it just needs to have three propositions and be valid.

Validity

An argument is **valid** if each deduction is guaranteed by the preceding propositions. Consider this "typical syllogism" (this one is typical in that it has two premises and one conclusion):

1. All dogs have four legs.

2. My pet is a dog.

3. My pet has four legs.

The third proposition (the syllogism's conclusion) is a deduction from the preceding two propositions. This conclusion is guaranteed by the preceding two propositions. The premise proposes an attribute or quality ("four legs") held by all members of a category ("dogs"). The second proposition proposes that "my pet" falls in the same category ("dogs"). Given these two propositions, logically we know two things about dogs: Each of them has four legs; and my pet is one of them. Thus, logically we can conclude that my pet has four legs.

We must not reverse the direction of a categorical proposition in order to reach a conclusion. This would be the equivalent of claiming that the attributes of one member in a category must be shared by all members of the category. For instance, the following syllogism is invalid:

1. All dogs have four legs.

2. My cat has four legs.

3. My cat is a dog.

Just because both categories ("dogs" and "cats") share the same attribute or quality ("four legs") does not mean that the two categories are the same. They could be categorically different in all other respects. For instance, males and females of a species share most attributes in common but not their sex.

The invalid argument above does not propose that dogs and cats have no differences, so we cannot deduce that they have no differences, so we cannot conclude that they are the same. The conclusion is not guaranteed by its premises.

The argument above may seem obviously wrong to you because you are familiar with the empirical reality that cats are not dogs, so consider this abstract version of the illogical syllogism:

1. All A-types (all things in Category A) have the attribute or quality x.

2. All C-types have x.

3. My A-type is a C-type.

The argument above is invalid because the argument does not guarantee that my A-type is also a C-type just because both A-types and C-types share the attribute designated as x.

Now consider this abstract logical argument:

1. All D-types have a y.

2. My F is a D-type.

3. My F has a y.

In the above argument, my F must have a *y* because my F is a D-type and all D-types have a *y*.

Non Sequitur

A conclusion that is not guaranteed by the argument's propositions is known as a **non sequitur** (Latin: "does not follow"). Consider the argument below:

1. All humans are mammals.

2. The weather will change.

The conclusion is a non sequitur. It is not guaranteed by the premise. The argument is invalid. When reading somebody's argument, do not assume that if you could not follow it, then the argument must be cleverer than you are—the argument might pretend to be clever but contain non sequiturs (see Research in the Real World 7.2).

The non sequitur in the above argument is obvious because the propositions are unrelated. Non sequiturs can be less obvious, such as when the conclusion is possible but not guaranteed by the premise, as in the following argument:

1. No reasonable person would behave as alleged.

2. I do not believe the allegation against my client.

In the above argument, the conclusion is not guaranteed: For the arguer to conclude that the client would not behave as alleged, the client must be reasonable. The client might be reasonable or unreasonable; the argument does not include a proposition that clarifies whether the client is reasonable or unreasonable. Since the arguer failed to explicitly clarify this, the conclusion is a non sequitur, although you could add the implicit proposition ("My client is reasonable") to make the argument valid.

You should describe a proposition as the non sequitur and describe an argument as invalid, rather than describe a whole argument as a non sequitur.

Since a premise does not need to be guaranteed by a preceding proposition, a premise might sound like a non sequitur, but a non sequitur is an unguaranteed conclusion, which is not valid, while a premise is an unguaranteed founding proposition, which is allowed.

Antinomy

Antinomies are propositions that contradict each other even though they are deduced from the same propositions or induced from the same observations.

The Illogical Argument Behind the "Paradoxical Logic of Strategy"

Edward Luttwak claimed "that *the entire realm of strategy is pervaded by a paradoxical logic* very different from the ordinary 'linear' logic by which we live in all other spheres of life" (Luttwak, 2001, p. 2; emphasis in original). Luttwak acknowledged his debt to Basil Liddell Hart, who had argued that the "indirect approach"—the longer, most difficult, or least expected approach—is usually the preferred strategy. Like Liddell Hart, Luttwak argued that the "indirect approach" could avoid a competitor's defenses or surprise the competitor.

> To move toward its objective, an advancing force can choose between two roads, one good and one bad, the first broad, direct, and well paved, the second narrow, circuitous, and unpaved. Only in the paradoxical realm of strategy would the choice arise at all, because it is only in war that a bad road can be good *precisely because it is bad* and may therefore be less strongly defended or even left unguarded by the enemy. (Luttwak, 2001, p. 3, emphasis in original)

Any claim that something can be "good because it is bad" is literally contradictory. Fortunately, in this particular example the intended paradox is clear enough. What Luttwak was nonliterally proposing is that advantages come with disadvantages, or that adversaries adapt and adjust to the material context, but none of this is paradoxical.

Similarly, Edward Luttwak claimed that an ancient Roman proverb—"Prepare for war in order to achieve peace"—is "paradoxical." Luttwak compares it to the imagined advice to lose weight by eating more, but the Roman phrase is a linearly logical statement about deterrence. It is therefore incompatible with his analogue, which is the converse of a real causal relationship.

In any case, the logic itself of "paradoxical logic" breaks down. If the "paradoxical" or "indirect" choice is an accurate description of a consistently preferable choice today, then competitors can adapt to those approaches tomorrow. Thus, the strategy of indirect approach is self-defeating.

The self-defeating cycle described above does not normally occur, because each side would need perfect information and perfect agility. The choice between the straight but potentially well-defended road and the circuitous but potentially weakly defended road must be concluded from inductions, not just deductions. If we were to know that the enemy was defending the straight road, we would, logically, take the circuitous road. Similarly, if we were to know we lacked the capabilities to navigate the circuitous road, we would logically take the straight road. Practical, strategic choices are never deterministic, but always inductive (Newsome, 2007, pp. 59–60).

Imagine that we propose that someone would behave in a very aggressive way given the premise or observation. Now imagine that we propose that someone could behave in a very cooperative way given the same premise or observation. These propositions seem to contradict each other—they are antinomies.

An antinomy is not a non sequitur: A non sequitur cannot be valid (it does not follow from the preceding prepositions), but each antinomy is valid (it does follow). Since antinomies are valid deductions or inductions, the discovery of antinomies does not automatically invalidate an argument, but does make the argument look less valid than it would without antinomies (see Research in the Real World Boxes 7.1 and 7.3).

True Arguments

Logic and Truth

A valid argument is not necessarily true. **Truth** is the accurate understanding of things as they really are. An argument's validity is independent of its truthfulness. An argument could be valid but untrue, true but invalid, untrue and invalid, or true and valid; as long as a conclusion is guaranteed by its premises, the argument is valid, but if the premises are untrue, the argument is untrue.

An argument is only as true as the propositions in it. If only one proposition in the whole argument is untrue, the conclusion must be untrue.

Consider the premise that all dogs have four legs. If I propose also that my friend has a dog, I must logically conclude that my friend's dog has four legs. My conclusion would be valid, but not necessarily true. I know by observation that some dogs have fewer than four legs because of genetic abnormality, accident, or illness. My observations prove the premise untrue.

The truth of an argument is important if you are arguing about the real world. Truth is less important if you are arguing philosophically, for the sake of argument, or even to mislead others about the real world.

In social science, we are usually developing an argument in order to better understand the real world, unlike in philosophy, where arguments are developed for the sake of argument. Thus, social scientists should be aiming to develop arguments that are both logical and true.

As explained in the following four subsections, good social scientists help their arguments to be realistic by:

Research in the Real World Box 7.3

Antinomies in Arguments About Why Democracies Win Wars

Source: ©iStockphoto.com/stockcam.

Dan Reiter and Allan Stam (1998, 2002) proposed that democratic leaders face a higher chance of electoral punishment for failed wars. They proposed that democratic leaders are incentivized to choose wars that they can win.

They concluded that democracies are more likely to win wars—this outcome became known as a "selection effect" because democratic leaders would be winning wars that they had selected as winnable.

Michael Desch (2002, p. 6; 2008, p. 5) criticized the "flawed logic" in this theory. Desch (2008, pp. 20–25) argued that autocrats should be more incentivized to pick wars that they can win because autocrats could lose their entire political career and even their lives if they are overthrown, while democrats would lose only their office as punishment for losing a war.

1. Using propositions that are necessarily true and avoiding things like beliefs that are not necessarily true

2. Using assumptions to escape unproven propositions

3. Using conditional propositions to avoid unrealistic categorical propositions

4. Using probabilistic propositions to avoid unlikely cases

Avoiding Propositions That Are Not Necessarily True

Some propositions are assumed to be true in the absence of evidence, for the sake of argument, but they cannot be proven as true without evidence. Few propositions can be said to be absolutely true. A proposition is absolutely true if it is proven to be true in all cases in perpetuity, but such a level of proof is difficult to achieve. In practice, many propositions are described as true because the bulk of evidence or the balance of evidence suggests that they are true. In other words, they are probably true but not certainly true.

None of the following six things can be claimed to be necessarily true: prejudice, belief, trust, faith, opinion, or assumption.

Prejudice

A **prejudice** is a premature judgment not justified by observation or reason, such as an unfounded judgment that today will be a bad day.

Belief

A *belief* is a proposition held as true but not necessarily proven as true. The term *belief* is neutral in the sense that a particular belief might be justified or not. One person could believe something to be true given evidence, while another person could believe something else to be true without evidence. Each person has a different belief, where one is easier to justify as true than the other, but both things are beliefs.

Trust

Trust is the confident expectation of something positive being fulfilled. **Distrust** is doubt about whether something positive will be fulfilled.

Faith

Faith is belief or trust without evidence. Whereas belief could be based on evidence or faith, faith implies the absence of evidence. You could trust that someone is protecting your best interests—if your trust occurred in the absence of evidence, your trust would be faith. Similarly, you could believe that someone is still alive, but if you had no evidence, then your belief would be faith. Faith is justifiable in lots of situations, such as religious or emergency situations, but has no justification in arguments that claim to be true.

Opinion

An **opinion** is a subjective proposition. An opinion is differentiated from facts. Facts are objectively verifiable, but opinions are not, because they are inherently subjective.

You can have opinions except where they challenge the facts. A useful phrase that has emerged in political discourse in recent years is that "everyone has the right to an opinion, but not to their own facts."

An opinion carries more weight in an argument if it is offered by a credible witness or expert (**credible opinion**), it is held by the majority of the public (**public opinion**), or it is held by a majority of experts (expert **consensus**).

Opinions are relevant in hypothetical arguments where perceptions take the place of facts. For instance, I could criticize a hypothetical expectation of how a consumer would behave if offered a hypothetical service by reporting that my interactions with consumers never gave me the perception that they would want the service.

Opinions in the sense of perceptions contrary to the facts are sometimes allowable defenses in courts of law. For instance, someone might escape a conviction for murder of an innocent person if he or she were to convince the court that his or her opinion at the time was that the other person was armed and dangerous.

Assumption

Assumptions are premises that are treated as if they are true without there being a claim that they are necessarily true. Assumptions sound a lot like hypotheses, but whereas hypotheses are subject to testing, assumptions are treated as if they are true so that they do not need to be tested. For instance, we could assume that people are rational in order to simplify our propositions about how people would behave.

If a reader of such an argument were to agree with you that the assumption is true, then he or she could not criticize the argument as purely assumptive. Another reader could disagree with your assumption, in which case this second reader could declare the whole argument as untrue because it is based on an untrue assumption—also known as a **bad assumption**.

Making Assumptions to Escape the Burden of Proof or Argument

While you should avoid assumptions if you are trying to develop a perfectly true argument, sometimes you cannot prove every proposition. You may solve an unproven proposition by assuming that it is true. An assumption is always inferior to a proven proposition, but such an assumption is justifiable if proving it as true would be overly burdensome or if the argument would be excessively complicated without the assumption.

Imagine that you are arguing about how the current president would behave in a hypothetical economic crisis. Any proposition about how anyone would behave in a situation that has not occurred cannot be tested. Where a test is impossible, an assumption is warranted. Sometimes a test is not technically impossible but impractically burdensome. Where proof becomes practically more difficult, an assumption becomes more justifiable.

An assumption is justifiable also to simplify an argument. Imagine that you are arguing about why the previous president acted as he did. One argument might attempt to propose all the different emotions, psychological influences, and cognitive thoughts that influenced the president's choice, but such an argument would become so complicated that many researchers and readers would prefer a simpler argument that assumes rationality and does away with emotions and psychology.

Be mindful that your readers might challenge your assumptions (see Research in the Real World 7.4), so you help yourself by improving your argument.

Many social scientists assume rationality at the start of arguments about decisions and behaviors, particularly medical, criminal, organizational, political, and economic decisions and behaviors. **Rationality** is used in the sense of a self-interested or optimal decision. If we assume that people or other actors would make optimal decisions, and we can determine the optimal decision, then we can conclude how the actors would behave rationally.

Rationality is an attractive assumption because it allows for simpler expectations and allows us to reach prescriptions about the optimal choice. However, rationality is less attractive where we want to reach realistic descriptions.

Empirically, we know that rationality is a poor assumption except under unlikely conditions, such as perfect information, sufficient time and capacity for consideration of the information, fewer choices, and stark choices. Even under extreme conditions, people may not behave rationally. Consider a person who awakes in a house that is burning. Rationally, the person should escape the fire, but in panic, haste, or confusion, the person could forget the best escape route or could spend too long considering his or her options. A conclusion about how all actors would behave rationally is valid given an assumption of rationality but is not always realistic.

Making Propositions Conditional to Escape Unrealistic Categorical Propositions

So far we have considered avoiding any propositions that are not necessarily true and making assumptions in order to simplify our burden of proof or simplify our argument. In this section, we will consider the use of conditional propositions to avoid unrealistic assumptions and unrealistic categorical propositions.

Propositions can be structured in two main ways: categorical and conditional. A **categorical proposition** proposes some expectation about all members of some

Criticizing a Bad Assumption in an Argument Over Democratic Wars

Source: http://commons.wikimedia.org/wiki/ George_W._Bush#mediaviewer/File:Blair_Bush_ Whitehouse_%282004-11-12%29.jpg.

Dan Reiter and Allan Stam (1998, 2002) proposed that democratic leaders face a higher chance of electoral punishment for failed wars. They proposed that democratic leaders are incentivized to choose wars that they can win.

Alexander Downes criticized what he characterized as a bad assumption in Reiter and Stam's expectations for electoral censure:

> One mechanism maintains that leaders choose wars they think they can win, while two others contend that leaders start wars they believe will be popular. But what is popular is not always what is strategically sound, and although the theory seems to assume that all good things go together, sometimes they do not. (Downes, 2011, p. 68)

category, class, or group—for instance, "All dogs have four legs," "All planets revolve around a sun," or "All ogres smell."

Many categorical propositions are inherently unrealistic but are used to make the propositions simpler or to make the argument easier to deduce. For instance, many of the syllogisms that you read in preceding sections have premised that all dogs have four legs, but you know that some dogs do not have four legs because of genetic abnormalities, accident, or illness. The premise is not always true, even though the proposition is mostly true and convenient to the argument.

One solution to an unrealistic categorical proposition is to change the categorical proposition to a conditional proposition. A **conditional proposition** proposes some expectation if something else is true—for instance, "If the administrators perform well, they will be reelected" or "Given perfect information, they would have behaved differently." Instead of proposing that all dogs have four legs (a categorical proposition), you could propose that all dogs have four legs absent any genetic abnormalities, accidents, or illnesses (a conditional proposition).

A conditional proposition can be disaggregated into its antecedent and its consequent. A logical **antecedent** is an expression that logically precedes and gives meaning to the consequent. The **consequent** is the expression that describes the result of the antecedent. Consider the following conditional proposition: "If I had wanted it, I would have bought it." Here, wanting something is the antecedent to buying it; buying it is the consequent of wanting it.

Similarly, a solution to unrealistic assumptions is to change them to conditional propositions. For instance, good social scientists can preserve the assumption of rationality while allowing for more realism by conditionally proposing rationality rather than assuming rationality. Consider the following conditional proposition: "Given perfect information about the speed of the fire, rationally they would have tried to escape earlier." This conditional proposition is more realistic than the following syllogism using only categorical propositions: "All people are rational. Rational people escape fires. People escape fires."

Making Propositions Probabilistic to Escape Unlikely Propositions

Social scientists who want their arguments to be both realistic and valid should adjust their arguments to be probabilistic rather than deterministic. Few things in nature are determined. Even if they were determined, they would be difficult to prove as determined. Consequently, probabilistic arguments tend to be more realistic arguments.

Deterministic propositions propose things as certain and do not allow for chance or randomness. If we were to propose that *all* dogs have four legs, then the quality of being a dog would determine that the thing has four legs (a deterministic categorical conclusion). If we were to propose that the administrators would be reelected *if* they were to perform well, then good performance would determine reelection (a deterministic conditional conclusion).

By contrast, a **probabilistic proposition** proposes something as likely, but not necessarily certain. If we were to propose that *most* people would behave rationally in a certain situation, our proposition would be probabilistic and more realistic than the deterministic proposition that *all* people would behave rationally in that situation.

Both categorical propositions and conditional propositions can be probabilistic. The probabilistic categorical proposition that most dogs have four legs is more realistic than the deterministic categorical proposition that all dogs have four legs.

Similarly, the probabilistic conditional proposition that people likely would escape a fire given perfect information about the fire is more realistic than the deterministic conditional proposition that if any person awoke in a burning house, then that person would escape the fire.

Strong Versus Weak Arguments

In popular discourse, people use the term "a strong argument" to describe anything that persuades them or that they agree with, but now that you are trained in argument, you should prefer to think of a strong argument as an argument that is truer or more logical (preferably both) than another argument.

Remember that truth and validity are independent, so you should not describe an argument as true just because it is valid, or vice versa.

Arguments can be compared as stronger or weaker relative to another. Stronger arguments are easier to judge where the probabilities are explicit. For instance, if one argument starts with the premise that most Americans speak English and concludes that the next American that I meet will speak English, then the conclusion is likely given the premise and the whole argument is strong. Now imagine another argument that proposes that the weather is sunny on 30% of days and concludes that tomorrow the weather will be sunny—this is a **weak argument** because the conclusion is unlikely given the premise.

An argument can be turned from weak to strong, or vice versa, by adopting the converse argument. For instance, take the premise that most Americans speak English. A conclusion that the next American I meet will speak English is a strong argument, while a conclusion that the next American I meet will not speak English is a weak argument. Nothing but the conclusion has changed in these arguments, but one is strong and one is weak because one conclusion is probable while the other is improbable.

Some arguments are poorly written or deliberately written so that they end up as unfalsifiable, in which case they should be regarded as weak; **unfalsifiable propositions**, by definition, cannot be proven or unproven. Reconsider the argument in which the author proposes that the target of the allegation is a reasonable person. The whole argument is:

1. No reasonable person would behave as alleged.

2. The accused is a reasonable person.

3. The accused did not behave as alleged.

The argument above is a valid argument because the first two propositions guarantee the third. This is still a dissatisfying argument because the threshold for what is reasonable remains unstated, so the whole argument seems prejudicial and unfalsifiable. While the argument remains a valid argument, it is weak.

The strongest argument would be one in which each proposition is proven to be true in all circumstances. Such strong arguments are rare in social science but are commoner in the hard sciences.

A strong argument might be described as a robust argument. A **robust argument** is one that has been re-proven by different testers or methods. Unfortunately, the term "robust" is used in ever looser ways, but try to restrict your use of it to academic meanings: It has survived challenges and new tests; each of its propositions has been proven, not just the conclusion; or it withstands variations in its premises.

Arguments appear to be stronger if they can be described as sound and cogent, or at least hypothetically sound, as described in the three subsections below.

Soundness

An argument is **sound** if the argument is valid and all of its propositions are true. Be aware that an argument can be valid but not true, in which case it cannot be sound (see Research in the Real World Box 7.5).

Consider this familiar syllogism:

1. All animals are mortal.

2. A man is an animal.

3. The man is mortal.

The above argument is both valid and true, so it is sound. Now consider this variation.

1. Special men are immortal.

2. Socrates is a special man.

3. Socrates is immortal.

The above argument is as valid as the preceding argument, but it is clearly not true, so it is unsound. No men are immortal, so the first proposition is untrue, although we could retain the argument as purely hypothetical.

Sometimes arguments are proven to be true after they have been developed. Reconsider the biological syllogism below:

1. An animal inherits exclusively from its mother all its mitochondrial DNA (deoxyribonucleic acid—a molecule recording genetic information).

2. All humans are animals.

3. Therefore, all humans must share mitochondrial DNA from a single prehistoric mother.

The above syllogism was argued before it was fully proven. With new techniques, biologists were able to prove every proposition, so now this argument is both valid and true—it is sound (Dawkins, 2011, Chapter 2).

Soundness is a fairer expectation of deductive arguments and categorical propositions than inductive arguments and conditional propositions. Deductive arguments and categorical propositions are deterministic—they claim to be always true as long as all the premises are true and all the deductions are valid. Inductions and conditional propositions are inherently probabilistic, so no argument with any inductions or conditional propositions should be expected to be always true (or sound).

The syllogism below illustrates why inductive arguments cannot be fairly described as perfectly sound, even though they could be described as probabilistic:

1. Most dogs do not bite people.

2. My pet is a dog.

3. My pet probably won't bite me.

Given the first proposition of what most dogs do rather than what all dogs do, the syllogism above concludes with a forecast of what is likely (probably my pet won't bite), not a statement of what is certain (my pet has never bitten me). This inductive argument cannot be described as perfectly sound—the conclusion is not certainly true. It would be fairer to describe it as cogent, as described in the next section.

Cogency

An argument is **cogent** if the argument guarantees that the conclusion is probably true.

An Everyday Argument That Lacked Soundness

Jackson Rees

"Once, at high school, I was in a literature class that was discussing the film *Apocalypse Now*, which depicts the Vietnam War, and is hailed as one of the first American war films to portray war as brutal and traumatizing. The teacher asked why the director might have chosen to portray war in such a way. An involved student, who often contributed intelligent input into discussions, raised a hand and proceeded to say, 'The director chose his portrayal as an attempt to enlighten the population to the realities of war and how brutal war really is, because during this time people were unaware of the experience of our soldiers abroad. And even though there were many protests during the Vietnam War they were protesting the concept of war, not because they knew explicitly what was going on in Vietnam.' Due to her conviction and authority, many accepted her argument, but while it could be described as valid it was not sound. Vietnam was the most televised war in American history, with images of violence beamed into living rooms every evening on the news. Moreover, the movie was made years after the end of the war." (Jackson Rees is majoring in political science at the University of California, Berkeley, class of 2016.)

Cogency is really a quality of inductive arguments—arguments that rely on inductions are inherently probabilistic. Deductive arguments are definitely true if all the propositions are true and the argument is valid. Strictly speaking, since inductive arguments cannot be definitely true, they cannot be sound in the same way as deductive arguments can be sound, but we still want them to be cogent. In a sense, cogency is the inductive argument's equivalent of the deductive argument's soundness.

In practice, certainly in everyday speech, soundness and cogency are used interchangeably. Indeed, people tend to use the words *logical*, *valid*, *sound*, and *cogent* interchangeably as synonymous adjectives to describe any argument they like. Be aware that the consumer of your research might not be as well trained in logical argument as you are now, so you should explain the differentiation between soundness and cogency when using these terms.

Hypothetical Soundness

A **hypothetical proposition** is a proposition that proposes something without claiming that it is true. Any premise, any conclusion, and any other proposition could be explicitly declared as hypothetical.

A hypothetical premise has implications for soundness, because so long as a premise remains unproven, the conclusion remains unsound. Remember: An argument could be logical but unsound, or sound but illogical; these are independent qualities of the argument.

Hypotheticals have no necessary implications for logic, only for truth. If you were to state a premise as hypothetical, you could make deductions in order to reach a conclusion, then claim that the conclusion is valid, but you could not claim that the conclusion is true. A reader of such an argument could justifiably point out that the argument is hypothetical until proven.

Whatever the truth of the other propositions, if the argument contains any hypothetical, then the conclusion also must be regarded as hypothetical. Imagine that we are arguing about how human beings would behave if aliens invaded. Since such an argument must hypothesize about an imaginary alien invasion, the conclusion must be hypothetical too.

We could try to prove a hypothetical proposition as true—this is essentially what all tests attempt (see Chapter 9). For instance, if an alleged criminal is proven to be sane, then the proposition that the alleged criminal is sane ceases to be hypothetical and can be admitted by a court as a fact, so that the court can prosecute the crime.

Sometimes an argument is meant to remain hypothetical—it imagines something that it admits as untrue, just for the sake of argument. How can we then evaluate the soundness of such a hypothetical argument?

You would not judge its empirical truth but its **hypothetical soundness**—the soundness of the rest of the argument, other than the hypothesis (see Research in the Real World Box 7.6). For instance, imagine that someone premises that people were immortal as part of a hypothetical argument about how immortal people would behave. Given an untrue premise, the rest of the argument remains hypothetical. As long as readers accept the concept of immortality, they can accept the argument as hypothetically sound.

One Hypothetical "State of Nature": Three Different Expectations of Behavior

Source: ©iStockphoto.com/adventtr.

Traditionally, social and political philosophers have imagined people living in a "state of nature" before civil society, before arguing about what sort of society would or should arise. These arguments are rarely criticized as invalid but are often criticized as unsound. Their propositions about how people would behave are inherently hypothetical but should be founded in how people actually behave in real situations. Depending on each philosopher's understanding of people, each philosopher could propose different expectations of how people would behave.

For instance, John Rawls (*A Theory of Justice*, 1971) imagined a group of rational people created without any rules or awareness of available assets, then proposed that it would agree to divide assets equally.

Robert Nozick (*Anarchy, State, and Utopia*, 1974) started with the same state of nature but argued that a rational individual would reject such an agreement in the hope of doing better alone.

Thomas Nagel (*Equality and Partiality*, 1991) argued that the group would agree on a lottery to distribute assets, since a rational person would rather choose the possibility of winning a majority share than choose the certainty of winning an equal share.

However, some concepts are so ridiculous, difficult to conceptualize, or difficult to describe that even their hypothetical soundness would be difficult to accept. For instance, imagine if someone premised an immortal rock. Since rocks cannot be mortal, an immortal rock is even more absurd than an immortal person.

Fallacious Arguments

This section will explain fallacy, circular argument, tautology, and some common fallacies.

Fallacy

A **fallacy** is a flaw in an argument. An argument containing a fallacy is a **fallacious argument**.

In logic, a **formal fallacy** is an unguaranteed or false deduction, leading to an invalid argument, as described already in the section on validity.

Informal fallacies are all the fallacies that are not necessarily illogical. Hundreds of informal fallacies have been identified, some of which overlap, some of which are contested. The sections below introduce the commonest dozen or so informal fallacies (see also Practical Advice Box 7.1).

Be mindful that informal fallacies can be contested, meaning that some people deny that their arguments are fallacious or at least allow for them to be nonfallacious under certain situations. Thus, you should not think of informal fallacies as unlawful, but as nonnormative. Formal fallacies are irrefutable when they disobey the laws of logic, but informal fallacies are not as clear. Sometimes fallacies are justified in particular situations.

Circular Arguments

A **circular argument** concludes with a premise. If A is B and I were to could conclude that B is A, then I would be offering a circular argument—the conclusion is essentially the same as the premise, even though I reversed its direction. If I argued that someone is a great speaker because he or she speaks well, that should sound circular.

Be aware that your premise and conclusion can sound different to you, but someone else could find them insufficiently differentiated and thus accuse you of circularity. A circular argument in sport would be an argument that one competitor won because that competitor is better than the other. Similarly, political scientists often argue that one political party wins because that political party is more powerful.

Circular arguments are often overlooked where they begin and end with the same thing but with different terms. Power is a concept that is routinely used in circular ways, because users both expect power to determine outcomes, such as victory in a fight, and expect power to result from victory. "Given the occurrence of war, the side possessing the greater power capabilities prior to the initiation of war will almost always be victorious" (Ferris, 1973, pp. 22, 25).

Tautology

A **tautology** in grammar contains an unnecessary repetition of meaning, such as "a male man" or "death due to a fatal injury" (see Chapter 11).

Practical Advice Box 7.1
Typical Analytical Fallacies

"*Ethnocentric bias* involves projecting one's own cultural beliefs and expectations on others. It leads to the creation of a mirror-image model, which looks at others as one looks at oneself and to the assumption that others will act rationally as rationality is defined in one's own culture. The Yom Kippur [1973] attack [by Egypt] was not predicted because, from Israel's point of view, it was irrational for Egypt to attack without extensive preparation.

"*Wishful thinking* involves excessive optimism or avoiding unpleasant choices in analysis. The British Foreign Office did not predict an Argentine invasion of the Falklands [in 1982] because, in spite of intelligence evidence that an invasion was imminent, they did not want to deal with it . . .

"*Parochial interests* cause organizational loyalties or personal agendas to affect the analysis process.

"*Status quo biases* cause analysts to assume that events will proceed along a straight line. The safest weather prediction, after all, is that tomorrow's weather will be like today's . . .

"*Premature closure* results when analysts make early judgments about the solution to a problem and then, often because of ego, defend the initial judgments tenaciously. This can lead the analyst to select (usually without conscious awareness) subsequent evidence that supports the favored solution and to reject (or dismiss as unimportant) evidence that conflicts with it." (Clark, 2013, pp. xxi–xxii; emphasis in original, boldface added)

A tautology in logic is inherently always true. Such a tautology arises where the argument becomes all inclusive, such as when someone declares his or her argument true "in any case." Definitions are often written in tautological ways where the definer is trying to be inclusive—for example, "a policy, whether authorized or not . . ." or "a car, whether with four or more wheels . . ."

False Analogy

A **false analogy** is an unwarranted induction across dissimilar categories, such as apples and oranges, as if they were the same. You can find similarities across different categories, but you should not assume that categorically different things share anything in common.

Examples of false analogies would include any claims that cats would bite humans at the same rate as dogs bite humans, young people have the same concerns as old people, deciduous trees suffer the same diseases as coniferous trees suffer, or men are as likely as women to be struck by lightning.

The dissimilar categories in these examples might seem obvious to you, but be mindful that a lot of arguments make false analogies without making their categories obvious and that it is up to you to realize the categories. For instance, if you heard someone claim that the rate of infection must be the same nationally as among a sample of people, you should be wondering whether the sample and the national population are alike. Perhaps the sample included only foreigners, men, the elderly, the affluent, tennis players, the unemployed, or some other subpopulation that is not representative of the national population.

Ecological Fallacy

The **ecological fallacy** is to make inferences from higher-level units about lower-level units. For instance, one might infer that the citizens of a polity are unusually belligerent because their polity is unusually belligerent, but this inference is fallacious without premises that guarantee it or observations that suggest it. The polity might be unusually belligerent because it is controlled by a belligerent minority that is opposed by a pacific majority.

You could prove that something is true at one level because it is true at another, but the ecological fallacy is to assume that the two are linked without logical or empirical warrant.

Reductionism

Reductionism is the process of reducing something to a part or a much simpler version.

In philosophy, reductionism can mean the view that each thing can be described by its parts. This is a justifiable view of mechanical systems, where parts of the system interact in predictable ways, but is not realistic in most domains, since some parts might not matter, some parts matter more than others, and some parts might interact in synergistic ways that are more than the sum of their parts.

Where reductionists are aware of their reductionism, they could justify reductionism as a solution to complexity, where describing the system in all its complexity would be impractical.

However, simplifying a thing is self-fulfilling; if you were to assume that a part can explain "the whole," and study only the part, you would find that the part explains "the whole."

Reductionism is clearly fallacious where it oversimplifies the thing but is used to reach conclusions about the whole. For instance, consider the parable of the many blind people observing an elephant for the first time: Each person touches a different part of the elephant (such as the tail, the trunk, an ear, a leg), each induces a conclusion about the elephant as a whole from just one part, and each has a uniquely inaccurate image of the elephant.

Reductionism sometimes leads to circular arguments where the findings depend on the reduction. For instance, where people assume that organizations or groups can be reduced to their leaders, people find that leaders determine everything about their organizations or groups. This reductionism ignores the many persons, organizations, and institutions between the leader and the outcomes of the leader's orders, not to mention how opposing entities interact to affect outcomes. This reductionism to the leader is so common that it has its own name: the "great-person theory," which claims to explain an organization's or group's great achievements as the result of a great person (Newsome, 2007, pp. 68–70). This reductionism can be justified for making the subject more manageable, but it also encourages unrealistic histories in which the subject's fortunes supposedly reflect its leader's talents (see Table 6.1).

Reductionists can be egotistical because they can blame or credit one person for everything, such as when the historian decides what the leader should have done given the historian's privileged retrospective information. This overlaps the historian's fallacy too (see below).

Reductionism is socially attractive because it allows the researcher to reduce everything to a single homogenous society, to which everyone can claim to belong, particularly in an era of increased popular representation. In the last half-century, many histories were produced as "**people's histories**"—the past from the perspective of the common person. Following the people's histories, many histories are told from the perspective of ever-smaller groups, usually defined by cultural, ethnic, religious, and political minorities.

Reductionism is politically attractive to people who favor centralized political systems, because they simplify the polity to a homogenous economy or society and its leader, which ignores the complexity of the relationships in between. For instance, Richard Overy argued that all Allied leaders showed skills of socioeconomic mobilization superior to those of their enemies in order to win

World War II. Even though the other Allied leaders represented very different societies and economies, Overy implied that their unification against fascism helped them to align around socialist ideals of centralized planning and social homogenization, that these ideals helped them to produce more armaments and more motivated people than their enemies produced, and that their superior productivity and motivations won the war (Overy, 1996; Overy, 1998, pp. xv, 328–330).

Critics have noted that historians routinely homogenize societies, economies, and polities as socioeconomic units that perfectly reflect the wishes of their leaders. For instance, some of the effective fields of diplomatic history include "war and economics" and "war and society," which study war in relation to an economy or a society, often both. The dominance of these fields encourages neglect of other relations, such as war and politics and war and organizations. These fields are psychologically attractive because they simplify and sanitize the subject—they allow the historian to escape the complexity of the polity and the "baseness" of combat (Cohen & Gooch, 1990, pp. 39–40).

Even for people for whom such reductionism is not egotistically or politically attractive, reductionism in these fields inevitably encourages them to imagine polities as homogenous units centrally controlled by a leader. These reductionist histories have four main explanations for victory in war:

1. A leader successfully mobilizes economic resources

2. The leader successfully justifies war to society

3. The society is compliant with the leader

4. The economy is centralized, helping economic compliance with the leader

Collectively, these four explanations might be termed a fallacious "socioeconomic mobilization" theory of victory in war (Newsome, 2007, pp. 64–66).

Applicatory Fallacy

Similar to reductionism, some researchers favor the traditional **applicatory method**—telling history from the point of view of the most prominent person. This reductionism imposes homogeneity on each society, group, institution, or organization. In other words, each is seen as a unitary actor whose performance perfectly reflects the performance of its most prominent person—usually a leader or commander. The applicatory method is a fallacy because it blames or credits the leader or commander for every respectively negative or positive event, but understates other variables, such as organizational performance in executing orders (Newsome, 2007, pp. 62–64).

The applicatory fallacy is associated with biased celebration of a particular person or persons. This is most obvious in military history, which is often written by people who aim to celebrate or memorialize a particular war, battle, commander, or side. Some disciplinary historians label such historians as **utilitarian historians** for their useful role in providing textual monuments honoring sacrifice and perpetuating pride. On the negative side, they perpetuate the great-person fallacy, reductionism, applicatory fallacy, and dogmatic principles of war based on exaggeration and myth-making (Alger, 1982, pp. 180–181; Cohen & Gooch, 1990, pp. 36–38; Paret, 1989, pp. 239, 255; Pennington, Hough, & Case, 1943, pp. 9–49).

Historian's Fallacy

The **historian's fallacy** is to assume that a person in the past had the same information or perspective as the historian. For instance, a historian might criticize a long dead leader for not investing in an invention that later revolutionized industrial production, without admitting that the leader's information at the time was that the invention would not work. Similarly, a historian might criticize a leader for defending traditional values and thereby losing the election, but perhaps the leader had valued tradition more than the elected position.

Presentism

Somewhat overlapping the historian's fallacy is **presentism**, which is the projection of present-day things, such as current morality or political ideology, onto the past. For instance, historians sometimes condemn previous generations for adhering to autocratic or oligarchic political systems, but at the time, when official bureaucracies were weaker and most people had no formal education, democratization seemed much riskier than it does today.

Narrative Fallacy

Presentism is inherent to historical study in the sense of **hindsight bias** or the *narrative fallacy*. History can seem inevitable and unavoidable in retrospect, but at the time the same events would seem like alternatives in a future that had yet to occur and still could be influenced by prior choices. Consequently, one critical definition of history is "any succession of events seen with the effect of posterity" (Taleb, 2007, p. 101).

Psychologist's Fallacy

The **psychologist's fallacy** is an argument in which the author of the argument projects his or her subjective self onto someone else. For instance, Sigmund Freud (Austrian, 1856–1939) famously founded psychoanalysis on his subjective interpretations of his own psychology and what others described to him as their psychological problems. Freud frequently projected onto others his own psychology, until he argued that practically everybody had the same repressed sexual urges, guilt, aggression, and other affects.

The psychologist's fallacy might cease to be fallacious if the author could claim that the author and the other person were so similar that their subjective perceptions could be assumed to be alike.

Naturalist Fallacy

The **naturalist fallacy** claims that something must be better just because it is natural, while something must be worse just because it is unnatural. For instance, a self-evidently fallacious argument would be to argue that we should allow a patient's own immune system to struggle with a disease unaided, just because the immune system is natural, while rejecting an artificial chemical compound just because it is unnatural, even if it would certainly save the patient's life with no harmful side effects.

Worse would be to favor a naturally occurring but toxic plant as a medical treatment over the harmless and effective but unnatural treatment. More common and less obvious is the commercial appeal of products, such as soaps, with inactive traces of natural ingredients over practically the same products with no natural ingredients at all.

The naturalist fallacy ceases to be a fallacy when we have other reasons to favor naturalism, such as a claim that we can be more certain about the risks of a natural ingredient that has been used for millennia over an unnatural ingredient that has just been invented.

Argument to the Person

The *argumentum ad hominem* (Latin: "argument to the man") is an attack on the author of the opposing argument rather than on the opposing argument.

Arguments to the person are clearly fallacious when they are abusive without being relevant to the substance of the argument.

An argument to the person is justifiable if the attack is on the other side's credibility, such as the other side's lack of honesty in their argument, their lack of direct knowledge of what they have claimed to observe, their lack of authority to judge, or their self-contradictions within the argument. These sorts of arguments to the person are routine in courts of law and politics in order to undermine the credibility of testimony. They are not routine in academic discourse, but could be used to undermine the credibility of a primary source, for instance.

Argument From Silence

The **argumentum ex silentio** (Latin: "argument from silence") is an induction from an absence of evidence. If a primary source does not mention something, an argument from silence would conclude that the primary source was ignorant of it. However, this should be regarded as fallacious, absent other grounds, because the lack of mention could have other explanations, such as the source's lack of interest in recording the thing or lack of opportunity to record the thing. For instance, some historians described the Phoenicians as lacking literature, but we now know that they wrote on a particularly perishable papyrus. Now imagine that a primary source does not mention a lunar eclipse: Perhaps the source never experienced a lunar eclipse or perhaps the source did experience a lunar eclipse but felt no need to record it.

The argument from silence could be justified if one had other grounds to expect the source to have been exposed to the thing and to describe everything in the category to which the thing belongs. For instance, imagine we pick up a diary supposedly written by someone who claimed to have circumnavigated the world and visited every continent in the Medieval period; if this source described an oceanic journey from Europe to Asia without mentioning the Americas or Africa, we could easily accuse the source of making up the story.

Biases

A *bias* is favor toward something. Some biases are somewhat inevitable. For instance, you inevitably have a bias toward sources in the languages that you can read. You can correct for it by becoming aware of it, learning a language pertinent to your research, or accessing a translation of a foreign language source.

Many researchers start out their careers properly mindful of bias, but gather biases while thinking of themselves as unbiased. For instance, many new fields or disciplines have emerged in recent decades with agendas to study things that were under-attended in the past, such as women, peace, and ethnic minorities, but these studies often reverse the biases that they claim to be correcting.

Be mindful that bias is not static. In practice, bias is highly variable across persons and groups and is dynamic within the life cycle of actors as they react to the environment and mature (see Research in the Real World Box 4.3). Some of the variance and dynamism is objective. For instance, a person who is exposed to a risk should be more sensitive to it than a person who is not exposed. Most people are subjective, so their sensitivities are likely to be exaggerated or neglected for parochial or even irrational reasons.

The subsections below explain allowable biases, unallowable biases, and nine common biases: proximity bias, anchoring bias, availability bias, unrepresentativeness, base-rate neglect, maturation, trust and distrust, fundamental attribution error, and group bias.

Allowable Biases

A bias is not necessarily a negative thing—it could be allowable or natural. For instance, rational people should have biases toward things that make them happy, do not harm them, are related to them, or that they value. In scientific research we should have some bias toward other scientific research.

In arguments, some bias is inherent and justifiable and could be declared as such. For instance, an argument must be biased toward whatever falls within the scope.

Sometimes the bias does not matter to the scope. For instance, the researcher's linguistic skills restrict the researcher to sources in languages that he or she understands, and the availability of sources introduces biases too. These biases matter if most of the literature relevant to the scope is in other languages. Biases do not matter if they are not relevant to the scope. If the researcher speaks only English but studies only English-speaking subjects, then the researcher's linguistic bias does not matter.

Sometimes a bias is not desirable but still allowable so long as the researcher admits to the bias. By admitting to the bias, at least the researcher cannot be accused of deliberate deceit. Even better, perhaps the researcher can explain the bias as unavoidable. For instance, a researcher might set out to examine the experiences of Italian immigrants to Greece in the 17th century, but in the time available the researcher might find sources written by only male Italian immigrants, leaving the research with no primary sources written by female Italian immigrants. If the researcher were to present evidence gathered from the sources without admitting and explaining the bias, the researcher might be accused of neglecting female sources due to personal bias, but if the researcher admitted and explained before presenting the evidence, then a fair consumer should agree that the bias is natural and not personal.

Unallowable Biases

A bias becomes a negative thing when it seems unjustifiable or unfair. Biases are not justifiable where they favor something at odds with the project's fundamental expectations or with research ethics. For instance, if the project meant to understand the dispute between Israel and Arab neighbors and the researcher read only Hebrew sources, then that linguistic bias would introduce a bias toward sources narrower than the scope of the project.

Proximity

People will feel more sensitive to something that is more proximate in time or space (say, when they are traveling through a stormy area) than when they are remote (say, when the last storm recedes into the past). **Proximity** effects can arise vicariously where the source or medium seems psychologically or emotionally proximate. For instance, the experiences related by a close friend can seem proximate to you even if they were experienced on the other side of the world.

Anchoring

When people experience an event, they tend to be psychologically "anchored" in the experience. For instance, people who experience a road traffic accident today likely will be more sensitive to the risks associated with road traffic accidents tomorrow than they were yesterday. Over time, or with therapy or distractions or maturation, memory tends to deteriorate or become less salient, and the sensitivity declines, but a particularly formative or shocking experience may anchor the person's sensitivity forever, even manifesting as a medical condition, such as posttraumatic stress disorder.

People do not need to experience the event directly to become anchored in it, as long as the experience is available to them in some captivating way, such as personally related, emotionally delivered verbal accounts by those who have experienced it. Visual images tend to be more arresting than verbal information. More immersive or experiential media, such as movies and video games, increase the effect.

The **cognitive availability bias** is the overestimation of the things most available to our senses or memory. For instance, most people in the world were geographically remote to the terrorist attacks in the United States on September 11, 2001, but were shocked by the images and accounts and felt more sensitive toward terrorism risk. These reactions were understandable and rational, since audiences were learning about a real event with implications for risks everywhere.

Cognitive availability can mislead the audience. People are more likely to recall events associated with striking images or experiences than events that are less cognitively available, even if they are objectively more important. For instance, the great interest that popular culture takes in fictional violent crime and that journalists take in real violent crimes contributes to a general perception that violent crimes are more frequent than they really are. Survey respondents often report high levels of fear but are imprecise about the threats, although they blame crime in general, the surrounding area in general, or certain demographics, and they refer to a recent crime as evidence of increasing frequency.

Availability

Each of us has a bias toward information that is most available to us. For instance, people who receive their news from only one source are not receiving different information from other sources.

People can exaggerate information just because they become more aware of the information, not because the information is actually new or more important than other information. For instance, elderly people were found to be more fearful when they had frequent visitors; these frequent visitors tended to remind the elderly about all the things to worry about, whereas people with fewer visitors received fewer reminders and developed less fear. Similarly, the self-reported fears of violent crime among residents of Winnipeg, Manitoba, surged after they received broadcasts from a television station in Detroit, Michigan, 1,000 miles away, where the news reports were dominated by crime. Winnipeg's crime rate had not changed (Kennedy & Van Brunschot, 2009, pp. 31–32).

The **availability bias** is easy to manipulate by officials, journalists and their editors, and entertainers—anybody with the capacity to release striking images or conceptualizations to a mass audience.

Unrepresentativeness

People take cognitive shortcuts through their memory to cases that seem "representative" of a new case, even when the cases are not provably representative at all (**unrepresentativeness**). For instance, one person could blame a surge in youth crime on bad parenting because of a memory of bad parents whose child turned to crime, while another person could blame the same surge on poverty because of a memory of a deprived child who stole food.

Base-Rate Neglect

Worse, most people are naturally under-empirical: They react to the most available and proximate events rather than checking the longer-term rate or trend. This dysfunction is called **base-rate neglect**. For instance, if all your friends got an illness, you would be wrong to conclude that the illness is a national epidemic without checking the rate of the illness in the larger population outside your friends.

Maturation

Maturation is the process of improvement or aging. Maturation suggests less base-rate neglect, less anchoring, and more representative cases, although unfortunately most people do not mature as much as they think they do once they reach adulthood.

Maturation can be associated with cycles of biases, rather than a linear trend. For instance, adolescents tend to act more recklessly, particularly when it comes to thrill seeking and speculative risks. Part of this recklessness is hormonal; youth and masculinity are associated with testosterone, a natural hormone that has been shown (in females too) to peak at the same time as reckless behavior. As people age or mature, testosterone production tends to fall naturally and they tend to gather experiences of risks and responsibilities (such as dependent families) that encourage them to be more sensitive. Yet older people, like very young children, naturally focus on very short-term concerns and can even behave more recklessly. For instance, rates of sexually transmitted disease increase after retirement, after a trough in middle age.

Trust and Distrust

Human beings are generally remarkably trusting, in part because living in societies would be practically impossible if each of us generally distrusted every other person. In this sense, human beings have a trust bias. Most of us interact daily with society, trusting that we will not be murdered, extorted, or any of a number of other horrible things.

Trust increases when the speculative behavior is institutionalized within *trust settings* or *trust regimes* that the speculator perceives as fair and universal, such as policing and banking, in part because the system would break down if most of us did not trust it. When rule breaking is exposed, general trust quickly shifts to general distrust. For instance, decades ago most people had confidence in the banking system, but after financial crises and scandals in 2008, they became more sensitive to financial risks and more distrustful of the financial system (Kennedy & Van Brunschot, 2009, p. 10).

While people are generally trusting, they are less trusting of things that seem outside their control, particularly if those things could affect them without being under their control, even if they are favorably disposed to those things. For instance, people are happy to complain about all sorts of pure risks and how poorly they are controlled by higher authorities, but they also complain when controls are imposed without consultation, affect personal freedoms, or use up resources that could be used elsewhere. Surveys can produce contradictory responses, such as majority agreement that a risk is too high and needs to be controlled, but majority disagreement with any significant practical controls that might be proposed.

Fundamental Attribution Error

The **fundamental attribution error** is the attribution of another person's behavior to intrinsic causes while one's own behavior is attributed to extrinsic causes. In more colloquial terms, we tend to make more excuses for our own behavior than we would make for another's behavior. For instance, when walking down the street, we must navigate other people. Most people, if they were absentmindedly to bump into another person, would excuse themselves with some extrinsic reason (such as a rain puddle or a third person to avoid), while blaming the other for intrinsically not paying enough attention.

Group

When individuals join groups, they tend to pick up the dominant biases in the group. For instance, if you socialize mostly within a certain gender, ethnic group, or nationality, you must inevitably be biased toward the views, needs, beliefs, information, and so forth within that group. If you think about it, every one of us is exposed to biases within many groups, unless we eschew all groups and live alone.

Individuals outside groups tend to develop their own parochial biases. Generally, people outside groups tend to be biased against those groups. Competing groups are particularly biased against each other.

Within groups, individuals tend to be vulnerable to social contagion or **peer pressure**. Individuals are apt to pick up the biases within the group, and this is especially the case for individuals who are keener to join the group. Groups tend to encourage members toward reckless behavior, particularly if the majority is unaffected.

Dialectic Arguments

The section will explain dialectic arguments, dialectic traditions, the appeal of the dialectic, and its fallacies.

What Is a Dialectic?

A **dialectic argument** essentially models each thing as the result of a clash between opposing or inversely related other things. For instance, a **dialectic** might imagine that a rock is the resultant of the clash between weather and earth or that a child's personality is the resultant of parents in opposition.

The two opposing things in a dialectic are known as the **thesis** and **antithesis**; their product is the **synthesis**. For instance, the ocean (the thesis) might clash with the coastline (the antithesis) to produce sand (the synthesis).

Be aware that these terms have many other meanings in intellectual life. For instance, a *thesis* can also mean an argument.

You need to recognize the dialectic form of argument so that you can critique it, but you probably should not use it yourself, unless you feel entirely confident in your understanding of it, because it has less formal justification than logic and has fewer uncontested rules. The dialectic model is simple and intuitive, which helps to explain its appeal, but also misleading.

Dialectic Traditions

The dialectic form of argument is a form with ancient philosophical, political, and psychological roots, so much so that it is used more often than admitted. It is used routinely in everyday argument without most people knowing the term or realizing the alternatives. Consequently, it may be used by researchers too without commensurate admission or training.

The dialectic is a formally recognized form of argument in some strands of philosophy, particularly metaphysics, from where many people pick it up or get the impression that it is a logical form of argument, which it is not. In ancient philosophy, the dialectic was an attempt at logical resolution of an argument, and many people continue to use the term as a synonym of argument or logic, but the modern dialectic was revised by the German philosopher Wilhelm Friedrich Hegel (1770–1831) as a deterministic model of ideas. Hegel modeled ideas as a clash of thesis and antithesis producing synthesis. Another German philosopher, Karl Marx (1818–1883), anchored his political philosophy in an explicit development of the Hegelian dialectic that came to be known as *dialectical materialism*, because Marx criticized Hegel as too ideational. Marxists came to regard dialectical materialism as so universal that they founded many arguments on otherwise unproven dialectical models of material things. These Marxist arguments have popularized the dialectic across more cultures than Hegelian philosophy ever could.

The Appeal of the Dialectic

The dialectic has psychological appeal because the image of each thing arising from a clash of opposing things has egotistical appeal. As individuals, each of us is constantly interacting with everything around us in an effectively binary interaction: On one side of the interaction is the individual, and on the other side is everything within the individual's observation. From this egotistical perspective, nothing is tangible except when within the individual's observation, and nothing is more observably affected than when the individual does something to it.

The dialectic has philosophical appeal because the early concerns of philosophy—ethics, spirituality, and politics particularly—are easily conceptualized as contests between two things. If you study ethics, you might imagine right and wrong in an eternal struggle.

The dialectic has spiritual appeal for similar reasons. Religions often conceptualize human life as a constant struggle between right and wrong, good and evil, heaven and hell, faithful and faithless, religion and secularism, or one religion and another religion.

If you study politics, you might imagine one political party clashing with another political party and producing legislation that reflects some compromise between them.

In a single-issue, two-sided war, political dispute, or ethical dilemma, the dialectic imagery may be useful, but otherwise the dialectic is misleading.

The Dialectic's Fallacies

The first problem with the dialectic is that it encourages reductionism—it reduces complex things to simple binary clashes. The dialectic tends to conceptualize just two things in the clash, whereas in real life an effect is usually caused by more than two things. For instance, most political outcomes have many more than two actors. Even if we assume a two-party system, just because two parties are much more powerful than any other parties, the parties are not the only actors. In reality, legislation is a resultant of partisan positions, particular personalities within those parties, precedents, the current context, issue linkage, the public mood, and so forth. Similarly, people do not negotiate between one partisan position and another or between right and wrong alone, but negotiate peculiar stimuli, situations, moods, interpersonal relations, groups, and societies too complex for the dialectic model.

Second, the dialectic's reductionism allows for other biases and fallacies. Many self-interested people want to reduce human choices to a perfect competition between opposing ethical choices rather than imperfectly competitive factors, such as cost, effectiveness, efficiency, and risk. Spiritual gurus and religious extremists like to pretend that life is a simple choice between their way and every other way. Politicians have self-interests in presenting life as a simple clash between their preferred politics and the opposition. Even familial relatives, romantic partners, and business partners tend to recall their relationships as single-issue clashes rather than more nuanced interactions of imperfectly competitive and cooperative interests.

Third, reducing an issue to a simple dialectic is appealing to the lazy or simplistic because it would avoid more complex modeling.

Fourth, the dialectic tends to conceptualize the resultant as incorporating something of both of the clashing things, such as a compromise that reflects some of what each side wants or a product of two inputs. However, sometimes opposing parties clash without reaching a compromise: The opposing parties might clash without any result; or one side might just get everything it wants because the other side gives in. One day a person might choose completely unethical behaviors, the next day completely ethical behaviors, perhaps as psychological compensation for the first day's behaviors. This psychological outcome is less of a clash than a vacillation.

Fifth, the dialectic tends to conceptualize things as always clashing, when in fact entities interact to produce things in all sorts of ways that are not best described as a clash. They could cooperate to produce things. Moreover, many things are produced in ways that are really too complex to be described as either a clash or a cooperation, things such as biological reproduction or industrial manufacturing.

Describing and Critiquing Arguments

Ideally, you should be informed and aware enough to use any of the terms above to describe an argument, but not all terms apply to all arguments. For instance, induction and cogency are not useful terms for describing an argument that is entirely deductive.

In order to analyze someone else's argument or to prompt you to write your own argument, use the framework in Table 7.3. This gives a more stylistic framework for understanding how the argument was written or should be written and thence for understanding its components.

Table 7.3	A framework for creating and analyzing arguments	
Argument's component	Purpose	Ask these "What? How? Why?" questions
Inspiration	To justify the topic to the reader	What is the topic? How does it aim to fill a gap in current/previous knowledge? Why is it important?
Claim	To assert some proposition or observation	What is the claim? How is the claim asserted? Why does the claim matter?
Evidence	To validate a claim or to refute a claim	What is the evidence? How does the evidence support or refute a claim? Why was this evidence appropriate or inappropriate?
Link	To clarify the evidence for a claim, the cause of an effect, or the observation for an induction	What are the two things that are being linked? How does one thing affect the other? Why was the clarification necessary or unnecessary?
Conclusion	To conclude the argument	What is the conclusion of the argument? How is the conclusion reached? Why does the conclusion matter?

For a more technical analysis of an argument, ask the following questions about it:

1. What type of argument is it? The main terms of relevance here are:

    a. Hypothetical

    b. Counterfactual

 c. Prescriptive

 d. Normative

 e. Descriptive

2. What is the approach of the argument? The two main alternatives described in this chapter are:

 a. Logical

 b. Dialectic

3. If the argument is dialectic, what are the thesis, antithesis, and synthesis?

4. If the argument is logical, what are the propositions?

5. Can you find any implicit propositions that need to be made explicit?

6. Of the propositions, which are the premises, conclusions, or propositions in between?

7. Of the propositions, are they all deductions or are some inductions?

8. Are the deductions valid?

9. Do the inductions contradict each other?

10. Is the conclusion (or any other proposition based on the premises) a non sequitur?

11. Can you find any antinomies?

12. Are the assumptions realistic?

13. Are the other propositions unlikely?

14. Is the argument strong?

15. If the argument is purely deductive, is the argument sound?

16. If the argument is inductive or conditional, is the argument cogent?

17. What are the explicit hypotheses?

18. Does the argument contain any fallacies?

19. Do you have any reason to suggest bias?

20. If you find bias, is it allowable or not allowable?

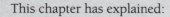

CHAPTER SUMMARY

This chapter has explained:

1. Argument
2. Hypothetical arguments
3. Counterfactual arguments
4. Prescriptive arguments
5. Normative arguments
6. Descriptive arguments
7. Logical arguments

   a. Propositions
   b. Premises
   c. Deductions
   d. Inductions
   e. The structure of arguments
   f. Syllogisms
   g. Valid arguments
   h. Non sequiturs
   i. Antinomies

8. True arguments

   a. True propositions
   b. Prejudices
   c. Beliefs
   d. Faith
   e. Opinions
   f. Assumptions
   g. Making assumptions to escape the burden of proof or argument
   h. Making propositions conditional to escape unrealistic categorical propositions
   i. Making propositions probabilistic to escape unlikely propositions

9. Strong and weak arguments

   a. Sound arguments
   b. Cogent arguments
   c. Hypothetical soundness

10. Fallacious arguments

    a. Circular arguments
    b. Tautologies
    c. False analogies
    d. Ecological fallacies
    e. Reductionism
    f. Applicatory fallacy
    g. Historian's fallacy
    h. Presentism
    i. Narrative fallacy
    j. Psychologist's fallacy
    k. Naturalist fallacy
    l. Argument to the person
    m. Argument from silence

11. Biases

    a. Allowable and unallowable biases
    b. Proximity
    c. Anchoring
    d. Availability
    e. Unrepresentativeness
    f. Base-rate neglect
    g. Maturation
    h. Trust and distrust
    i. Fundamental attribution error
    j. Group

12. Dialectic arguments

KEY TERMS

QUESTIONS AND EXERCISES

1. How does an argument differ from a theory?

2. Take the following four propositions:

   - If Shannon had eaten the candy at the party, she would have had an allergic reaction.

   - If Shannon had had an allergic reaction, she would have missed her physics test.

   - If Shannon had missed the physics test, she would have dropped a whole letter grade.

   - If Shannon had eaten the candy at the party, she would have dropped a whole letter grade.

   a. Which of these terms could be used to describe this argument: hypothetical, counterfactual, prescriptive, descriptive, or normative?

   b. Which of the propositions could be described as premises or conclusions?

   c. Are the propositions categorical or conditional?

   d. Is the argument valid?

3. Take the following four propositions:

   - If there were to be a fire in the apartment, our smoke detector would alert us.

   - If our fire alarm alerted us, we would evacuate in time.

   - If we evacuated in time, we would be safe.

   - Thus, if there were to be a fire in the apartment complex, we would be safe.

   a. Which of these terms could be used to describe this argument: hypothetical, counterfactual, prescriptive, descriptive, or normative?

   b. Which of the propositions could be described as premises or conclusions?

   c. Are the propositions categorical or conditional?

   d. Is the argument valid?

4. Take the following three propositions:

   - Society protects the private property of an individual by enforcing property rights.

   - Assuming people are rational, it is in an individual's best interest to protect his or her private property.

   - Individuals should willingly enter into society to protect their private property.

   a. Identify the type of argument: hypothetical, counterfactual, prescriptive, descriptive, or normative.

   b. Which of the propositions could be described as premises or conclusions?

   c. Are the propositions categorical or conditional?

   d. Is the argument valid?

5. What is necessary for an argument to be valid?

6. Construct a valid argument that a Black Raven is not a White Shoe. Is your argument inductive or deductive?

7. Take the following argument:

   • Poor people tend to vote for Political Party A because its candidates are more likely to represent their social or religious beliefs.

   • Political Party A tends to economic policies that are harmful to the poor.

   • It is in the best interests of poor people to vote for Political Party B.

   a. What are the flaws in this argument?

   b. How could you change the argument to be valid?

   c. What would you need to do to claim this argument as true?

   d. What would you need to do to claim this argument as sound?

8. For each of the following statements, explain why it is true or false:

   a. Deductive arguments present conclusions that are probabilistic, while inductive arguments are deterministic.

   b. In order for an argument to be valid, it must be true.

   c. There are times when biases are acceptable.

d. *Argumentum ex silentio* refers to the fallacy made when personally attacking another with an opposing view in the argument.

e. The truer the argument, the sounder the argument.

9. Identify the fallacy committed in each of the following statements.

   a. "President Reagan was a great communicator because he had the knack of talking effectively to the people."

   b. "The U.S. government can justify its treatment of foreigners because the U.S. government did the same thing to Native Americans."

   c. "If you were to sell armaments, you would be a murderer."

   d. "This man cannot prosecute my client for drug use, as he himself has been known to take drugs!"

   e. "I have three friends named Kevin, and each is a very good dancer. All people named Kevin are great dancers."

   f. "Unmodified foods are better."

   g. "I can't understand how anyone once supported slavery."

   h. "They won because they clearly wanted it more."

   i. "As we now know, she was wrong to choose that option."

Theorizing and Modeling

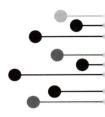

Opening Vignette: Same Observations, Different Models

Source: ©IStockphoto.com/rwarnick.

"If two models agree with observation, neither can be considered more real than the other. A person can use whichever model is more convenient in the situation under consideration. . . . A famous real-world example of different pictures of reality is the contrast between Ptolemy's Earth-centered model of the cosmos and Copernicus' sun-centered model. Although it is not uncommon for people to say that Copernicus proved Ptolemy wrong, that is not true, as in the case of our view versus that of the goldfish; one can use either picture as a model of the universe because we can explain our observations of the heavens by assuming either Earth or the sun to be at rest" (Hawking & Mlodinow, 2013).

Learning
Objectives
and
Outcomes

At the end of this chapter, you should be able to:

1. Critique theories

2. Develop theories

3. Develop hypotheses

4. Design and specify different types of models

Theories

What Is a Theory?

A *theory* is an explanation for the facts.

A theory is not the same as an argument (Chapter 7), even though these terms are often conflated. While an argument does not need to fit any facts, such as a purely hypothetical argument, a theory must fit some facts.

A theory may be derived from philosophy (Chapter 2), but while philosophy needs to be reasonable, it does not need to be factual. Be aware that these terms too are often mixed up. For instance, many political scientists continue to refer to "political theory" and "political philosophy" interchangeably as a field, but these terms are not literal synonyms.

Imagine that someone claims that the world was made by an enormous alien from dirt found hanging around in the universe. This claim could be counted as a theory in the sense that it fits one fact—a world exists. However, this theory must be judged as the poorest of theories, since it fits no other facts and is contradicted by other facts. It may have value as entertainment or tradition, but it has no value as a theory of how the world was created.

Causes and Effects

A theory inherently explains something. Theories explain why something exists, occurs, grows, shrinks, or otherwise interacts with something else.

Theories are causal in that they explain something as a cause or an effect of something else. A **cause** is something that affects something else, perhaps by creating it or changing it. An **effect** is a change or the thing that is changed by the cause.

We could observe the fact that people marry, then ask, why do people marry? A theory that answers this question would treat marriage as an effect and explain the causes of marriage.

Instead of causes and effects, we could theorize about inputs, outputs, drivers, or products. An *input* is something that enters a system. An *output* is something that exits a system. A river is an example of a system with inputs (such as rain and minerals) and outputs (such as flood water and evaporation).

We might refer to drivers and products. A **driver** is something that is directing something else. A **product** is something created from or by some inputs or drivers. In manufacturing, materials and labor are inputted into a production system; some fabrication is outputted.

When comparing two potential causes, try to contrast the strength of their effects. For instance, people might marry for love or money. This proposition gives us two potential causes (love and money) of the effect (marriage). To differentiate these two causes, you might propose that one is stronger than the other.

You could differentiate the **operable conditions**—the conditions under which a cause operates or is dominant. For instance, if two people have more money than either needs, then perhaps the money has no effect and they marry only for love. Under conditions of abundant money, money would no longer *operate* as a cause of marriage and love would have more causal strength.

You could differentiate the causes by whether they are necessary or sufficient. A **necessary cause** must be present for the effect to operate. A **sufficient cause** is sufficient on its own to have an effect. For instance, if the metamorphosis of a tadpole into a frog demands the presence of a specific hormone, that hormone is a necessary cause for the change to happen. If that hormone alone can cause metamorphosis, then it is sufficient. Yet perhaps the hormone is not sufficient on its own because two hormones are necessary for metamorphosis—both hormones are necessary but neither is sufficient.

A cause might be necessary but not sufficient. For instance, to construct a building I need both labor and building material, meaning that labor is a necessary cause and the building material is a necessary cause—the product (the building) has two necessary causes. Each is insufficient but necessary. Together they are sufficient.

A cause might be sufficient but not necessary. For instance, to finish a building I might need 100 laborers or a special machine. With 100 laborers I could finish the building, so they are sufficient. With the special machine I could finish the building, so it too is sufficient. Since either is sufficient, neither is necessary.

Value

A theory does not need to explain all the facts or explain any fact perfectly; it just needs to explain some of the facts. Explaining the facts is not the same as proof. Just because a theory attempts to explain a fact does not mean that it is proven by the fact. As long as it continues to explain some facts, a theory does not cease to be a theory just because it does not explain one fact. A theory is a form of argument and thus, like any argument, could be a strong argument or a weak argument.

A theory becomes more valuable as it

1. explains more facts (parsimony),

2. explains each fact more completely or deeply (depth), and/or

3. becomes simpler (simplicity).

Ideally, a theory should explain all facts, explain each fact completely, and consist of just one proposition, but this ideal is impractical. In practice, parsimony, depth, and simplicity trade off against each other. Normally, the more parsimonious a theory, the shallower the theory; the more completely that the theory explains some fact, the fewer other facts that it explains; the more that a theory explains, the more complicated it becomes.

Often we must make conscious choices about what sort of theory we want. Do you prefer a theory that explains everything in general but nothing in detail? Do you prefer a theory that explains one case perfectly but explains no other case? Do you prefer a theory that can be argued as a simple syllogism but explains little, or do you want a theory that explains more, even if its argument would run to hundreds of pages?

Improving Theory

Remember that a theory is an imperfect trade-off between parsimony (superficial explanation of all the facts), depth (deep explanation of some of the facts), and simplicity, so imperfections alone are not grounds for rejecting a theory. We could judge that the imperfections are too numerous or great for the theory to be useful, but to describe a theory as imperfect is not profound. Almost every theory is imperfect.

To improve knowledge, we must inherently challenge theory, but our objective should be to improve theory rather than simply destroy theory (see Chapter 4). Perhaps a theory needs more depth or breadth. Perhaps a theory needs to be adapted given new facts.

In practice, disproving a theory can be difficult as well as misplaced. Two theories could have completely different arguments, but so long as they explained the same facts and neither was more illogical, false, fallacious, or biased than the other, neither theory could be rejected as inferior to the other (see this chapter's opening vignette). We would be left to find some other way to suggest that one theory was superior to the other, perhaps by showing that the argument behind one was better than the other, perhaps by using a better method or gathering better evidence to test one theory against the other.

Falsifiability

For a theory to be truly scientific, it must be *falsifiable*, meaning that we should know how to prove it wrong, what evidence we would need to prove it wrong, or what it is that we are testing.

Often theories that attempt to be parsimonious end up being so superficial or simple that they are unfalsifiable. Some theorists claim to explain everything but refuse to explain anything in sufficient detail that we could test the theory.

Some theorists deny exceptions as only exceptional in the details. Some theorists claim that their theories are probabilistic and that anything unexplained must be in the minority. These claims are tautologies; they are all-inclusive and thus cannot be disproven (see Chapter 7). For instance, realism, a traditional theory of international relations, is sometimes criticized as so parsimonious as to be nonfalsifiable, because it reduces everything that a state does to a result of its quest for power and conceptualizes every cause and effect of any state behavior as a form of power. Some realists admit criticisms such as these but are unwilling to abandon the parsimony of realism (Baylis & Wirtz, 2002, p. 6).

In your own theorizing, you do not necessarily need to show or state that your theory is falsifiable, but falsifiability should be inherent to your theory. You should be mindful of the demand for falsifiability and be prepared for critics to contest the falsifiability of your theory. This mindfulness should make you more attentive to building a theory with tangible concepts and tangible propositions that can be falsified.

Replicability

Theories become unfalsifiable when they rely on assumptions or concepts that are too intangible to be operationalized—we cannot test anything that is intangible except with personal impressions, which are not replicable. "Power" is the frequent example. Traditional sociologists, political scientists, and diplomatic historians—as well as nontraditional postmodernists—have conceptualized social phenomena, such as rape, as resultants of "power." For critics, power theorists reduce everything to power but do not routinely attempt to disaggregate power. When they offer tangible correlates of power, they often claim that measures cannot truly capture everything about power, so they characterize any proof against power theories as unfair. If nobody can measure power, then power cannot be tested replicably (Baldwin, 1989; Claude, 1962; Rothgeb, 1993).

Influences and Biases

Theories are supposed to explain facts and could be induced from facts alone, but in practice almost all theories have influences and biases. Some are in the arguments (see Chapter 7), some in the methodologies (Chapter 9), some are traditional (Chapter 2), and some are situational or personal to the theorist (see Chapters 4 and 7).

You are not obliged to admit your influences or biases, but you should be aware of them so that you remember to explicitly justify the justifiable influences or biases and steer your theory away from unjustifiable influences or biases.

Sometimes you should admit your influences, so that you have an early opportunity to justify them and you cannot be accused of trying to hide them. For instance, you might admit that you are more knowledgeable about Western history than Eastern history, so your inductions are mostly from Western history. By admitting your bias, you have shown yourself a self-aware and honest theorist and you have deflected (but not eliminated) criticisms of your bias. By admitting your bias, you have effectively admitted that your theory is not parsimonious but is a theory that fits only Western history. If you are lucky, your inductions from Western history might fit inductions from Eastern history, but by admitting your bias you give somebody else the opportunity to prove this wider fit rather than provoking that person to disprove your claim that your theory fits Eastern history.

For example, some critics have complained about the political, philosophical, and methodological biases in American theories of international relations. In the Western tradition, the dominant paradigm has been realism. Realism reflects Western experiences from the ancient world through at least the 19th century, although Western experiences are not representative elsewhere, particularly Asia. Realism is reinforced by expectations of human nature as self-interested and violent, and is attractive because of its parsimony and simplicity. In the early 20th century, more positive expectations of human nature grounded alternative paradigms known as liberalism or institutionalism, which expected states to cooperate and share institutions that would encourage more peaceful and mutually beneficial relations. For realists and other critics, these new paradigms were grounded in unrealistic expectations or simple optimism; hence they used the term *idealism* to describe these new paradigms. The collapse of peace and institutions after World War I seemed to confirm realism. However, during World War II, institutions were reasserted. Moreover, at this time many political scientists were asserting behavioralism—the study of tangible behaviors—in contrast to the realist's traditional instrumentalism. Still, views of international relations and diplomacy generally are split between realism and liberalism. Ironically, liberalism and realism have been most extreme in the same country: the United States (Guilhot, 2008).

Hypotheses

A *hypothetical proposition* is a proposition that proposes something without claiming that it is true. Social scientists should develop arguments that are logical; then they should test whether they are true (see Practical Advice Box 8.1). They could declare any of the propositions as a **hypothesis**—a proposition that is subject to testing. A **proven hypothesis** has evidence that it is true. A **working hypothesis** or a **provisionally accepted hypothesis** is one that is not yet proven but has not been falsified by the tests to date.

You do not need to declare any proposition as a hypothesis until you are looking to test your theory. Your research could be purely theoretical, meaning it will just build or review theory. At some point you or someone else should try to test the theory, at which point a hypothesis must be chosen.

At its simplest, your research so far might consist of some question about a phenomenon and a single proposition about the phenomenon, which you could declare as your hypothesis. When building a more complex theory or reviewing another's theory, you would progress through its various propositions, from which you would choose at least one hypothesis. In a complete social scientific project, you would write a section dedicated to the theory, at the end of which you would be looking ahead to the next section dedicated to testing the theory, so the typical place to declare your hypothesis is at the end of the theory section—before the start of the test section.

Source: ©IStockphoto.com/marekuliasz.

A theory could consist of just one hypothesis. Theories often contain lots of propositions, so you face the choice of which proposition to declare a hypothesis. You could test any proposition within an argument. Ideally, you would test every proposition within the argument, although this is usually less efficient than testing only the conclusion.

Often the hypothesis is the theory's final proposition—its conclusion. Many social scientists deduce propositions until they reach some conclusion that is not yet proven or is easier to prove, and then they declare the conclusion as the hypothesis and proceed to test it. Proving the conclusion implies that the whole argument is true.

For instance, biologists once proved that the genetic materials in the mitochondria of animal cells are inherited exclusively from the animal's mother. They also knew that all humans are animals. Therefore, they concluded that all humans must share mitochondrial genetic material from a single mother. This conclusion remained a hypothesis until proven by samples of the genetic material from lots of humans—they prove that we are all descended from a single mother who lived in Africa more than 100,000 years ago, when other family trees died off to leave her as the one bottleneck ancestor of all of us alive today (Dawkins, 2011, Chapter 2).

Sometimes you have a choice of propositions—you could test all of them as hypotheses, but they would become more burdensome, so you could choose whichever proposition is easiest to test. Look for a hypothesis with a simple causal relationship—with a potential cause and a potential effect that are easy to measure.

You might test another proposition before the conclusion if the conclusion is too difficult to test. Indeed, you might move back through several propositions in the argument if the later propositions are too difficult to test or have been tested elsewhere. Imagine that we are arguing about how people would behave in a fire. The argument might conclude that people would not escape a certain type of fire, but this would be difficult to test realistically without starting fires and unethically exposing human subjects to risks. Instead of testing the conclusion, we could test an earlier proposition, such as the proposition that fire would spread through a particular building faster than someone could escape it.

Models

This section will explain models, show you how to specify a model, and compare different types of models.

What Is a Model?

A **model** is an imperfect representation of something. If it were a perfect representation, it would be the same as the thing. Something that is the same as something else is really a copy, not a model.

This is important to remember, because to criticize a model as imperfect would be unfair. We could criticize a model for being too simplistic or inaccurate to be useful, but we should not criticize a model just for being imperfect.

Be aware that models and theories are similar but are not the same. Be aware too that linguistically, people often use the terms interchangeably, sometimes by convention. For instance, "game theory" is a misleading term with too many meanings; it is mostly a branch of applied mathematics that studies strategies of competition and cooperation. In fact, most game theory is made up of mathematical or formal models, not theories. Yet, by convention, we use the term *game theory* to describe all these things.

Specifying a Model

This section will show you how to specify the variables and constant, how to specify their relationships, how to develop a model, and how to specify its boundaries.

Variables and Constants

While a theory should refer to causes and effects, or perhaps inputs and outputs or drivers and products, a model should refer to variables and constants. Variables and constants are things we use to represent real attributes. Variables represent attributes with varied values, whereas constants do not change.

A **constant** is a representation of an attribute whose value does not change. Gravity and the speed of light are examples of constants.

In social science, few attributes are constant. One could assume that very large or slow things are constant, such as the circumference of the earth, a coastline, or the border between countries. However, not even these things are constant. The earth's circumference varies depending on where you measure it. Coastlines move due to the physical effects of water, seismic activity, and human activities. Borders shift for physical and political reasons. For convenience, we can assume that these things are constant. Anything that does not vary significantly can be assumed to be constant for modeling convenience, without claiming that the attribute is constant in reality.

Constants do not vary in theory, even though measures vary in practice. Nominally, an inch is constant. Human height varies, but a nominal inch does not vary. In practice, the measuring devices that we use to measure an inch in the field are imperfect, so measurements of an inch in the field do vary, even though a nominal inch is constant.

Just because something is constant does not mean that it has no effect, just that its effect is constant. You cannot assume that a constant has less effect than a variable, only that a constant effect does not vary, while a variable effect does vary. For instance, gravity has a constant effect on each of us, even though we take it for granted. Note that while gravity is constant on earth, each person's weight varies.

A **variable** is a representation of an attribute with varied values. For instance, one human attribute is height, another is weight. A variable represents height with nominal values, such as a certain number of inches or centimeters. These values vary between people: Some people are taller than others; the variable representing their height varies between the shortest and the tallest values.

Be aware that you could look at a single item with some quality that does not change, such as a person's gender, but you would be wrong to describe gender as a constant—the value may be constant for one item, but the attribute is actually variable across many items in a population.

While theories refer to causes and effects, models should refer to independent or explanatory variables and dependent variables. The **independent variable** or **explanatory variable** models the cause, driver, or input, while the **dependent variable** models the effect, product, or output. A simple theory might explain marriage as an effect of love. Love is the cause, marriage is the effect, and the causal relationship is directed from love to marriage. A model of this simple theory would refer to love as the independent variable, marriage as the dependent variable, and the relationship as positive.

A **mediator** or **intervening variable** is a variable between other variables. It mediates the relationship between those other variables: A mediator represents both the effect of one of the variables and the cause of the other. Imagine that a simple theory proposes that better teachers help students to better understand the subject. This theory has an independent variable (the quality of teachers) and a dependent variable (the quality of student understanding) but no mediators. A more complex theory proposes that better teachers are more likely to plan their teaching or to produce better teaching plans, which in turn help students to understand their subject. The lesson plan is now an intervening variable between the quality of the teacher and the quality of the student understanding.

A **moderator** moderates the direction or strength of a relationship. For instance, hunger is one cause of eating, but sometimes we are both hungry and too distracted to eat. Our distraction moderates the relationship between hunger and eating by weakening the relationship.

If you suspect that a relationship could switch directions or switch signs, you should consider a moderator. If you suspect that the relationship can change if the conditions change, you probably need to model the conditions as a moderator. For instance, if you suspect that more democratic governments produce superior policies only where the public is paying attention to policies, you should model public attention as a moderator.

If you are uncertain about a variable, first consider whether the variable could be a cause or an effect of any other variable in your model. You might realize that it mediates other variables or is truly an independent variable or a dependent variable. Otherwise, consider whether it could be a moderator. If you still cannot place it, it may not belong in your model.

Relationships

While specifying your variables or constants, you should specify the relationships between them, at least by direction and sign.

As soon you have modeled an independent variable and a dependent variable, you have effectively modeled a causal relationship from the independent to the dependent, which is to say that the **direction** of the relationship is from the independent to the dependent.

You might wonder if the variables have relationships in both directions, as if one variable sometimes affects the other variable but sometimes is the effect of the other variable. You should avoid modeling a relationship in opposing directions at the same time. Instead, you should find conditions under which the relationship has one direction, and conditions under which the relationship is directed the other way. These conditions should lead you to a moderator. For instance, given access to healthy foods, we should expect the consumption of food to be associated with declining obesity, but given access to unhealthy foods, consumption should be associated with increased obesity.

In addition to specifying the direction of the relationship, you should specify its sign: the relationship could be positive, negative, or null. A **positive relationship** or **direct relationship** is one in which one variable increases in value as the other variable increases. For instance, micro economic theory expects price to increase as demand increases. A **negative relationship** or **inverse relationship** is one in which one variable increases as the other decreases. For instance, micro economic theory expects price to fall as supply increases.

A relationship could be **null** in the sense that it is neither positive or negative—in which case no relationship exists, at least under the particular conditions of the particular model. For instance, micro economic theory has nothing to say about the relationship between gravity and price—we can assume a null relationship.

Developing a Model

You probably realize already that you can make choices about the variables to include in the model, so by your own choice a model could be very simple (just two variables) or very complex (many variables, of all types: independent, dependent, mediating, and moderating).

We are incentivized to keep our models simpler. All other things being equal, a simpler model is a better model. Yet at the same time, we want models to be parsimonious and deeply explanatory, so we are incentivized to try to explain everything. Simplicity and explanation are somewhat opposing, so we face a trade-off between simplicity and explanation. We are likely to start with simple models that we would make more complicated. You should add variables for one of three main reasons:

1. To consider the validity of the model or of the argument on which the model is based

2. To expand the model's explanatory breadth or depth

3. To expose new variables that you could test

In developing a model, you should start with one variable that represents a cause, then add a variable representing an effect, or start with a variable representing an effect, then add a variable representing a cause. Once you are satisfied with this simplest model, you could look for more variables.

Adding variables to the modeled process is called **process tracing**. Between an independent variable and a dependent variable, you could add intervening variables. You could add variables after a variable; these new variables represent effects of the variable and are called *consequents*. You could add variables before a variable; these new variables are *antecedents*. The final consequent becomes the dependent variable. The ultimate antecedent becomes the independent variable.

You could trace the process from a dependent variable to an independent variable or vice versa. Every time you add a consequent after a dependent variable, the old dependent variable ceases to be dependent and becomes intervening, while the new variable becomes the new dependent variable. Similarly, every time you add an antecedent before an independent variable, the old independent variable becomes an intervening variable, while the new variable becomes the new independent variable.

Do not forget to consider potential moderators too. Perhaps the independent variable and dependent variable do not need a mediator, only a moderator, in order to expand the model's explanatory scope.

Be aware that you could model more than one independent variable or dependent variable. In nature and in theory, some effects have multiple causes, while some causes have multiple effects. If two causes are necessary in the theory, you should be modeling two independent variables. If one cause affects two other things in the theory, you should be modeling two dependent variables.

Models actually allow you to model contradictory theories. For instance, some theories expect democracies to win more wars, while other theories expect autocracies to win more wars. These theories are contradictory, but you can model both theorized causes (democracy; autocracy) without any fallacies.

Your model can also capture contradictory observations. Empirically, the Correlates of War dataset suggests, during the last 200 years or so, 62% of the victors in major wars (defined by more than 1,000 combat fatalities on all sides) were democratic states, while 38% were autocratic. A model can have just one dependent variable (victory) while expressing these frequencies/probabilities by different relationships with the dependent variable (Newsome, 2007, pp. 10–11).

Boundaries

You should be explicit about what is within the model; in other words, you should be declaring what you are modeling. This is important for our understanding and your communication of the model. In effect, you should acknowledge the boundary between whatever is within and whatever is without the model. Things within the model are **endogenous**, while anything without the model is **exogenous** or **extraneous**.

Explicitly specify the variables and constants that are being modeled. Implicitly, nothing else is being modeled, but to avoid any confusion, sometimes you should be explicit about whatever is exogenous, especially when your audience might expect you to model something that you want to keep exogenous.

For instance, if I were to declare that I was modeling the effects of individual psychology on the individual's choice to marry, then individual psychology and marriage would be explicitly endogenous, while implicitly everything else would be exogenous.

Perhaps our audience expects models of marriage to include individual wealth as well as individual psychology. To help my audience's understanding, I should declare that individual wealth is exogenous to my model.

Alternatively, given that my audience expects me to model individual wealth, I could include individual wealth in my model (making it endogenous).

Sometimes we should include something in order to explain it, but we cannot reach a satisfactory theory for it or perhaps it is too difficult to measure. One solution is to declare it exogenous.

Declaring something exogenous is not the same as declaring something irrelevant. We could theorize about something and conclude that it has effects on the things that we want to model, yet we could choose to keep it exogenous for simplicity or in order to avoid the methodological problems of measuring it. If you make any of these choices, you should be honest about them, effectively declaring that you did choose to keep some things exogenous in order to reduce your own burden. This keeps critics from accusing you of failing to consider something. Critics could still complain that your model is too simplistic, but this would be a contest about the trade-off between parsimony and simplicity. You should feel justified in declaring something exogenous if one of the following is true:

1. Its relationship with any of the endogenous variables is trivial (null or too weak to significantly affect it).

2. The thing is constant, not variable. (If something is constant, it cannot be used to explain variance in the variables.)

One methodological solution to any exogenous variable is to hold the exogenous variable constant. For instance, we could combine different explanations for marriage until we have a model with wealth, love, and the availability of chocolate as independent variables, but we are most interested in the relative importance of wealth and love. In our test, we could hold the availability of chocolate constant by choosing to study marriage in societies where the availability of chocolate is the same. We could nullify the availability of chocolate by studying marriage in societies that have never known chocolate.

Types of Models

Models exist in various forms and for various purposes. The subsections below will compare descriptive and prescriptive, tangible and conceptual, static and dynamic, deterministic and stochastic, solvable and simulated, linear and curvilinear, and linear and cyclical models.

Descriptive or Prescriptive

Models can be descriptive or prescriptive. In basic research, you will come across mostly descriptive models; in applied research and ethical research, you will come across more prescriptive models.

Descriptive models describe something. For instance, medical students often look at drawings of human organs in order to learn about those organs—these drawings are effectively descriptive models of the organs.

Prescriptive models show how the user should behave. Meanwhile, medical students could learn how they should behave ethically or use a certain technology by looking at a diagram of the process they are supposed to follow. Decision-support advisories, standard operating procedures, guides to using a system, and ethical advisories are all forms of prescriptive models.

Tangible or Conceptual

Descriptive models can be tangible or conceptual.

A **tangible model** (also known as a **physical model**) observably represents something. For instance, a map represents terrain or routes, a plan represents how something is built or developed, a clock and a calendar are representations of time, and scale models are conventionally used to represent houses, vehicles, or molecules.

A **conceptual model** is less observable than a tangible model. The border between a conceptual model and a tangible model is subjective. A written, formulaic, or statistical description of something is usually considered a conceptual model. Drawings and scale models are normally considered tangible models, but as they become more abstract they tend to be considered conceptual, and as they become more realistic they tend to be considered tangible.

Static Versus Dynamic Models

Static models have no variables, only constants: All inputs are fixed and do not vary, and thus the outputs cannot vary. For instance, a static model of insurgency might assume 100 insurgents with perfect intent to attack a target, which has the defensive capability to deter or prevent 90% of insurgents from attacking, leaving 10 insurgents to attack the target with the capacity to cause $1 million of damage per insurgent, or $10 million of total damage.

Dynamic models allow for changes in the inputs and thus changes in the outputs. A dynamic variant of the example static model above would allow you to vary the number of insurgents, the deterrence or prevention rate, and the damage rate.

Deterministic Versus Stochastic Models

Deterministic models do not allow for uncertainty: given the same inputs, the model would produce the same outputs every time. Note that deterministic models can be static models but are not necessarily static models, since deterministic models allow for variables, while static models have constants but no variables. Whatever the inputs, given the same inputs a deterministic model will produce the same outputs.

Stochastic or **probabilistic models** include uncertainty, usually in the form of some random variable or some variation of probability: The model might allow for either of two possible outcomes from one input, depending on a random choice; or it might assign a probability to an input.

A perfectly realistic model would be deterministic, because a perfectly realistic model would include everything that affects the outputs, in which case the outputs could be predicted from the inputs.

Most social scientific models end up as probabilistic models. As you have seen already, most social scientific arguments are probabilistic (see Chapter 7), so most social scientific models are probabilistic. Researchers struggle to describe all the relationships accurately, so they end up modeling things so imperfectly that they can only say what might happen, not what will happen.

Solvable Versus Simulated Models

Solvable models describe something in a formal way that can be solved logically or mathematically. For instance, I could theorize that each hen would produce

Source: ©iStockphoto.com/Krugloff.

one egg per day. Given 50 hens, a mathematical model would predict 50 eggs per day. Given 50 hens and 50 days, the model would predict 2,500 eggs. This model is perfectly solvable—given the inputs, the outputs can be solved in only one way. **Formal theory** is the misleading term used to describe mathematical representations of logical processes. Formal theory is really a model, rather than a theory, and is not necessarily more formal than any other model.

A **simulation** is an operable model, meaning that it can be operated like a machine. Usually simulations are operable in the sense that they can be operated in imitation of something. For instance, I could simulate the various causes of marriage by asking people to pretend to face a choice about marriage under various imaginary conditions.

Formal logical solutions are regarded as deterministic if the formal logic is based on a purely deductive argument (see Chapter 7). However, simulated solutions must be regarded as probabilistic because they lack the deductive certainty of formal logic.

Linear Versus Curvilinear Models

Linear models assume only linear relationships, in which the two variables change at a constant rate in proportion to each other.

For convenience of explanation, let us assume that the two variables are an input and an output, although the two variables might be a frequency and a performance. In a linear relationship, the outputs are directly proportional to the inputs, meaning that the outputs change with the inputs at a constant rate or factor. On a graph, the plot would be a straight line. For instance, if the outputs are three times the inputs, then they are directly proportional by a factor of three. If the inputs go up as the outputs go up, then the relationship is positive. If the outputs go down as the inputs go up, then the relationship is negative.

Curvilinear models allow for both linear and **nonlinear relationships**. An **exponential model** is one in which the output changes at an accelerating rate. The output rises quicker than the input rises. For instance, births tend to rise exponentially as new organisms reach maturity and reproduce.

If outputs decelerate with increasing inputs, we would be seeing **diminishing returns**, such as when initial increases in rewards lead to dramatic improvements in performance but the effect declines as people become satiated.

A **threshold model** is one in which the outputs change only once the inputs have breached some threshold. For instance, rebellions and other forms of political violence against government suddenly break out not upon the first provocation but after many provocations, such as after a government abuses rights, raises taxes, or starts wars.

A **normal distribution** or **bell curve** (so called because of its shape on a graph) is one in which the outputs do not increase much for a while, dramatically increase like an exponential curve, flatten off like diminishing returns, dramatically decrease, then flatten off. This is called a normal distribution because many natural behaviors normally look like this. For instance, student performance is normally distributed in that a few students perform very poorly, most perform very close together, and a few perform very well.

A normal distribution is **unimodal** in that it has a most common value or item (the **mode**). A **distribution** could be **bimodal**—it has two modes: On a graph, the distribution would rise once and fall away, then rise a second time—it would have two peaks. Bimodal distributions occur often in nature, such as in political disputes, where most people choose one party or the other. Distributions can be trimodal—with three modes. Distributions can have as many modes as you could identify statistically, although more modes become meaningless.

These nonlinear relationships are difficult to model statistically, so most academic models are actually linear. For instance, a political scientist might model rebellions by describing human rights abuses as causes of rebellions, effectively assuming a linear relationship rather than modeling a threshold relationship. However, in social science, probably most relationships are nonlinear while most models are linear. You should be aware of such linear biases and be aware of more realistic alternatives, even though many statistical models would force you to assume linearity. Statistical solutions do exist for curvilinear models, but this book has no space to introduce them to you.

Where you discover nonlinearity, you should try to disaggregate the variables or add variables. One variable may be conflating too many things, each with a different linear relationship with the other variable, but together, when conflated, they look like one curvilinear relationship. Imagine that we observe that a certain crime-fighting practice seems to reduce crime quickly, but promote crime in the long run. We should disaggregate the independent variable (the practice) or the dependent variable (the crime). Perhaps the practice reduces only one kind of crime quickly but promotes other crimes slowly. Perhaps the modeled practice conflates several real practices, some of which reduce crime quickly while others promote crime slowly.

Given nonlinearity, you should consider also mediators or moderators. Imagine that a particular policing practice has previously reduced crime but suddenly no longer works. Look for a mediator or moderator that could explain the change. Perhaps some neighboring jurisdiction has changed its policies and now allows criminals to shelter there where your policing practice cannot affect them. This neighboring jurisdiction is a moderator. Perhaps the criminals have acquired some defensive capability that reduces the effectiveness of your policing practice. This defensive capability is a mediator.

Linear Versus Cyclical Models

Linear models have a single direction, from the independent variable to the dependent variable. In practice, many things are modeled as **cycles**, such as life

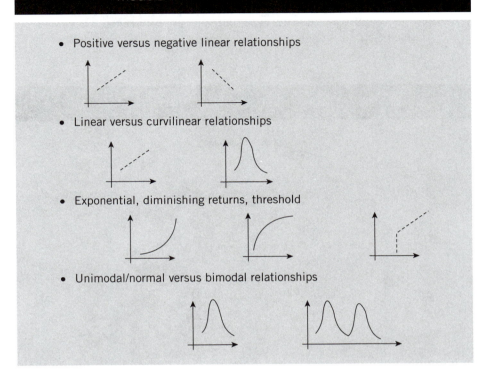

Figure 8.1 Graphical depictions of different distributions and models

- Positive versus negative linear relationships

- Linear versus curvilinear relationships

- Exponential, diminishing returns, threshold

- Unimodal/normal versus bimodal relationships

cycles, regulatory cycles, and feedback loops, where the process ultimately leads back to its start.

Arguments and theories are difficult to complete as cycles: Any such argument or theory could be criticized as a circular argument—a logical fallacy (see Chapter 7). Thus, cyclical models are difficult to justify on theoretical grounds.

Yet cycles are routine in prescriptive models. For instance, a regulatory cycle could begin with a policy, an inspection of subjects to check compliance with the policy, a review of the policy's effectiveness, and development of a new policy (see Figure 8.2).

These cycles are difficult to model linearly, but you can easily do one of two things:

1. You could model each of the individual steps as separate linear models, so that you could test each individually. In the example above, you could model any step, such as the relationship between a review of the policy and the development of a new policy.

2. You could model the whole process as a linear process from the start to the end, without returning to the start. The main problem with this approximation is that your linear model would ignore the step between where one cycle ends and a new cycle begins, although you could separately model this too as a linear process.

Figure 8.2   A cyclical model of the policy process

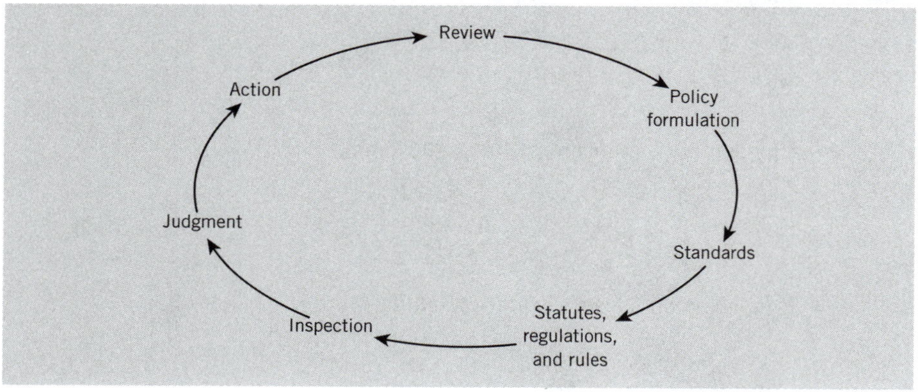

CHAPTER SUMMARY

This chapter explained:

- Theory
- Causes and effects
- What makes a theory more valuable
- How to improve theory
- The principle of falsifiability
- The principle of replicability
- Influences and biases in a theory
- Hypotheses
- Models

- Variables and constants
  - o Independent
  - o Dependent
  - o Mediating
  - o Moderating
- The relationships between variables or constants
- How to develop a model
- How to specify a model's boundaries

- Endogenous and exogenous variables
- Types of models
  - Descriptive
  - Prescriptive
  - Tangible
  - Conceptual
  - Static
  - Dynamic
  - Deterministic
  - Probabilistic
  - Solvable
  - Simulation
  - Linear
  - Curvilinear
  - Cyclical

KEY TERMS

QUESTIONS AND EXERCISES

1. What is the difference between a theory and an argument?

2. If you have a theory that explains multiple cases, what term describes the value of this theory?

3. If you have a theory that explains one case thoroughly, what term describes the value of this theory?

4. If you have a model with only two variables (the independent and the dependent) while another model has three variables, what term describes the comparative advantage of the former?

5. In order for a theory to be considered scientific, it must fulfill which two standards?

6. Read this text: "Let's imagine that during a political election we placed voters along a spectrum from left to right depending on their political attitudes (the most left being extremely liberal and the most right being extremely conservative). As we continued to plot voters, a 'normal' or 'bell' distribution would begin to form, with the highest frequency of voters being located in the very middle. During elections, a conservative candidate would attempt to attract the median voter in order to gather the most votes. This same strategy applies to the liberal candidate. Candidates should prefer to place themselves as close to the middle to secure the most votes." What parts of the text above are best described as a theory or a model?

7. Read this text: "One field of sociology seeks to explain the various social institutions that exist within the world of sports. Two sociologists have presented evidence that soccer is popular amongst girls and women in the United States, while opportunities for females to participate in soccer are lower in nations where football is more popular, such as Brazil and England. They observed that more popular sports in America (such as American Football) offer fewer opportunities for women to participate than for men to participate. They characterized their observations as evidence for 'hegemonic masculinity' in sports" (Markovits & Rensmann, 2013).

a. Identify the independent and dependent variables in the above text.

b. Draw a graphical model with these two variables.

CHAPTER 9

Methods

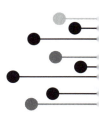

Opening Vignette: Expectations for Social Scientific Methods

Carl Sagan

Source: http://commons.wikimedia.org/wiki/File.Carl_Sagan_Planetary_Society.JPG.

"At the heart of science is an essential balance between two seemingly contradictory attitudes—an openness to new ideas, no matter how bizarre or counterintuitive they may be; and the most ruthless skeptical scrutiny of all ideas, old and new. This is how deep truths are winnowed from deep nonsense" (Sagan, 1997, p. 304).

Methods and Methodologies

A **method** is a technique for investigating or testing. A **methodology** is a collection of methods that is prescribed or used as appropriate for particular conditions.

A **test** is any attempt to establish something. Some people use this term loosely to describe everything a researcher does, but the useful specific meaning is the testing of hypotheses, which is why you should get in the habit of referring to your test separately from the method chosen for the test. For instance, you could be testing a hypothesis with several methods—a survey, an experiment, a historical case study, in which case you would have one test and three methods.

Learning Objectives and Outcomes

At the end of this chapter, you should understand:

1. The difference between methods and methodologies

2. How to research history

3. How to study cases

4. How to survey cases or respondents

5. How to research in the field

6. How to experiment

To get to the hypotheses that you will test, you should ensure that the argument is logical and true (Chapter 7), then develop hypotheses (Chapter 8). Remember, under scientific principles, these hypotheses should be falsifiable.

Replicability

Under scientific principles, methods should be **replicable** in the sense that other people could perform the same method in order to confirm or falsify your results. In practice, this implies two obligations:

1. You should be testing in such a way that others could replicate it for themselves.

2. You should describe your test in sufficient detail that a reader would understand how to replicate the test.

Practically, the first obligation mostly means that your test should not rely on you personally or subjectively. The second obligation can become impractical if the test is very complex—for instance, in an article of 10,000 words, you probably would not spend more than 1,000 words describing your method.

If you are short of space for a description of your method, you should refer the reader to any or all of the following three things:

1. An appendix containing the original **instrument** (that is, something used to measure something else) or a fuller description

2. A publicly accessible archive (this could be your own webpage or a cooperative library)

3. Your own contact details, so that the reader can request more information from you directly

Most scientists would be happy to observe that your method could be replicated, without going to the trouble of actually replicating it. In fact, few results are ever replicated, mostly because publishers and readers prefer novel research. However, recent revelations of fraudulent results in top journals have encouraged more attention to replication. For instance, a survey of the top 100 education journals found that only 0.13% of replication studies were actual replications. More alarming, attempted replications were much likelier to replicate the original results if the article was published in the same journal (89%) or was authored by the same authors (71%) than if the attempted replication was by different authors (54%) (Makel & Plucker, 2014). Junior researchers, including likely readers of this book, should expect more attention to replication in the future.

Quantitative and Qualitative

Before we examine different methods, we need to acknowledge a common differentiation of methods into quantitative or qualitative methods. This is a somewhat vague differentiation; the difference remains poorly defined.

Sometimes it is set up as a difference between large-n or small-n datasets (see Chapter 10), but this is a differentiation by the number of data, which does not necessarily have anything to do with methods. You could survey five people or 5 million people, but the method is still a survey.

Sometimes quantitative and qualitative methods are set up as a contest between statistical and nonstatistical, but this is another false differentiation, since any use of numbers is essentially statistical. Just because a dataset is smaller does not mean that we could not apply statistical analysis to it.

Sometimes quantitative and qualitative methods are set up as a contest between objective methods and subjective methods, but this is another false differentiation. Large datasets or small datasets could be populated with subjective or objective data. Both subjective and objective data can be analyzed statistically.

The most literal way to differentiate quantitative methods from qualitative methods is to say that the qualitative methods are more sensitive to the qualities of the subject and proximate to the subject, while quantitative methods are less sensitive to the qualities and more remote from the subject. Thus, quantitative methods tend toward large datasets, statistical analysis, remote correlates, and objective measures, while qualitative methods tend toward small datasets, proximate attention to the qualities of the subject, and subjective measures. Qualitative methods, in this literal differentiation, include personal interviews with individual persons. Examples of literal quantitative methods include automated analysis of online consumer behavior.

Qualitative methods are historically dominant because they are more accessible and less burdensome. This changed greatly in the modern period, when bureaucratic capacity and information technologies enabled more quantitative methods. Quantitative methods were certainly dominant by the 1960s but have suffered crises of confidence after their failures to predict the Latin American debt crisis in the 1980s; the collapse of communist economic and political systems around 1990; the Asian economic crisis in the late 1990s; the surge in terrorism around September 11, 2001; and the global economic and fiscal crisis beginning in 2008 (Suder, 2004, p. 178). Since then, some social scientists have again criticized the dominance of quantitative methods. For instance,

Kristin Luker, a sociologist, referred to the 2008 crisis as evidence for a failure of supposedly "rigorous" methods. She criticized the trend in social science toward ever "more abstractly mathematical" methods. She blamed "money and power since World War II"—meaning the alleged political and commercial elites' use of quantitative methods to separate themselves from ordinary people with access to only more qualitative methods. At the same time, she criticized qualitative methods: "My main complaint about qualitative methods is that they so often lack a method." She advocated a "sweet spot" between these two extremes (Luker, 2008, pp. 25, 31–32).

Control and Naturalness

While the differentiation between quantitative and qualitative methods is often vague or misleading, the differentiation between control and naturalness is always insightful. A **control** is something we do to maintain or change a condition. Without our control, everything would be **natural**—existing in nature without us affecting it. Controls are useful in helping us to test what we mean to test and to replicate a test, but naturalness is desirable so that we observe something as it is naturally rather than as we have affected it.

The ideal method is completely controlled by the researcher, and entirely unaffected by the researcher's control (it remains natural). This ideal is practically impossible. As we impose more control, we tend to affect the thing we are observing. For instance, in order to observe how nurses perform in their medical roles, we could rely on our own eyesight, ears, touch, conversations, and thoughts as we follow them around performing their roles. Our observations would seem natural, but we would be affecting our subjects by following them around, getting in their way, making them self-conscious, and interacting with them. If we wanted to be sure that the thing remained entirely natural, we would withdraw in order to avoid affecting the thing, but total withdrawal would leave us no opportunity to observe. This trade-off is between control and naturalness.

The ideal controlled method would involve our observation of something in the **laboratory** (an artificially controlled environment), where we can perfectly control the conditions and the measurements. The ideal natural method would involve our observation of something in its natural state in the **field** (an uncontrolled environment) without affecting the thing—perhaps we would need to remain invisible and unreactive to the thing and its environment. Whereas perfectly natural observations must occur in the field, historical research can occur in any **repository** of information—an archive, a library, a fossil layer, or wherever artifacts from the past or past observations are deposited or reposed.

Thus, control and naturalness can be summarized in three contexts:

1. Laboratory research allows more controlled observations.

2. Field research allows more natural observations.

3. Repository research allows observations of things in the past.

Triangulation

In practice, we can try to combine sufficient control and naturalness in one method, or we can combine a more controlled method with a more natural method. **Triangulation** is the use of more than one method in the study of the same thing. (In some professions, triangulation is known as "validation.") Triangulation is used (a) to get the best out of multiple methods and (b) to reduce exposure to the weaknesses of any one method. All methods are imperfect; each has advantages and disadvantages. By triangulating, we could maximize the advantages. For instance, by triangulating a case study with a survey, we would combine the depth of a case study with the **generalizability** of a survey.

However, if we triangulate poorly, we could maximize the disadvantages. Moreover, sometimes some methods are clearly superior to others, so to triangulate with inferior methods is not scientifically advantageous.

As you should realize by now, triangulation is open to abuse. One researcher could be dissatisfied with the results of your research but be unable to challenge your method. He or she might attempt to disprove it with an inferior method while claiming to triangulate your results.

The main principle of triangulation is to offer some advantage over the other method. Usually, triangulation is a combination of a very natural and uncontrolled method with a very controlled but unnatural method. For instance, Richard E. Nisbett and Dov Cohen (1996) wanted to test whether a culture of honor drives violence. They triangulated their tests by experimenting with subject reactions in the lab, and by measuring honor and violence in the field.

The following sections explain the main methods: historical research, case study, survey research, direct observation in the field, and experimental research.

Historical Research

Historical research collects past observations. Past observations are natural in the sense that the researcher cannot control what happened in the past. However,

Source: ©iStockphoto.com/urbancow.

the observer and thence the historian can select which observations to study or report. Moreover, the observer or the historian could interpret these observations in ways that misrepresent the past. Thus, although past observations in themselves are natural, historical research cannot be as natural as direct observations of things in the field as they occur.

Historical research involves studying past observations of what happened—these past observations are found in memoirs, artifacts, and other primary sources. These past observations are more natural than any experiment in the laboratory, but they are not direct. Historical research is not field research because we cannot travel back in time to observe the thing in the field in the past, so historical research cannot be as natural as current observations. At the same time, historical research cannot be controlled either, because we cannot control the past, although we can control how we study the past.

Note that subjects of historical research are not the same today as they were in the past, so historical study is inherently less natural than direct observation in current time. A fossilized animal is a stone representation of biochemical material (such as bones and tissues) that no longer exists. Similarly, a letter that someone had written in the past must have aged by today—age does not necessarily matter unless the content has been damaged due to decomposition, rough handling, graffiti, or suchlike.

So far as the historian imposes control, it should be to avoid bias or error. The historian has the responsibility to choose observers or artifacts that are unbiased and error free, and to report findings without error or bias.

Historical research is most natural where it randomly collects unfiltered anecdotes and artifacts, but is then also least controlled. The historian could use more controlled instruments, such as case studies, to control what is being studied, and common survey instruments, in order to collect recollections from people who experienced the event under study.

Case Study

A **case** is one of many examples of a thing. For instance, the marriage of Prince Charles and Lady Diana Spencer is one case among many marriages.

Historians commonly study historical cases; legal researchers commonly study legal cases; environmental scientists study cases of environmental change; geologists study examples of different rocks; and anthropologists study social or cultural cases.

As soon as a researcher chooses a case for further study, the researcher has imposed some control. If the researcher chooses a case with particular attributes, the control has increased, but beware of selection bias. The case should be selected as the fairest test, not because it is the case in which the researcher expects to find what the researcher wants to find.

Case studies should be important cases or least likely cases:

1. An **important case** or **key case** is more important than the average case, implying that if the important case cannot prove the hypothesis, then the theory cannot explain important facts. For instance, according to the Correlates of War dataset, around 65 major wars (defined by at least 1,000 combat fatalities on all sides) have occurred in the last 200 years. Hundreds of smaller wars have occurred in the same period. Researchers can justify their study of only the major wars on the grounds that major wars are more important.

2. A **least-likely case** is selected by attributes that make it least like the sort of case that the theory is best at explaining. For instance, imagine that someone has theorized about why people marry, and has induced only from heterosexual marriages, or has proven the theory with only heterosexual cases. Another researcher could justify a new test using only homosexual marriages as least-likely cases. The researcher might hope that if the theory explains even these least-likely cases, then the theory has been empirically strengthened. Note that a tester could take the least-likely principle too far and select a case that is unlike anything the theorist intended to explain. For instance, testing a theory of marriage using cases of romantic relationships short of marriage is probably an unfair test.

Ideally, you would select a case that is both important and least likely. If you could not find such a case, you could study two cases: an important case and a least-likely case.

Survey Research

A **survey** is a study of lots of cases from the same category. To conduct **survey research**, we could survey tigers, tigers of a certain age, tigers from a certain region, democracies, ash trees, criminals, politicians, or civil wars—any set of things that can be defined as falling within the same category. A historian could survey all the politicians involved in a certain historical event. A legal researcher could survey all the constitutional cases heard by the Supreme Court. A biologist could survey all the diseased trees in a forest. A geologist could survey all the seismic fault lines under a city.

Most surveys are a mix of naturalness and control; they can lie anywhere on the spectrum from extremely natural to extremely controlled. Surveys gather purely natural data if they survey unspoiled things in the field without affecting them. Imagine that we could survey the health of trees in a forest from afar without touching them. This would seem as natural a form of survey as one could expect.

We still need the survey to be somewhat controlled to be replicable. If someone walked through a forest and then reported his or her subjective impressions, that person would count as a primary source, but the method would not be truly replicable.

To explain replicability, the following subsections introduce different survey instruments and explain how to design surveys in general.

Survey Instruments

Survey researchers affect the thing they want to observe whenever they construct an instrument to gather the data they want. Most surveys are tangible instruments, such as a piece of paper or a webpage issued to a person (the respondent) who is asked to respond to questions or prompts within the document.

Surveys look more controlled when they start to use instruments. Most survey researchers value the control offered by some sort of **survey instrument** that prompts observations and controls the responses. These instruments could be as simple as documents with questions or prompts to respond with information; sometimes the instrument is a system of automated sensors, computers, and software. The subsections below explain direct surveys, questionnaires, and Delphi surveys.

Direct Surveys

A **direct survey** is the direct observation of lots of cases. Even direct observers in the field could use survey instruments to guide what they observe and record.

Most survey instruments specify the desired observations and control the allowable responses. For instance, a book describing the different species of trees is a useful guide to the researcher of trees. From this book, the researcher could specify the trees to look for and the healthy attributes to look for.

A survey should proceed according to some coding rules. A **coding rule** is an instruction as to how to judge the observation. If a researcher designed a survey instrument as a series of prompts for what to observe and measure, such as the height of the tree and the presence of fungus, another researcher could use the same instrument in a replicable way.

How do we know if a tree is diseased? A coding rule could instruct you to code a tree as one of three things: healthy if you can see no fungus, diseased if you can see any fungus, or dead if you can see no new growth since the previous year.

Coding rules have three main benefits:

1. They help the method to be replicable.

2. Different researchers using the same instrument are more likely to produce the same codes.

3. The coding rules are tangible evidence of your method.

Two researchers could use the same coding rules without needing to develop their own. Their codes are more likely to agree if they use the same rules. Their codes might differ, but at least their instruments are common.

Coding rules offer two main problems. One downside of coding rules is that they can be too exclusive—they could restrict the observer to things that do not fully capture the phenomenon of interest, or they could restrict how the observer reports the observation.

A second downside is that the coding rules can taint the response. Coding rules reflect the designer's biased or narrow understandings of the phenomenon. For instance, someone might decide to study sexism in a country. The designer might instruct survey researchers to survey women on their experiences of sexism, but this would be a biased instrument—it would not survey men who live in the same country and could have experienced sexism. Another designer might write the coding rules in such a way that the coding rules exclude all sorts of behaviors that another researcher would regard as examples of sexism.

Questionnaires

A **questionnaire** is a survey instrument with questions that the subjects are meant to answer.

Source: ©iStockphoto.com/wdstock

Questionnaires are relatively controlled and cheap instruments. They are used routinely to measure human attributes because directly observing natural human behavior is very burdensome, particularly across large populations.

However, questionnaires are problematic. One of the problems is that the questionnaire is a very controlled instrument that can be a vector for the designer's biases.

Highly controlled methods tend to be highly unnatural methods. People often think of questionnaires as natural methods because they interact with the subjects directly, but this is misleading. A questionnaire is not necessarily an accurate survey of the respondents—respondents have their own biases; respondents can be inattentive or dishonest.

Questionnaires do not directly observe natural behaviors. You could use a questionnaire to survey people on their attitudes, values, beliefs, opinions, motivations, incentives, past behaviors, or intended behaviors, but you cannot use a questionnaire to directly observe their actual behaviors. A questionnaire relies on the respondent to report to the researcher, so it is actually an indirect instrument from the researcher's perspective, in the sense that it does not directly observe the subject; it is just the instrument by which the subject observes itself.

While a direct nonparticipant observer could observe how people behave naturally when they cross the street, a questionnaire is not directly observing any behavior when it asks people how they would cross the street.

Respondents could claim to behave differently than they really behave, perhaps without realizing the difference. In hypothetical situations, people tend to claim more recklessness or bravery than they would exhibit in real situations. For instance, if asked how they would behave if they saw a stranger being robbed, most people would claim to defend the victim, but in practice, most people would not (Newsome, 2014, p. 161).

Sex, gender, race, religion, politics, ethics, and crime are notoriously unreliable subjects for questionnaires, so ideally should be studied in more natural ways.

People tend to be dishonest about topics that they consider private or sensitive. For instance, few people admit to racism when asked directly, but most people claim to have experienced racism.

Social expectations also cause people to exaggerate or understate certain behaviors. For instance, in most questionnaires women report more depression than men report, leading some researchers to conclude that women suffer more depression, but other researchers have wondered whether men are less willing to admit depression or conceptualize depression differently. Indeed, when asked whether they have regrets, anxieties, dismay, and other negative feelings, men respond affirmatively at about the same rate as women. Similarly, in surveys men tend to report many more sexual partners than women report, but many researchers have noted cultural expectations for men to overreport their sexual activity and for women to underreport it. When questioned while connected to what they think are lie detector machines, women and men report about the same number of partners (Fisher, 2013).

To make a questionnaire more natural, the questions need to be framed and phrased in ways that encourage the respondent to respond realistically. For instance, a question should carefully specify a hypothetical but realistic situation and ask how the respondent would behave. This would give a more behaviorally realistic response than a response to a question about whether helping a victim of crime is right—most people would say that helping the victim is right, but fewer could claim that they would help the victim.

A questionnaire is *valid* if it accurately measures what it intends or claims to measure. It is *reliable* if it performs in the same way each time it is used. You should be concerned about the reliability of a survey if respondents answer similar questions differently. Imagine that you ask respondents (a) whether they agree with a certain political party and (b) whether they would vote for that political party. If respondents tend to answer these two questions in opposing directions, then something must be wrong with the questions, and the survey must be unreliable. Reliability can be measured statistically by analyzing agreement between each respondent's answers to similar questions. This book does not have space to explain statistical analysis, but be aware of how reliability is reported statistically so that you can read other people's reports on their surveys: Reliability is reported statistically as a number between 0 and 1, where 1 suggests perfectly reliability and 0 suggests absolute unreliability.

Delphi Surveys

The survey itself can be structured in more reliable ways. The least reliable surveys are informal discussions, particularly those between a small number of people under the leadership of one person, such as those commonly known as focus groups. Informal discussions tend to be misled by those most powerful in the perceptions of group members, and by mutually reactionary, extreme positions.

Delphi surveys encourage respondents away from narrow subjectivity by asking them to re-forecast a few times, each time after a revelation of the previous round's forecasts (traditionally only the median and interquartile range are revealed, thereby ignoring outliers). Interpersonal influences are eliminated by keeping each respondent anonymous to any other. This method helps respondents to consider wider empirical knowledge while discounting extreme judgments, and helps them to converge on a more realistic forecast. It has been criticized for being nontheoretical and tending toward an artificial consensus, so my own Delphi surveys have allowed respondents to submit a written justification with their forecasts that is released to all respondents before the next forecast.

The Survey Design Process

As explained in the subsections below, survey design should follow the following eight steps:

1. What information is required?

2. Who are the target respondents?

3. How will they be contacted?

4. What survey item would generate the necessary information?

5. What response format would give enough control without invalidating the responses?

6. How should the items be ordered?

7. What other content does the survey need?

8. How should it be pretested?

What Information Is Required?

The hypotheses under test should guide you as to what information you need. If the hypothesis proposes that job security drives private spending, we need to measure job security and private spending.

Who Are the Target Respondents?

The required information should guide you to the target respondents. To operationalize job security, we could survey corporations on their expectations for retaining or reducing their current employee population, or we could survey employees on how secure they feel about their jobs. In the former cases, our target respondents are corporations; in the latter, they are employees.

Representativeness. You could survey every case so that your survey is entirely **representative**, but surveying more cases becomes more burdensome, so you might survey only a sample. Sometimes you might attempt to survey all cases but fail to access all cases. For instance, you might want to survey all cases of a diseased tree, but one foreign jurisdiction might prevent you from visiting cases within its jurisdiction lest you spread the disease. Similarly, you might try to survey all the leaders of companies in a certain industrial sector, but only a few leaders comply.

Generally surveys of large populations capture only a sample. For instance, lots of people want to know what Americans think, but surveying more than 300 million people would be impractically ambitious (except when mandated for national democratic elections), so surveyors conventionally survey a sample. The sample should be representative of the whole population by important attributes, such as gender. Statistical methods are available for assessing when a sample achieves representativeness—this book has no space to explain these methods, but just be aware that a sample can be surprisingly small yet still representative of a much larger population, as long as the selection criteria are valid. Most surveys of American opinion actually survey only around 2,000 Americans, yet can statistically claim to represent more than 300 million Americans. In any case, whenever you present a sample as representative of a larger population, this claim must be justified in the product of your research.

Expert Opinion. You might be able to survey a representative sample but still might want to survey an unrepresentative subpopulation. This is likely where you do not need to know majority opinion, but rather you need informed or expert opinion. Democratic elections are essentially surveys of majority opinion, but information and expertise are not evenly distributed or democratic.

A survey of people selected for their peculiar expertise or insight or honesty is most appropriate where you want informed forecasts or prescriptions. Surveys of experts or selected subpopulations are sometimes known as **expert panels** or **expert opinion**.

However, expert surveys have their own problems. Some surveys with smaller populations of respondents can start to look like interpersonal conversations or interviews. They can attract new titles like "structured surveys," "roundtables," and "focus groups," which some researchers unfortunately use to indicate some sort of exclusive method. These methods can start to look unreplicable because of the leading role played by the researcher.

The main problem with any survey is that objective experts are rarer than most people realize. Generally, procurers and surveyors report that they have surveyed experts or **subject-matter experts**, but do not measure or report expertise. Selection of experts involves choices: the more respondents, the more diversity of opinion, but adding more respondents also suggests wider recruiting of inferior experts. Our statistical confidence in the average response increases as we survey more people, although surveying more nonexperts or biased experts would not help.

Subject-matter expertise can become disengaged from wider knowledge. Probably everybody is subject to biases. Even experts are subject to these biases, as well as political and commercial incentives.

Worse, the researcher might select certain respondents over others—thereby introducing a selection bias. For commercial, political, and personal reasons, many supposed experts are just the cheapest or most available or friendliest to the procurer. At the highest levels of government, assessments of risk often result from informal discussions between decision makers and their closest friends and advisers, contrary to rigorous official assessments. Politicians often are uncomfortable accepting influence, especially with methods that they do not understand.

Political, social, and commercial incentives help to explain failed surveys. In recent years, public confidence in experts of many types has been upset by shocks such as financial crises and terrorist attacks, suggesting that we should lower our expectations or be more diligent in choosing our experts. For instance, in tests, most political experts performed little better than random when forecasting events five years into the future. Confident experts with deep, narrow knowledge ("hedgehogs" in Isaiah Berlin's typology of intellectuals) were less accurate than those with wide and flexible knowledge ("foxes"), although even foxes were not usefully accurate in forecasting events years into the future (Tetlock, 2006). Political scientists have a poor reputation for forecasting, perhaps because the phenomena are difficult to measure, they rely on small populations of data, they reach for invalid correlates, or they rely on unreliable judgments (unreliability may be inherent to political science, if only because the subjects are politicized). Consequently, political scientists are highly polarized between different methods. While conscientious scientists attempt to integrate methods in order to maximize the best and minimize the worst, many political scientists form isolated niches (McNabb, 2010, pp. 15–28). Similarly, economists have received deserved criticism for their poor awareness of financial and economic instability in recent years.

This is not to say that we should doubt all experts, but that we should be more discriminating than is typical. We should carefully select the minority of all experts who are objective, evidence-based, practical interdisciplinary thinkers. We should also structure our surveys in more functional ways. Any consumer faces some basic methodological choices and statistical choices (for instance, we should select the median rather than mean response because medians are less sensitive to outlier responses).

How Will They Be Contacted?

The target population affects our communication options. For instance, private consumers of telecommunications could be accessed by their private telephones, but a government is not as accessible by private telephone as is a private consumer.

Available forms of communication have trade-offs, mainly between response rate, response speed, accuracy of targeting, and the burden of execution. The response rate is the proportion of approached targets who supply the requested information. You can improve response rates by offering payment or by passing the survey through somebody who has authority over the respondent, but these options increase the burden, could bias the results, and have ethical implications.

Four main methods of communication are available, with different advantages and disadvantages:

Table 9.1 Different ways to communicate a survey

Communication	Response rate	Response speed	Accuracy	Problem getting...
Email or fax	5%	Fast	Good	Email address
Telephone	10%–20%	Fast	Medium	Numbers
Postal	5%	Slow	Medium	Address
Focus group	20%	Fast	Medium	Space
Face to face	25%	Medium	Good	Space

a. Email is very cheap and fast and normally can be targeted well at the desired recipient. However, collecting email addresses can be materially and ethically challenging, and the response rate is poor (around 5%).

b. Telephones are quick forms of communication, reasonably accurate (although some telephones are not exclusive to one recipient), and show a reasonable response rate (10% to 20%), but you face material and ethical challenges in identifying the recipients' telephone numbers and calling them without invitation.

c. Postal communications are reasonably accurate (although several people can share the same address), and addresses can be obtained from public records, but the response rate is slow and low (around 5%).

d. A personal verbal approach can be accurate or not, depending on whether you approach an identified target or randomly approach people on the street. This method has a high response rate (around one quarter of people will agree to answer questions), but a high burden in terms of time and sometimes space, if permission or license is required before using a space.

What Survey Item Would Generate the Necessary Information?

A **survey item** is whatever is used to generate an item of information. Survey items are mostly questions or similar prompts for information. The required information should drive the number and design of particular questions. In general, a question needs to trade off its specificity with the burden of answering it. Generally you want to over-specify what you need so the inattentive or uninformed respondent knows what you mean, but you need to reduce the respondent's burden so that he or she does not give up on the question.

The words should be chosen to minimize misunderstanding. Clarify the context, such as the period of time. Define important concepts, such as "job security." Avoid ambiguous words, slang, and contested concepts.

Avoid **leading questions**. The grammar of the question and the given choices of answers or the space available for answers lead the respondent to answer each question in certain ways. For instance, you would be leading the respondent if you asked, "Do you think the current government is stupid, given its stupid decisions to date?" A less leading question would be "How do you rate the government's decisions to date?" Avoid loaded questions, such as "Given how insecure we all feel, how insecure do you feel about your job?"

Consider whether the question should be direct or indirect. Respondents tend to be dishonest about subjects that they regard as private or sensitive, such as sex and politics. You can encourage more honest responses by avoiding direct questions (such as "Are you racist?") in favor of indirect questions (such as "Do you think race influences how Americans vote?").

What Response Format Would Give
Enough Control Without Invalidating the Responses?

The design of the instrument forces the respondent to respond in only the ways that you allow, except for any free space for the respondent to submit his or her own comments. You face four main choices of response format: open or closed, different media, comparative or noncomparative, and scale.

Open or Closed. An open response gives space for the respondent to choose his or her own response, such as text or drawing or even (depending on the media) a verbal message or a physical message. An open response allows a more natural response, but is more difficult to code. A closed response is a prescribed response—you would give the respondent a choice of a limited number of responses, such as "yes" or "no." Controlling the answers speeds up the response and helps you to analyze the responses. Even if most of your items have closed responses, you could still mix in open responses when you want to allow for explications of closed answers, or for final thoughts or reactions to the survey.

Medium. You could restrict the medium of response. Sometimes the instrument restricts the medium. In a telephone interview, you would be limited to verbal responses. In a personal interview, you could allow verbal, drawn, or written responses.

Comparative or Noncomparative. This format requires a referent, such as the current rate of employment. The responses are framed in relation to that referent, such as whether the employment rate would increase or decrease in the future.

Scale. A scale is a series of degrees, points, or categories on a single dimension, such as degrees of agreement, friendliness, wealth, employment, and height. In most controlled responses, you would offer a choice between two points (such as "yes" or "no") or among five choices (such as "excellent," "good," "neither good nor bad," "bad," "terrible"). A two-point scale is acceptable when the possible responses are binary (such as "old" and "young"). A five-point scale is a common scale because it has a clear middle, bottom, and top; it is not so truncated as to leave the respondent wanting more choices (such as a three-point scale); and it is not so broad that neighboring points become difficult to differentiate (as on a 10-point scale).

Scales are conventionally known in four types:

a. A nominal or categorical scale has mutually exclusive categories, but no relativity is implied, such as a scale with oranges, apples, and pears.

b. An ordinal scale has categories in an order (such as increasing fruitfulness, exposure, or friendliness), but the categories are not necessarily of equal size (such as "least important," "most important"). See Table 9.2 for an example; here the United Nations prescribes an ordinal scale for the impact of disasters and catastrophes.

c. An interval scale is an ordered scale where each subsequent point on the scale is proportionally different in scale, such as "10%," "20%," "30%," and so forth.

d. A ratio scale is an interval scale starting from zero.

How Should the Items Be Ordered?

The first questions should be simple enough to encourage the respondent to proceed. They should avoid anchoring the respondent in any concepts or values that might prejudice later questions. Often the first questions are simple demographic questions. The later questions should proceed from the general to the specific, or from the least private and least sensitive to the most, or from the simplest to the most complex. The questions otherwise should be grouped in themes.

What Other Content Does the Survey Need?

By design, the survey needs survey items as the main items in the central bulk of the survey; instructions for the respondent to read at the start; instructions to guide the respondent's submission at the end; and spacing between questions and between sections so that questions are not broken across pages.

The format of each item should be consistent except to accommodate changes in the response format. Some methods of coding demand special accommodation, such as when you expect the responses to be scanned by some machine.

How Should It Be Pretested?

A **pretest** is a test of something before it is implemented for its intended purpose. Pretesting is useful for testing whether the instructions are clear, whether the items are understood, which items might be most challenging, the response rate, the response time, how burdensome the responses are to code, and how burdensome the codings are to analyze.

Direct Observation in the Field

Field research is the direct observation of current phenomena under natural conditions, with little to no controls.

Table 9.2 The UN's standard scale of impacts

Critical	Death or severe injury	Total loss of assets	Loss of programs and projects
Severe	Serious injury	Major destruction of assets	Severe disruption to programs
Moderate	Non-life-threatening injury and high stress	Loss or damage to assets	Some program delays and disruptions
Minor	Minor injuries	Some loss or damage to assets	Minimal delays to programs
Negligible	No injuries	Minimal loss or damage to assets	No delays to programs

Source: United Nations, Department of Peacekeeping Operations. (2008). *United Nations peacekeeping operations: Principles and guidelines.* New York, NY.

Field research is most natural where it makes observations without affecting the thing being observed, but perfect avoidance of any effect is practically impossible.

Field research has two main methods:

1. Direct nonparticipant observation

2. Ethnography or participant observation

Nonparticipant Observation

Nonparticipant observation is the direct observation of natural phenomena without participating in the subject. For instance, biologists and anthropologists might travel into the field and hide in an attempt to watch animals or humans behaving naturally without affecting them.

Ideally, the observer would observe directly but remotely to ensure that nothing interrupted the observer's direct sense of the subject, while also ensuring that the observer did not affect the subject. In practice, the observer aims to maximize observation while minimizing interaction with the subject. For instance, an ornithologist hides in order to observe how birds behave in their natural environment without human interaction. The method offers natural observations, but the principle of nonparticipation restricts how closely the observer can observe.

Note that the choice between nonparticipant and participant observation applies mostly with human subjects, a little with animal subjects, and practically not at all with inanimate subjects. Some subjects are practically impossible for the human observer to affect, such as a mountain, so any personal observation is practically nonparticipant—the observer simply could not participate in the mountain. On the other hand, a single researcher can still affect apparently inanimate subjects—the researcher who climbs a mountain to study might think that he or she is not affecting such an enormous piece of geology, but in fact he or she is eroding the surface and carrying contaminants.

Ethnography

Ethnography or **participant observation** is research where the observer is participating in the thing under observation. The term *ethnography* emerged from anthropology, where the method became routine in the study of living ethnic rarities, but "participant observation" is the more accurate term (see Practical Advice Box 9.1).

Participant observation is inherently more burdensome than nonparticipant observation, if only because of the time necessary to observe and participate.

Ethnographers often justify their method as natural, but it is less natural than nonparticipant observation because the observer inevitably affects the thing. Some ethnographers claim that participation leads to more natural observations because participants can learn to describe their subjects in the same way the subjects themselves would. These claims to superiority can become egotistical ("my interpretations are better than yours"). At best, ethnography is natural but not perfectly replicable. Worse, it is corrupted by all sorts of subjective biases. At worst, the lack of replicability and embrace of subjectivity creates an unaccountable and irresponsible research environment.

For instance, Napoleon A. Chagnon (1938–) spent all his career studying the Yanomamö people in the Amazon. His doctoral dissertation (*Yanomamö Warfare, Social Organization, and Marriage Alliances*, 1966, University of Michigan) and book (*Yanomamö: The Fierce People*, 1968) claimed that their life was naturally violent, and that the most violent men were genetically dominant. The book became the bestselling anthropological text of all time and was made more famous by 22 documentary films released in the 1970s and 1980s alone. However, Jacques Lizot (*Tales of the Yanomami*, 1985) countered that the Yanomamö were mostly peaceful and unexceptional. Brian R. Ferguson (*Yanomami Warfare: A Political History*, 1995) found that their wars were infrequent and on the fringes of their civilization, partly related to pressures from outside civilization, which had interacted with them since the 1700s.

Source: ©iStockphoto.com/Alija.

"I see these methods as a continuum, running from specific and delimited observations to answer a specific question ('How do little boys and girls play differently, if at all, in the school yard?') to understanding an entire way of life. On the far end of the continuum lies anthropology, since sociologists rarely feel so bold as to take on an entire society.

"I tell my students, only half in jest, that if you get to go home at night, it's participant observation, and if you don't, it's ethnography." (Luker, 2008, p. 155–156)

In 2000, Patrick Tierney's *Darkness in El Dorado* accused Chagnon and his colleagues of encouraging their belligerence and deceiving them about blood samples that exacerbated a measles epidemic. The American Anthropological Association had received complaints about Chagnon's work since 1993. It convened a task force in February 2001. Its report in May 2002 found that Chagnon had failed to obtain proper consent from both the government and the groups, although the Association's members voted to rescind parts in 2003 and the whole report in 2005. The two sides continue to feud, with little resolution, in part because the methods on both sides tend to be weak (Borofski, 2005).

Experimental Research

In everyday speech, an experiment is any test under somewhat controlled conditions. As a truly differentiated method, an **experiment** is a comparison of two cases, of which one is exposed to something, the other is not, and everything else is ideally the same for both cases. A **controlled experiment** is an experiment under largely controlled conditions; a **natural experiment** is an experiment under natural conditions.

The subsections below will explain the different types of experiments, how to design experiments, and the experimental process with human subjects.

Types of Experiments

Three types of experiments will be explained here: controlled experiments, natural experiments, and simulations.

Controlled Experiments

The most controlled research is a *controlled experiment*. Here the researcher controls the conditions so that the conditions are understood or manipulated. The downside of the controlled experiment is that no controlled conditions can be perfectly natural, so the results can be criticized as artificial. However, the researcher can still seek to design the experiment in ways that maximize both control and naturalness despite the inevitable trade-offs. For instance, the experimenter could invite subjects into the laboratory but pretend that the invitation is for a purpose other than experimentation and administer some treatment that pretends to be natural, such as a deliberate collision that pretends to be accidental, in order to test how people react to apparently accidental collisions.

The design of controlled experiments is explained more in the following section ("Experimental Design").

Natural Experiments

Experiments can be *natural* when something occurs naturally that the research would otherwise want to create artificially. For instance, perhaps the researcher is interested in what would happen if two leaders were to cooperate to solve climate change. The researcher likely has no control over what the two leaders do, so the researcher cannot experiment with the two leaders. The researcher's only hope is that the desired event occurs naturally. From the researcher's perspective, this event would be a natural experiment, even though for the two leaders the event would just be a natural event in the course of their careers.

Simulations

Simulations can be highly controlled with no naturalness, or can allow natural behaviors. For instance, you could design a completely mathematical model with no human interaction except from you the designer, or you could design a role-play simulation, where all the actors are played by real people.

Remember from Chapter 8 that a *simulation* is an operable model, meaning that it can be operated like a machine. These operations allow you to control the conditions. You can simulate things completely artificially, such as when a mathematical model forecasts how the economy would behave given certain conditions and starting values. You can simulate things more naturally, such as when you observe how people behave when playing roles.

Simulations can give you lots of options for trading control and naturalness, but are often ignored as methodological options because they are still unconventional in much of social science and are often implemented poorly. Most social simulations are either completely artificial, such as mathematical models of human behaviors that are uselessly oversimplified, or claim to be natural but do not admit their artificiality. For instance, many role player simulations actually impart the designer's biases through the framing of the roles, the instructions given to the role players, and the rules for how role players interact, rather than allow the role players to actually behave naturally. Many role player simulations end up as circular—they confirm the designer's expectations because the design restricts the role players to the designer's expectations. Others are just games or experiences—they give the illusion of natural experiences to the participants, and the illusion of pedagogy to the designers.

Having said that, with proper attention to instructional design, game design, and experimental design, simulations can be both reasonably controlled and natural. For instance, I once designed a simulation of terrorism and counterterrorism as a controlled experiment with two otherwise identical counterterrorism groups responding to the same terrorist role players, where all the simulated human actors were played by real humans, while the environment and all other materials were modeled on computers (Newsome, 2006).

Experimental Design

How should you design an experiment? The subsections below will explain to you comparison of cases, internal validity, constancy, and the experimental process.

Comparison of Cases

The most basic way to design an experiment is to expose one case or group of subjects to the intended independent variable (the **treated group** or **manipulated group**) while another case or group is not exposed (the **comparison group** or **control group**). This would allow us to compare these two cases or groups with the expectation that the one exposed to the treatment would show the effect, while the unexposed other would not show the effect. A **treatment** or **manipulation** is anything deliberately applied to the subject in expectation of some effect.

In a controlled experiment, we would separate two groups, treat one group without treating the other group, and keep everything else the same. For instance, we could take one group into a room and expose them to some newspaper content that is negative about the current government before surveying their opinions about the government, then bring another group into the same room with the same survey but without the newspaper content.

In a natural experiment, we want to compare one case with another, where the intended independent variable operates in the first case but not in the other case, and keep everything else the same (as long as all these things occur naturally). For instance, by accident a newspaper might print a negative story about the government in a batch of newspapers that are sold in one district of a city, but send another batch of newspapers without the negative story to another district of the same city, where the districts are otherwise the same and the newspaper buyers are of the same demographic diversity.

Internal Validity

The experiment should be internally valid. An experiment has **internal validity** if only the intended independent variable could explain the effect.

Experimental designers attempt internal validity by:

1. Accurately operationalizing the intended independent variable

2. Removing or keeping constant any other potential independent variables

3. Ensuring that the intended independent variable is the only thing operating

4. Avoiding any biases or other influences other than those absolutely necessary for the practicalities of running the experiment

Constancy

The groups should be constant. **Constancy** means that the groups are effectively the same, and their sameness remains constant through the experiment, apart from any treatment.

Apart from treatment, the conditions should be the same for both groups:

1. Ideally, the groups should start off the same in all respects except the upcoming treatment.

2. Both groups must be untainted by the intended independent variable until any of them is given the treatment.

3. Even though the groups differ by treatment, we can minimize this difference by applying a placebo to the untreated group. A **placebo** is something as similar as possible to the treatment without being the same as the treatment. For instance, if we want to test the pedagogical effectiveness of a new educational program, we would treat one group with the new educational program while treating the other group with a different educational program that pretends to be equally "new" to the subjects.

For the groups to be effectively the same, we should try one of the following three strategies, which are ordered from the most ideal to the least ideal.

1. Select two identical groups. This is easier with nominally identical inanimate objects, such as industrial products manufactured to the same design, but is difficult with biological and social subjects.

2. Match the groups by their attributes. For instance, we could select two groups of humans with the same ratio of males to females, old to young, opposing political viewpoints, and as much else that might affect the results.

3. Randomly assign the members. We could take a large population of subjects and randomly assign each to one of the two groups in the hope that randomly assigned groups mimic identical groups or at least avoid any other form of selection bias.

Inconstancy means that the groups are not effectively the same. This can arise from any of the following six things: selection bias, differential attrition, regression to the mean, event history, inconstant testing, or inconstant instruments.

Selection Bias. *Selection bias* arises when subjects are selected into a group, with the result that the group is not the same as it would have been otherwise. **Self-selection bias** occurs when subjects choose to join a group in such a way that the group is not the same as it would have been otherwise. Selection bias can arise unconsciously, such as if you were to form one group in one city and another group in another city without realizing the different demographics. Self-selection bias also can be unconscious, such as when friends want to be in the same group. Be aware that selection might be justified if the experiment requires a particular type of subject. For instance, if you want to experiment with the effects of a back-to-work training program on the unemployed, you should select unemployed subjects.

Differential Attrition. **Differential attrition** arises when certain types of subjects drop out of the group at a higher rate than other types, leaving the group biased to the types that remain. For instance, you might form two groups that look identical thanks to careful matching of the groups by the attributes, including the ratio of employed to unemployed members. However, if you were to schedule the experiment during a workday, more employed than unemployed members would fail to show up or leave the experiment early.

Regression to the Mean. Some members of a group will show **regression to the mean**—they will tend to adjust their behavior to fit the average member or the dominant member, rather than retain their initial attributes. One solution is to run the experiment very quickly so that the members do not have time to adjust. Another solution is to limit the subjects' awareness of each other or interaction with each other.

Maturation. **Maturation** is the process of change in the subject during the experiment. By convention, we refer to this change as maturation, although we should not imply that the change leads to more mature people, just that the people change. For instance, if we run an experiment over years, we should expect human subjects to change emotions, knowledge, beliefs, values, and a host of other attributes. We should run the experiment quickly or in a way that minimizes the subject's exposure to things outside the experiment.

History. Events during an experiment could change the subjects. These events become part of the history of the experiment; thus, by convention, we refer to this form of inconstancy as *event history* (or just *history*), even though the events are current during the experiment. For instance, imagine that we survey one group of people about their attitudes toward terrorism before news of a major terrorist attack, after which we survey another group; we should expect the second group to be changed by the news.

Inconstant Testing. Subjects are changed by the experiment itself. For instance, if we test a human skill, we should expect the subject's skills to improve each time the subject undergoes the test. Solutions include exposing the test to each member only once, ensuring that the test is unlike anything else the member might have been exposed to, and ensuring that members cannot teach each other about the test.

Inconstant Instruments. The tester or the instrument can change in ways that could influence the subject. For instance, if the treatment involves a role player, that role player should remain the same and behave the same every time the role player is involved in the treatment. If the role player were a different person each time, or the role player were the same person but acted out the role differently, then we would have an inconstant treatment. To avoid inconstant instruments, we should use perfectly replicable instruments, and replicate each use the same way.

Experimental Process With Human Subjects

Controlled experiments with human subjects have a predictable prescription, shown by the following 10 steps: Design, pretest, recruit subjects, ensure compliance, assign subjects to groups, introduce the subjects to the experiment, treat, check for the intended treatment, measure results, and close.

Design the Experiment

Design the experiment as prescribed in the section above.

Pretest the Experiment

Pretest the experiment to check its design. Your primary interest is whether subjects understand the content, how long the experiment lasts, and whether the controls perform as expected. A pretest is not normally focused on constancy, although a pretest can indicate problems such as maturation and differential attrition. Additionally, a pretest is not intended to collect results. Given this allowance, you could pretest with a group of subjects who would not be candidates for the experiment, such as your friends or other subjects that would not pass the constancy principle.

Recruit Subjects

Recruiting involves specifying the required subjects, such as a group of industrial products or a group of laborers; advertising for, approaching, or gathering potential subjects; evaluating potential subjects; and selecting subjects (for constancy, but not any other selection bias).

Ensure Compliance

All human subjects have rights to informed consent and other things, as defined by law and ethics (see Chapter 3). These rights affect how the experiment is designed, how you recruit, what you communicate to your subjects, and how you treat them. You may be required to file for permission from the requisite ethical authority.

Assign Subjects to Different Groups

Having recruited subjects, assign them to the treatment group or the control/comparison group. Remember to assign subjects by the experiment's requirements, without otherwise violating the constancy principles (see the section above on constancy).

Introduce the Subjects to the Experiment

The introduction is an opportunity to communicate or disclose anything necessary, such as the subject's expectations for compensation. You also have the opportunity to instruct the subjects in behaviors that would keep them constant, such as avoidance of the news and avoidance of attrition. Many aspects of the experiment can be communicated here, such as the duration of the experiment, but some things should not be communicated, such as any expectation of the treatment, since you should remember the principle that the subjects should be the same up to any treatment.

Treat/Manipulate

Treat one group, but not the control/comparison group.

Check for the Intended Treatment

Did the subjects take the intended medication but avoid the disallowed medications? Were the subjects paying attention to the intended news report and not watching other news? Did they complete the survey instrument, or did they ask someone else to do it for them?

Measure Results

Whatever the expected effects, you need some way to measure those effects. For instance, if you were interested in the efficacy of a new educational program, you should make sure that the treated group's members were paying attention and were awake during the program.

Close

Closing the experiment is an opportunity to fully disclose to the subjects anything necessary that was not yet disclosed, such as the true nature of the treatments; provide any instructions for the post-experiment phase; and provide opportunities for the subjects to give feedback or ask questions.

CHAPTER SUMMARY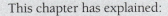

This chapter has explained:

- Methodologies and methods
- Quantitative and qualitative methods
- Control and naturalness
- Historical research
- Case study
- Survey research, including:
  - Survey instruments
    - Direct surveys, including coding rules
    - Questionnaires
    - Delphi surveys
  - The survey design process
- Direct observation in the field
  - Nonparticipant observation
  - Ethnography or participant observation
- Experimental research
  - Types of experiments
    - Controlled experiments
    - Natural experiments
    - Simulations
  - Experimental design
    - Comparison of cases
    - Internal validity
    - Constancy
  - Experimental process with human subjects

KEY TERMS

QUESTIONS AND EXERCISES _____

1. What is the difference between a method and a methodology?

2. What makes a method scientific?

3. Why should a method be natural?

4. Why should a method be controlled?

5. What is the difference between the field and the laboratory?

6. In what way is historical research natural but in need of control?

7. Each of the notional examples below of a method has a flaw. For each example, is the flaw best described as: selection bias differential attrition, event history, inconstant testing, or inconstant instruments?

   a. A historian is searching for a connection between race and rates of criminal arrests in the 1960s. She surveys only cases where minorities were arrested.

   b. In trying to determine if people could trace a shape on a piece of paper while looking at everything in a mirror, the researcher allowed each subject to make five attempts.

   c. The experiment is scheduled at a time and place where no public transportation is available.

   d. A researcher surveys two groups of people about sensitivity to crime. One group is recruited from a high-crime city, the other group from a low-crime city.

   e. The subjects of a study are asked to divide themselves into two groups.

   f. Halfway through a test, in which half of the participants are female and half are male, about half of the females drop out.

   g. The researchers survey several groups of people about their opinions on obesity. Afterward, broadcast journalists air a report on the obesity epidemic. Finally, the researchers survey some new groups of people.

8. For each of the notional examples below of research, is the type of research best described as historical, survey, case study, direct observation, or experiment?

   a. The researchers follow the education of low-income children compared to high-income children. The researchers measure the students' standardized test scores, graduation rates, and dropout rates.

   b. Your friend studies the rate of mortality due to malaria in a foreign country by visiting patients in their hospital beds.

   c. Another friend studies mortality due to malaria by reviewing reports on a foreign country with a uniquely high mortality rate.

   d. A group of researchers travel to Africa to record photographic images showing the natural behavior of meerkats.

   e. A researcher mails (posts) the same list of questions to every resident of a village and asks each resident to respond with answers to the questions.

   f. A local politician is running for reelection. Her staff telephone constituents in order to gauge their feelings and opinions about political issues.

g. From the 1960s to 1980s, Dian Fossey studied gorillas while living among them.

h. Researchers want to study the capacity of crows to remember skills. They place food in a box that can be opened with no less than three biomechanical actions.

i. An ornithologist uses binoculars to watch the in-flight mating ritual of eagles.

j. Your friend is reading the professional journals of police officers working in the city of Dallas during the 1920s.

k. A public health agent is studying the medical records of residents who live near high-tension electrical power lines, compared to others who live remote from such lines.

l. Your mentor wants to study the influence of violent images on public perceptions of personal security. You form two groups of subjects. One group is shown images of violent crimes; the other group is shown images of nonviolent crimes. After these images, both groups are asked the same questions about their sense of security.

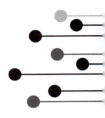

CHAPTER

10

Evidence and Data

Opening Vignette: Invalid Operationalization

Source: ©iStockphoto.com/wdstock.

"Here's an embarrassing story to prove the point about operationalization. I once gave a sample of abortion clinic patients a questionnaire and, being a 'political correct' sociologist, I listed 'Native American' (that is, a person of American Indian heritage) as one of the ethnicities that people could choose. Imagine my surprise when 90 percent of my sample said they were 'native' Americans, which to them meant people born in the United States" (Luker, 2008, p. 43).

Observations and Data

The term **observation** has two meanings:

1. The process of gaining information through the senses or instruments

2. One item of information produced from the observing process

Note that the second meaning of *observation* (one item of information) overlaps the term *datum*. A **datum** is one item of information. **Data** are items of information. An observation is not quite the same as a datum, because an observation is a product of the process of observation, while a datum is one item of information, irrespective of how the datum was produced. A datum can be produced by combining other information, while an observation must be observed. If you choose to use the term *observation*, you are implying that the information was gathered by observation; if you use the term *datum*, you are not implying anything about how the information was gathered.

Remember from Chapters 2 and 6 that *phenomena* are things we can observe. Note that phenomena are not the same as observations or data. When we observe phenomena, we gain an observation, which contributes information to a datum. For example, imagine that a new biological organism (a phenomenon) is discovered in some remote area. Once we have traveled to it, we can observe this phenomenon, and thence we can generate observations, such as our visual observation of what it looks like or its behaviors. These different observations can be combined as new data, such as the conclusion that the animal is categorically a mammal.

Note too that variables and constants are not the same as observations or data. As Chapter 8 showed, variables and constants are representations of the attributes of something. For instance, the weight of biological organisms varies. The weight is an attribute. We represent weight as a variable by allowing it to occupy a range of nominal values, such as grams or ounces. When we weigh something, we are observing its weight (perhaps using an instrument that measures it in a verifiable way). Our process of observing the nominal value of weight produces one observation. The information from this observation or several observations, such as the average weight of various observed examples of this particular organism, produces one datum.

Operationalization

Operationalization is the process of defining how we could observe something. Given the scientific principle of replicability, the data used or produced should be **verifiably observable**, meaning that someone else should be able to observe what we observe, given the same method. The data produced by verifiable observations are known as **empirical data** as distinct from unverifiable data, such as subjective experience.

Many phenomena are not directly observable or perfectly observable, in which case we must work out how to operationalize them.

We could choose a broad definition that captures too much that is exogenous to the thing in which we are interested, or we could choose a narrow definition that captures only a part of the thing in which we are interested. Sometimes researchers operationalize things in biased ways. For instance, official crime rates run about half the rate of victimization (the rate of self-reported victims of crime in a survey population). The true crime rate is difficult to induce, because official authorities are sometimes incentivized to under-investigate and under-report, while victims both fail to report some of the crimes that they have experienced and overestimate crime in general. If you were to measure crime by either the official crime rate or the victimization rate, you could be accused of bias. Thus, you should consider both (Newsome, 2014, p. 19).

A **valid operationalization** measures something that is as much like the thing that we want to measure as possible. Ideally, we would observe the target directly, but if we cannot observe it directly, we must measure something that is as similar as possible to the target. Definition is crucial; in order to know what you should be measuring, you should review definitions of the target and identify things that best fit the definitions and yet are still measurable. Ideally, your target is both

1. as like the target as possible, and

2. as practically measurable as possible.

You should immediately realize a trade-off in the above. Sometimes the target is too abstract to measure directly, in which case you could justify choosing something that is like the target but easier to measure, although then you could be accused of measuring something other than the target (**invalid operationalization**). Data become *invalid* if they do not accurately describe what they are supposed to describe.

In practice, if we cannot observe something directly, we must find a correlate that is as like the thing as possible yet easier to measure. **Correlates** are things that vary together, such as sunshine and sunburn. We are forced to choose a correlate when the subject is too difficult to measure directly. To identify a correlate, choose or develop the best definition of the target, then identify something as like the target as possible.

Be aware that correlates that are close in definition are known as **conceptual correlates**, as distinct from **statistical correlates**, which statistically vary with each other. For instance, imagine that you want to measure aggression. Aggression is a behavior with varied definitions—it is not an undisputed discrete phenomenon that is easy to measure directly. Thus, researchers must find correlates of aggression. For instance, one researcher might measure the aggression of a human being by measuring the concentration of a hormone in the person's blood, knowing that the hormone is statistically correlated with aggression (a statistical correlate). However, the researcher could be accused of measuring a remote correlate—a hormone rather than the behavior that is the ultimate target of the research. Another researcher might choose to observe physical fighting as a correlate of aggression, knowing that many definitions of aggression refer to fighting (a conceptual correlate). However, this researcher could be criticized for measuring only fighting, which is not exactly the same as aggression conceptually. Aggression is a propensity to be offensive or hostile, which could be manifested in many ways other than physical fighting, such as verbal abuse.

If you are confronted with multiple correlates, of which none is clearly the best, you should measure a few that are justifiably better than the others. Be prepared to challenge other researchers' correlates—perhaps a normative correlate is not conceptually justified; perhaps another correlate is conceptually justified, but is not strongly correlated statistically, suggesting that the definitions need to be revised. These dilemmas are better explained in the next section, on measurement.

Measurement

Measurement is the process of collecting observations. Measurements should be:

- **Replicable**: Other researchers should be able to reproduce the observation using the same processes and instruments.

- **Valid**: The measurements should measure whatever you intended or claimed to measure.

- **Reliable**: The process of measurement and its performance must not vary between different measurements. **Systematic measurement errors** are inherent to the process or instrument, such as a weighing instrument that is incorrectly calibrated and thus under-reports weight. **Nonsystematic measurement errors** are random errors, such as an unpredictable cut in electrical power to the instrument during measurement. An **observation error** is the difference between the measured value and the true value, perhaps due to a misrecording.

- **Recorded**: All measurements should be stored just as they were produced by the process.

- **Reported**: The process and the products should be reported accurately in sufficient detail that consumers could understand and replicate what you did.

Observations can be measured in many technically different ways, but the main differentiation is between objective correlates and judgmental correlates. The subsections below explain objective correlates, judgmental correlates, triangulation of different measures and correlates, multiple measures, and meta-analysis.

Objective Correlates

Objective correlates are collected without subjective involvement, although this ideal is practically impossible, so objective correlates are often more subjective than admitted. The ideal objective correlates are those measured with perfectly reliable instruments without any human interaction. For instance, computers can be programmed to record which websites are visited by the computers' users, how long they spend on different websites, and what purchases they make online. These observations could be used as correlates of consumer preferences.

The objectivity of some correlates can be challenged. For instance, perceptions of crime, as reported in victimization surveys, are subjective. By contrast, the officially recorded frequency of crime is often described as objective, but the frequency of crime is not perfectly objective. All crimes are defined and recorded with human involvement; sometimes humans make errors or deliberately misrecord, such as when police forces under-record crime to appear successful in fighting crime (Newsome, 2014, p. 19).

Judgmental Correlates

Judgmental correlates are subjectively coded, meaning somebody (the coder) must make a judgment as to what the code should be. To make your coding replicable, you should code using coding rules that are consistent and declared. A common way to code judgmentally is to use a five-point scale, as is common in surveys (see Chapter 9), in which each step or point is associated with a coding rule. For instance, an educator could aim to judge the attentiveness of a class of students to each of succeeding teachers by choosing a scale of codes from 1 to 5, with coding rules from "Most of the students are looking at material other than course material most of the time" to "Almost all the students are looking at the teacher or the course material almost all the time."

Good design of the coding rules (see Chapter 9) helps the codes to be as objective as possible, but judgments are always somewhat subjective. Having improved the coding rules, you are left to improve your coders. Your human coders should be objective people, trained in the coding rules, constant performers, and have other qualities that fulfil the design rules associated with surveys (see Chapter 9).

You could choose to ask only external experts to judge. External experts are remote from the researchers' biases, and they are expert, so they should be more objective and informed (see Chapter 9). At the least, external experts are useful for checking for external agreement with your internal analysis.

Triangulation

As defined in Chapter 9, *triangulation* is the use of more than one method in the study of the same thing.

In addition to triangulating different methods, you could triangulate different datasets, different measures, or different sources of your data. For instance, perhaps one researcher was criticized for using only secondary sources. You could triangulate his or her data by gathering new data from primary sources.

As well as triangulating primary and secondary sources, you could triangulate different sources. For instance, if you require data on international trade, you could extract data from the United Nations Conference on Trade and Development, but you might worry about relying on a single source, while other researchers might claim that the source is biased, is incomplete, or measures trade in a way that does not capture something important about trade. Thus, you should seek data from another source, such as the World Bank. You would be seeking another source here not because you want data on a different phenomenon, but because you want to triangulate sources.

You could triangulate different instruments. Perhaps one researcher has offered data gathered from memoirs that have been criticized as biased. You could attempt to measure the same thing using direct observations instead of memoirs.

You could triangulate different scopes. For instance, perhaps a researcher has studied marriage in Western culture. Another researcher could offer to study marriage in another culture.

Multiple Measures

Ideally, you should measure the same phenomenon in multiple ways, each of which might capture some part of the phenomenon but not all parts. **Multiple measures** help us to capture all the parts rather than some. For instance, in measuring trade, you could measure the financial value of trade, the number of transactions, the material goods traded, the services traded, the imports, the exports, or the balance of trade (imports relative to exports). Each of these measures is capturing something about trade but not in the same way as any other measure. You could decide that just one of these measures is the best conceptual correlate of something in particular about trade that you want to observe, or you could use all these measures to capture as much about trade as possible.

You could compare different measures to see if they agree (statistical correlates). For instance, if the financial value of trade were growing and the number of transactions were growing, these two measures would suggest the same direction in trade—trade is growing.

If you have a lot of different measures, say dozens, you would face problems handling so many measures, and a problem of multidimensionality.

Too many measures become unmanageable: You would struggle to communicate meaning in each measure, and your consumers would struggle to understand the nuances between them. In this situation, you could combine the measures into an index. An **index of measures** is a statistical combination of multiple measures. Common indices with which you should be familiar from popular news include gross national product and gross domestic product, which are used as measures of the value of economic activity in an area. Similarly, the consumer price index and the producer price index are used as correlates of inflation. A less familiar example is the Global Peace Index, which claims to capture the wider symptoms and indicators of a country's peacefulness, both internally and internationally, by year (Institute for Economics and Peace, 2012).

Indices are often controversial. Any measure can be challenged for not capturing everything about the phenomenon; some measures may be better than others; some measures may capture some part of the phenomenon, but not capture all of it; some measures may capture too much from exogenous phenomena.

The statistical way in which the measures are combined can be criticized. Many indices weight some measures, meaning that they give those measures a larger proportional role in the formula.

Any index can be criticized for **multidimensionality**, which is the measurement of more than the intended phenomenon. For instance, the Global Peace Index includes three broad indicators of peacefulness: high safety and security in society; low conflict, domestic or international; and low militarization. Across these three themes are 23 measurable criteria, including foreign wars, internal conflicts, murders, prisoners, human rights, democracy, and the arms trade (Institute for Economics and Peace, 2012). However, some measures, such as military expenditure, are ambiguous correlates of peacefulness. High military expenditure could result from either aggressive policies or defensive responses to aggressive neighbors. Additionally, high military expenditure could result from either selfish belligerence or generous, responsible commitments to the enforcement of peace and other peace operations.

The solution to multidimensionality is to throw out the less valid measures. An extreme solution is to throw out all but one measure—this one measure is sometimes known as the **figure of merit** or the most valid measure.

Meta-analysis

Meta-analysis is the combination of results from several studies of the same thing, without gathering new results. For instance, three studies could study the same behavior but report their measures over different periods of time: 15 minutes, 2 hours, and half a day. We should align these data in minutes: 15, 120, and 720 minutes. Then we should summarize the data, such as the average duration (in minutes) of the behavior.

The process of meta-analysis involves the following five steps:

1. Collect all studies of the thing

2. Collect all data from these studies

3. Categorize the data by variable

4. Align the data within each category by a common unit (for instance, standardize all the seconds, minutes, and hours into just minutes)

5. Summarize the data

Meta-analysis is allowable in science; do not confuse meta-analysis with philosophical metaphysics or similar-sounding terms (see Chapter 2).

Classifying Data

Once you have operationalized and measured, you should classify the data to help your analysis of the data and to help you communicate your analysis. As explained in the subsections below, researchers commonly classify data by units of analysis, groups and scales, types of data, and levels of analysis.

Units of Analysis

You could classify the data by the **unit of analysis**—the discrete entity that is being observed. For instance, if you were to count people in each of several cities, then the unit of analysis would be the person. Similarly, if you were to count the number of people with a disease, or the number of people who earn above a certain income, or the average weight of people, the unit of analysis would still be the person. Note that the unit of analysis is the entity (such as the person) being observed, not the entity's attribute under observation (such as weight). You would be changing the entity if it were aggregated or disaggregated. For instance, you could look at families instead of individual persons (an example of aggregation) or at the intestinal parasites within human hosts (an example of disaggregation). If you looked at the cities with populations of at least 1 million people, the unit of analysis would be the city. By contrast, if you looked for some human attribute within each city, the city would not be the unit of analysis, but the city would be the scope for each study.

Units of analysis can be categorically different, even if related. For instance, males are categorically different from females. We cannot count males as females or vice versa. Yet we could aggregate two categories as subcategories of a higher category. For instance, males and females can be aggregated as people.

Units of analysis can be either discrete or continuous. **Discrete units** are not reducible. For instance, in counting the number of males in a population, we cannot count parts of males. By contrast, **continuous units** are reducible to fractions. For instance, steel production could be measured by weight or financial value. In measuring steel production, we could weigh different units of steel production (such as sheets, plates, and fabrications), then add their weights together on a continuous scale. This continuous scale could have nominal units (such as pounds or kilograms) with continuously reducible fractions (such as half a pound or 227 grams).

Groups and Scales

Data can be grouped or scaled, usually along a scale of the same continuous unit. The six main types of scales are:

1. Cardinal

2. Grouped

3. Nominal/categorical

4. Ordinal

5. Interval

6. Ratio

Cardinal data indicate the count or number of something, without any implied relativity or order. If you were to count the number of people in a city, you would be measuring the population in cardinal terms, such as "1.1 million people." By contrast, the same population could be described as "big"—this is not a cardinal number but an ordinal judgment (see below). Cardinal data are not necessarily grouped or ordered, except in the sense that numbers lie in quantitative order (for instance, from zero to infinity).

Data can be **grouped**, meaning that some data are placed in one group, some in another, without necessarily implying that they are categorically different. For instance, imagine that the data indicate where each person lives in a city. These data could be grouped by district so that we can count the people living in each district.

A **nominal scale** or **categorical scale** has mutually exclusive categories, but no relativity is implied. For instance, eye color can be coded categorically by colors; hair color also can be categorized by colors. You could categorize each of your friends by their hair color without necessarily implying that one color is better than the other. Categorical scales are most useful for analytical comparison. You could make a list of eye colors, then count the frequencies of each eye color within a city's population. You could compare the distribution of eye colors in each of several cities.

An **ordinal scale** is a stepped scale on the same dimension, such as population size, healthiness, or democraticness. For instance, public health could be ordered on a three-step (three-point) scale: healthy, mediocre health, unhealthy. These three categories can be coded with numbers: 1, 2, 3. Clearly these values are arranged in order. An ordinal scale could have any number of steps/points from 2 to infinity. Remember from Chapter 9 that a five-point scale (1, 2, 3, 4, 5) is typical because of its reasonable sensitivity without unreasonable complexity. The steps (points) are not necessarily of equal size—if they are of equal size, the scale is an interval scale (see below).

An **interval scale** is an ordinal scale where each point on the scale is equidistant in scale, such as "more than 10% to 20%," "more than 20% to 30%," "more than 30% to 40%," and so forth.

A **ratio scale** is an interval scale starting from zero, such as "zero to less than 10," "10 to less than 20," "20 to less than 30," and so forth.

Types of Data

Data can be differentiated by the type of phenomenon they describe. The six main types of data are:

1. Attributes data

2. Flows data

3. Structural data

4. Event data

5. Rates

6. Frequency data

Attributes data are observations of the attributes, characteristics, or qualities of entities at some point in time, such as the voting preferences of the national population at the time of a census.

Flows data are observations of movements, communications, or changes over a period of time, such as trade during a year, tourist visitors during a season, or emigrants.

Structural data are observations of authoritative relationships at some point in time, such as the number of international organizations to which a state belongs at the start of the year, or the number of agencies that report to a certain higher authority.

Event data are observations of discrete happenings. Events are recorded with data about each event, normally (a) when something happened, (b) what happened, and (c) where it happened. For instance, most data on accidents and crimes are actually event data.

A **rate** is a ratio of one thing to another, such as the number of children as a proportion of the total population, or the number of people who vote for one party as a percentage of the total population.

Frequency data are rates of the same event over a period of time, such as the number of accidents per year or the number of births per decade.

Levels of Analysis

A *level of analysis* is one level in a hierarchy. The food chain is an example of an analytical hierarchy, at the bottom of which are organisms that live without eating anything else but are eaten by other organisms, which in turn are eaten by other organisms, and so on up the food chain, until we reach the apex predator—the organism that eats other organisms but is not eaten by anything else. Within that hierarchy we could choose a single level of analysis, such as the bottom, the apex, or the middle, and look at the data within only that level, or we could compare data across levels.

However, remember the ecological fallacy, which involves inferences from data at one level about another level (see Chapter 7). Examples of the ecological fallacy are inferring anything about an apex predator given information about animals at the bottom of the food chain, or inferring a nation's behavior from how its citizens behave.

Datasets

Some choices about using data are driven by the size of the dataset, as explained in the following subsections, which explain the controversial differences between large and small datasets, how to use small datasets, and how to use large datasets.

Large-*n* or Small-*n*?

Data and methods are often differentiated by the size of the dataset, with a simple differentiation between **large-*n*** and **small-*n***, where *n* is short for *number*. Often the differentiation is used prejudicially in the contest between quantitative and qualitative methods (see Chapter 9). For instance, small-*n* datasets are often misleadingly described as "qualitative data" because fewer cases allow for deeper study of the qualities of each case, but a case study might be superficial, while an ambitious survey of lots of cases could involve deep analysis of each case.

We have no common standard for knowing how many data we need before a small-*n* dataset becomes a large-*n* dataset. The expectations vary by discipline and subject. In the hard sciences and applied sciences, datasets commonly have tens of thousands of data, but in the social sciences, where observations are more difficult to gather, a dataset can be considered large at 50 cases.

Another way to assess your *n* is to assess the *n* relative to the known total population. For instance, if the universe of cases were 50, a survey of all 50 cases would produce data on as many cases as possible. On the other hand, if you wanted to know what more than 300 million Americans thought, but you surveyed only 50 Americans, then you would have a small-*n* dataset relative to the total population.

Remember from Chapter 9 that a sample, if representative, can be very small relative to the total population but still be representative, so a survey of 2,000

Americans can be representative of all Americans even though it produces a small-*n* dataset relative to the total number of Americans.

When assessing the *n*, be mindful of the difference between cases and data. Imagine that we identified 50 different instances where a particular type of crime was committed; if you were to collect data on dozens of different attributes of each case, you would have a dataset of 50 cases and hundreds of data across the 50 cases. Owners and users of such datasets, in their descriptions of such datasets, would naturally focus on the hundreds of data in order to impress us, but critics would focus on the smaller number of cases.

Source: ©iStockphoto.com/Maxiphoto.

Be aware too that commitments to either large-*n* or small-*n* data are often driven by methodological prejudices, different skill sets, and access to or availability of data. For instance, some people regard large-*n* data as a vehicle for asserting power by restricting access to the data or to the skills for collecting or analyzing such data. Meanwhile, the same critics admit that some people prefer small-*n* data because they prefer more subjective observations (Luker, 2008, pp. 25, 31–32).

Too many people complain that the data with which they disagree is simply either too "quantitative" or too "qualitative." Such a complaint is always misleading and often more revealing of the complainant than the data. This is more likely in fields that are on the fringe of social science. For instance, I remember presenting to a conference a mix of objective correlates and judgmental correlates. A historian in the audience became increasingly uncomfortable with the evidence, but couldn't articulate his discomfort, until he suggested that I needed more "qualitative data," which he could not specify. Be prepared for biased audiences that blame your data rather than their own competences.

Small-*N*

A choice in favor of fewer cases implies deeper study of each case and the gathering of more data about each case. This depth allows fuller investigation of the variance between cases (see Table 10.1). Statistically, fewer data implies less confidence, although we might be more confident in the detail of individual cases, especially if cases are highly variable.

However, fewer cases implies that you are more exposed to the peculiarities of those cases and less able to generalize across all cases. If you were to select unrepresentative cases, you could be examining outliers. Remember from Chapter 9 how you should select cases for case studies.

Large-*n*

Data from more cases implies that your findings could be generalized across all cases, but also implies shallower investigation of each case and less understanding of the variance between cases.

Large-*n* datasets imply more statistical confidence. This is clearest in the analysis of frequencies. A **frequency** is the number of events per defined unit of time, for example, "100,000 deaths to cancer per year." For the more frequent, well-observed, and nonadaptive behaviors, such as common infections and accidents, statisticians can confidently assess future probabilities from past frequencies. For instance, if 1 million Americans die from a particular disease every year, we can confidently predict that 1 million Americans will die from that same disease next year. All other things being equal (ignoring all other risk factors and assuming no changes), the probability of an average American dying from that disease next year is the number of forecasted deaths (1 million) divided by the total population (315 million), the product of which is 0.3%.

We can be confident in frequency data where events are numerous and accurately observed and their causes do not change. For instance, car drivers are not remarkably adaptive (short of a shock, like a road traffic accident), in part because driving and accidents are regular enough that the risks are treated as familiar. Thus large-*n* data on car drivers are relatively reliable.

Table 10.1   Comparing small-*n* and large-*n* datasets

	Small-*n*	Large-*n*
Number of cases	Few	Many
Depth of cases	Deep	Shallow
Advantages	Explains outliers	Generalizable
Disadvantages	Overstates outliers	Understates critical cases

However, frequency data would be misleading evidence for dynamic or volatile phenomena. For instance, criminal behavior would seem stable until the advent of some innovation that rapidly spreads through the criminal population. Data on criminal behavior before the innovation would be misleading about criminal behavior after the innovation.

Data on terrorism are particularly problematic because terrorism is infrequent compared to most other crimes. Additionally, the data are corrupted by poor reporting of most terrorist events, official secrecy, and politicization. Finally, terrorism is an adaptive behavior. Consequently, relying on data from a previous decade to forecast terrorist behavior in the next decade is foolish. Many analysts prefer subjective judgments, based on more qualitative data, rather than relying on statistical modeling (Greenberg, Chalk, Willis, Khilko, & Ortiz, 2006).

The dilemma for the conscientious consumer of statistics is that longer-term historical data are suggestive of more confidence if we assume unchanging phenomena, but less confidence if we suspect fundamental change in the real world.

In any domain, due diligence includes checking the validity of the data. Sometimes, the highest authorities fail us. For instance, in April 2004, the U.S. State Department released its latest annual *Patterns of Global Terrorism*, which claimed that the frequency of terrorism had declined in 2003. The George W. Bush administration claimed that the data were proof of its counterterrorism policy and of reduced risks from terrorism. However, two independent academics showed that the numbers literally did not add up and that in fact terrorism had increased. After they published their findings in a newspaper and a journal, the State Department stopped the annual publication (Krueger & Laitin, 2004).

Larger-*n* datasets imply more opportunities and more need for analysis by statistics software. This book has no space to explain such software. You should investigate whether your institution holds a license for a particular product, whether researchers in your discipline normatively use a particular product, and which product you find most agreeable for your own purposes.

Statistics software reduces the burden of analyzing data. Indeed, it helps one analyst to perform several analyses in a few seconds that otherwise would take weeks on paper. Statistics software allows users to analyze models with:

- Different measures of the dependent variable

- Different variables as statistical controls

- Different sample sizes

- Different experimental conditions

- Different controls on interaction between variables

On the other hand, statistical software allow users to analyze new models until, by accidents of interactions between variables or by deliberately adding or dropping different variables of controls, they get statistically significant but **false-positive results** (results that claim to prove something but do not). These false-positive opportunities could be deliberate or accidental. They are coming under increased scrutiny by publishers and readers, so you should be prepared for more burdensome attention in the future. You can avoid unnecessary scrutiny—as either an author or a reviewer—by voluntarily complying with some recommended guidelines for avoiding false positives (see Practical Advice Box 10.1).

Uses of Data

You can use data in many ways:

- Evidence

- Information or intelligence

- Entertainment

- Illustration

- Analogies

- Anecdotes

- Inductions

Data become **evidence** when used to support some proposition. People often confuse data with evidence, because most of the time we are collecting data with intent to use them as evidence for something. Yet data are not the same as evidence, and you do not need to use data as evidence.

Data can be valuable enough as interesting information or *intelligence* (processed information). This information can be entertaining, such as a funny story, in which the entertainment is derived from some observation of something surprising or something that we would not have expected.

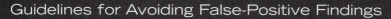

Source: ©Stockphoto.com/stevanovicigor.

Authors must:

1. Decide, before data collection begins, the rule for terminating data collection, and report this rule in the article

2. Collect at least 20 observations for each target or show that the cost would be prohibitive

3. List all variables measured

4. Report all experimental conditions, including failed treatments/manipulations

5. Report the results of any models in which observations are eliminated

6. Report the statistical results both with and without any variable

Reviewers must:

1. Ensure that authors follow the above guidelines for authors

2. Tolerate more imperfect results

3. Require authors to demonstrate that their results do not depend on arbitrary analytical decisions

4. Require authors to replicate their method if they cannot compellingly justify their data collection or analysis (Simmons, Nelson, & Simonsohn, 2011, p. 1362)

You can also use data to illustrate rather than to prove. When I provide an instance or example, I am doing so to illustrate the proposition, not to prove it. For instance, I could mention that a pine tree is an example of an evergreen tree. This instance is not being used as proof, just as an example.

You can use data as analogies. An **analogue** is something like the target but not the same. By claiming that the analogue helps to understand the target, I am making an **analogy**. For instance, I could claim that living through the global economic crisis of 2008 gave people a taste of the Great Depression of 1929.

Anecdotes are stories, usually from personal experience, that can be used to illustrate or entertain. Anecdotes are not necessarily data or of any other use, until you take some observation from an anecdote.

Remember too that you can use data to induce a proposition (see Chapter 7).

Evidence

Social scientists use most of their data as evidence. *Evidence* is information used to support some proposition. We could use evidence to justify our proposed topic, to suggest that the literature has failed to explain something, to show that a method does not work, or to prove a hypothesis.

Evidence can be presented in many forms, as explained in the subsections below: facts, proof, direct evidence, credible evidence, judgmental evidence, or a majority as evidence.

Facts

A **fact** is an item of information that is true. In practice, a fact is a datum proven true. While facts are special kinds of data, facts are not propositions, opinions, beliefs, assumptions, faith, or prejudices (see Chapter 7 for a reminder of their definitions).

The term *fact*, when used literally and properly, means something that is true without any reservation. In other words, a fact is literally true, so the term is not literally up to dispute.

Yet assertions of fact are up for dispute. An assertion of fact could be mistaken. Factual mistakes are not always deliberate. For instance, somebody could assert that his body weighs 200 pounds. However, perhaps he approximated his actual weight; perhaps his measuring instrument was mistaken; perhaps he had put on weight since he last measured his weight. If his claim proves to be mistaken, what he asserted as fact is not a fact, albeit a forgivable mistake or approximation.

While assertions of fact can be challenged, remember that the term *fact* is not up for literal dispute. When you use the term *fact*, you are claiming that the information is true. If the information is untrue, then your description of it as a fact is incorrect. Similarly, if you claim something as untrue but it turns out to be a fact, you have asserted incorrectly.

Unproven Propositions Masquerading as Facts About Torture

"I have little doubt—as a matter of *fact*, not *law* or *morality*—that presidents would condone some forms of torture if they truly believed it was the only option available to prevent an act of mass-casualty terrorism. Nor do I have much doubt that intelligence operatives on the ground would resort to torture under such circumstances. No law or proclamation would change this cruel reality.

"Some people have argued that the entire debate about torture is foolish and unnecessary because torture never works, because it always produces false and useless information from suspects who will say anything to stop the pain.

"It is in my view dishonest, though politically correct, to claim, as an empirical matter, that torture *never* works—that it *never* produces reliable and useful real-time information that could save lives." (Dershowitz, 2014, pp. 330–331, emphases in original)

Unfortunately, slippery arguments can be used to confuse people about facts. Somebody could use the term *fact* nonliterally. He or she might assert probable information as a fact, or assert an expectation, opinion, proposition, or assumption as a fact (see Research in the Real World Box 10.1). None of these things is a fact. Return to Chapter 7 for an explanation of what makes an argument true.

Proof

Proof is properly used to mean indisputable evidence (incontrovertible evidence), but sometimes is used inappropriately to mean evidence in general. You should clarify proof as either

1. proof, or

2. provisional evidence.

Proof is indisputable evidence—it is without doubt true. **Provisional evidence** does not disprove the proposition but is not yet indisputable proof of it.

Direct Evidence

Other than proof, evidence is relative and disputable, which is why people often talk about "good evidence," "bad evidence," "the best evidence available," "weak evidence," "strong evidence," and similar terms.

Some of these terms are vague. You can describe evidence as good or bad and still sound academic, but a more meaningful but still simple way to differentiate evidence is as either

1. direct evidence, or

2. indirect, circumstantial, inferential, or suggestive evidence.

Direct evidence is a direct observation supporting the proposition, whereas **indirect evidence** is consistent with the proposition. For instance, if we are investigating whether employees produced what they were ordered to produce, direct evidence would include testimony by people who directly observed the employees producing it. Indirect evidence would include observations of the employees being at work at the time, despite no observations of the employees actually producing it.

Now imagine that we are investigating the life of a famous historical personality, but we do not know when the subject was born. Imagine that we have failed to find direct evidence of the birth, such as an eyewitness report or a birth certificate. We could search instead for indirect evidence. We could discover direct evidence for the parents' departure on a journey without the subject, and direct evidence for the parents' ending their journey with the subject as a baby. These data give us indirect evidence that the subject was born during that journey.

Be aware that data can be presented as misleading evidence by errors of omission. Someone could fail to report evidence. Someone could present only the data that appear to support a proposition, without admitting the greater data that disprove the proposition. For instance, somebody could discover in the archives a birth certificate but fail to report this evidence to support their earlier claim that the subject had been born before the date of the certificate.

Credible Evidence

Evidence must be true, otherwise it is not evidence. Sometimes evidence is difficult to verify, such as when one person knows what he or she saw but nobody else saw it. Here we must often interrogate the credibility of the source. This task utilizes skills that you learned during your assessment of the ethics of research (Chapter 3), sources (Chapter 5), and the credibility of arguments (Chapter 7).

In English and American legal traditions, evidence is considered more and more credible if it fulfills more of the following three criteria:

1. It is true.

2. It is the whole truth.

3. It is nothing but the truth.

Source: ©iStockphoto.com/IS_ImageSource.

These criteria are enshrined in the oath that witnesses take before giving evidence to a court in law, in which they promise to each of these three things. Giving evidence under oath adds some credibility to oral evidence, but unfortunately we know how mistaken and deliberately dishonest witnesses can be.

Evidence becomes more credible if it corroborates other evidence. For instance, one person might testify to have seen something; if another unrelated and uncorrupted person testifies to have seen the same thing, then each of these witnesses is corroborating the other. A photograph might corroborate that a person was present where and when that person claimed. A sales receipt or telephone call might corroborate that the person was in the location around the time claimed.

Evidence becomes more credible if it leaves nothing out or makes no error of omission (see Research in the Real World Box 10.2). For instance, if a witness testifies that he or she observed a crime, but refuses to explain why he or she was present, then we have not heard the whole truth, so the testimony is not as credible as it could have been.

Evidence is more credible if it contains no falsities. For instance, if a witness testifies to having seen a crime, but has provably provided false testimony in the past, then the witness seems less credible. If the witness provably lies in his or her testimony, then the rest of that person's testimony is less credible.

Judgmental Evidence

Unfortunately, many data are inconclusive as evidence—they remain subject to interpretation or judgment. Sometimes the same case provides contradictory evidence if interpreted in a different way or if recoded more accurately. For instance, many people have argued that democracies produce more motivated soldiers; they often induce this argument from individual cases, such as the

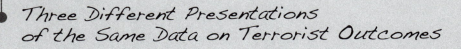

Research in the Real World Box 10.2

Three Different Presentations of the Same Data on Terrorist Outcomes

In 2008, the RAND Corporation published a seminal study of "how terrorist groups end." Of 648 terrorist groups that were active at some point between 1968 and 2006, a total of 268 ended during that period, another 136 groups splintered, and 244 remained active. Of the 268 that ended, 43% reached a peaceful political accommodation with their government. Most of these had sought narrow policy goals. The narrower the goals, the more likely the government and terrorists were to reach a negotiated settlement. In 10% of cases, terrorist groups ended because they achieved their goals. Forty percent were eliminated by local police and intelligence agencies. Seven percent were eliminated by military force (Jones & Libicki, 2008).

Secondary presentations of the same data varied widely:

"A recent RAND study focusing on how terrorist campaigns end found that roughly 10 percent of the 268 terrorist groups that have come and gone since 1968 disbanded after achieving all or some of their political objectives. A much larger percentage ended after being incorporated into the mainstream political process, which, for some of these groups, represented a partial victory in its own right" (McCormick & Fritz, 2014, p. 149).

"Of the 648 groups identified in the RAND-MIPT Terrorism Incident database, only 4 percent obtained their strategic demands" (Abrahms, 2014, p. 154).

success of the ancient city-state of Athens against the Persian Empire. However, Athens was actually oligarchic, not democratic; moreover, we have no direct evidence that Athenian soldiers were more motivated; we have indirect evidence in the form of Athenian victories over Persia, but Athens did not win all its battles; ultimately, Athens would be defeated later by despotic Sparta, and both would be defeated by despotic Rome (Newsome, 2007, p. 14).

A Majority as Evidence

If most cases conform with a theory, we have a majority as a form of evidence for a probabilistic theory. Remember from Chapter 8 that an inductive or probabilistic argument would conclude that most of the time something is true if most of the cases show that something is true. While deterministic arguments must be true for all cases, probabilistic arguments can be proven by evidence proving that most cases fit the probabilistic argument.

Contradictory cases do not challenge probabilistic arguments, because probabilistic arguments allow for some minority of cases separate to the majority of cases. However, important anomalies challenge the argument's "explanatory fit." Ideally, the argument explains everything. Its explanatory fit can be criticized if we find more cases that it cannot explain or if we find that it fails to explain the most important cases.

Causality and Correlation

In social science, we are usually looking for evidence of **causation**—the process by which a cause has an effect. Usually we model some causal relationship with an independent variable (IV), which models some cause, and a dependent variable or DV, which models some effect. Given this model, we should expect the IV and the DV to be *statistically correlated*—they should vary together; as the IV varies, so should the DV. If they vary in the same direction, they are **positively correlated**. If they vary in opposite directions, they are **negatively correlated** (**inversely related**). For instance, if our salary goes up and our productivity goes up, then salary and productivity are positively correlated. If productivity goes up even as our salary goes down, then they are negatively correlated.

You can use **correlation** as evidence for causation, but correlation and causation are not the same. Indeed, correlation can be misleading. If we were to prove correlation, we would not have proven causation—we would have proven only that two things vary with each other, but we would not have proven that one thing varies because the other thing causes it to vary.

Moreover, even if we were to assume a causal relationship, correlation does not prove the direction of causation. If we were to show that *x* varies with *y*, this could be because *x* causes *y*, *y* causes *x*, or a third thing causes them both to vary at the same time.

Spurious Relationships

If a third thing is causing two other things to be statistically correlated, those two things have a **spurious relationship**. For instance, ice cream sales go up when crime goes up; as people buy more ice cream, more people commit crimes. Ice cream and crime are statistically correlated. Is this because ice cream sales cause crime? Does crime cause ice cream sales? These absurd questions should remind you to be cautious of correlation. Ice cream sales and crime do not cause each other, but each varies with sunshine and climatic temperature. In sunny or hot weather, people buy more ice cream in order to cool down or as a traditional summertime treat; also in sunny or hot weather, people become more active and irritable, so commit more crimes.

Bivariate Fallacies

The **bivariate fallacy** is the claim to causation given correlation between just two variables. The bivariate fallacy usually begins with a **bivariate analysis**, meaning examination of only two variables or several independent pairs of variables. A bivariate analysis is a failure to control for exogenous variables. For instance, Richard Wilkinson and Kate Pickett claimed to prove that each of different types of social, economic, and political inequality leads to national problems (2009), but were justly criticized for presenting only bivariate analyses and not controlling for other potential explanations.

CHAPTER SUMMARY

This chapter explained:

- Observations and data

- How to operationalize what you want to observe

- How to measure

  - Objective correlates
  - Judgmental correlates
  - Triangulation
  - Multiple measures
  - Meta-analysis

- How to classify data by:

  - Unit of analysis
    - Discrete
    - Continuous
  - Groups and scales
    - Cardinal
    - Group
    - Nominal/categorical
    - Ordinal/ranked
    - Interval
    - Ratio
  - Types of data
    - Attributes
    - Flows
    - Structural
    - Events
    - Rates
    - Frequencies
  - Levels of analysis

- How to use small-n datasets

- How to use large-n datasets

- How to use data as:

  - Evidence
  - Information or intelligence
  - Entertainment

- o Illustrations
- o Analogies
- o Anecdotes
- o Inductions
- How to present evidence
  - o Facts, proof
  - o Direct evidence
- o Credible evidence
- o Judgmental evidence
- o A majority as evidence
- How to separate correlation from causation, particularly by recognizing:
  - o Spurious relationships
  - o Bivariate fallacies

KEY TERMS

QUESTIONS AND EXERCISES _____

1. Reread the opening vignette. How could the operationalization have been improved to avoid the respondents' confusions?

2. Why is an observation not quite the same as a datum?

3. Read the text in quotes: "According to the digital gauge on their thermostat, the temperature of the air in their room varies from 54 to 65 degrees Fahrenheit, with an average of 63 degrees, which to them feels too warm, although ice forms on some of the lower windows. Their children find the temperature just right." Identify in the text examples of:

   a. A variable
   b. An attribute (and of what this is an attribute)
   c. A nominal value
   d. A verifiable observation
   e. A measuring instrument
   f. A datum that is not an observation
   g. Unverifiable data
   h. Empirical data

4. Now identify in the quoted text above an objective correlate and a judgmental correlate of room air temperature.

5. Imagine that you are called upon to survey the air temperature in each of several rooms in a building. What would you be promising if you were to claim that your data are each of the following things?

   a. Replicable
   b. Valid
   c. Reliable

d. Recorded
e. Reported

6. Somebody else had already surveyed the temperature in each of the rooms; your data suggest that the rooms are warmer than reported by the other surveyor. What would you investigate if you were asked to check for each of the following three types of errors?

   a. Systematic measurement errors
   b. Nonsystematic measurement errors
   c. Observation errors

7. To improve on each of the scenarios listed below, choose the likeliest response from the following options: triangulate, index, figure of merit, or meta-analysis.

   a. A previous study of average room temperature in this city relied on one contractor for data.
   b. Two surveys have been carried out: one reporting in degrees Fahrenheit, one reporting in degrees Celsius.
   c. A new report has reported average temperature, maximum temperature during the summer season, minimum temperature during the winter season, average humidity, whether ice was observed on any windows, and the residents' comfort with the temperature on a scale from 1 to 10. Different consumers have criticized each of these measures for not capturing everything about the comfort of habitation, but agree that each captures something unique.
   d. An official consumer of the new report has criticized all but one of the measures for ignoring the residents' self-reported comfort.

8. In each of the scenarios below, what is the unit of analysis?

   a. The financial value of illegal drugs confiscated per year

   b. City residents who report that they pray at least once per week

   c. The number of buildings used for religious worship in each city

   d. The number of cities with at least 50 buildings used for religious workshop

   e. The average height of trees in the city's public parks

   f. The number of parks with trees taller than 60 feet

   g. The average weight of leaves shed by each tree per year

   h. The average weight of a leaf shed by a tree

9. In each of the scenarios above, is the unit discrete or continuous?

10. Imagine that a client wants to study parasitic diseases in the city's residents.

Now imagine an example of some data that would be useful to the study and that would count as:

   a. Cardinal

   b. Grouped

   c. Nominal/categorical

   d. Ordinal

   e. Interval

   f. Ratio

11. What are the comparative advantages of large-n datasets versus small-n datasets?

12. What is the difference between a datum and a fact?

13. Identify the unproven propositions masquerading as facts in Research in the Real World Box 10.1.

14. Explain the differences in presentations of the same data in Research in the Real World Box 10.2.

15. Why does the bivariate fallacy encourage spurious assertions?

CHAPTER 11

Writing

Opening Vignette:
How to Write in Social Science

Robert Axelrod

"The first thing I'd say is that for me writing doesn't come easily. In fact, of all the aspects of my job as a professor, I like writing the least, but when I write I feel like an arthritic basket weaver who knows the job can be done but every minute along the way feels the pain.

"In the case of my [1984] book *The Evolution of Cooperation*, I took almost a full year from the time I had finished the research (and published four articles that made up about half the book) just to write and rewrite.

"I was fortunate to have an outstanding high school education which taught me a lot about writing, including grammar.

"I find it helpful to give presentations of my work before I start writing. That way I can start to formulate the sentences, decide on the logical flow, and—most importantly—get feedback.

"I also recommend getting feedback on several drafts. Cultivate friends who will be willing to read those drafts by offering to read theirs ahead of time.

"Finally, good writing follows the answer to the violinist looking for directions, who asked 'How do you get to Carnegie Hall?' and was told, 'Practice, practice, practice.'" (Robert Axelrod, the Walgreen Professor for the Study of Human Understanding at the University of Michigan.)

Learning Objectives and Outcomes

At the end of this chapter, you should be able to:

1. Plan your writing

2. Structure a coherent text

3. Edit

4. Find your style of writing

5. Write efficiently

6. Properly structure your writing

Planning the Writing of Your Whole Product

Whatever you write has a **structure**—discrete parts, some superior or subordinate to others. At the least, any document must have a beginning and an end.

It should have parts, where each part has a separate theme, although each part should transition sensibly from the previous part and contribute to the whole. These parts could be termed chapters or sections. Within each of these parts is an internal structure, indicated by subsections of various levels (subsections can have subsubsections), further differentiated by titles or headings of different styles. (A **style** is a distinctive manner.) Within any of these parts, at any level, is a structure indicated by paragraphs, sentences, and the syntax of each sentence.

Let us begin with the structure of the whole document. A full report on any social scientific research would include at least four parts:

1. An introduction

2. A review of the theories

3. A test of at least one hypothesis

4. A conclusion

Every document varies, but every social scientific product must contain at least these four parts. You might be wondering about the proportions of the whole document occupied by these parts. While remembering that every document varies, the introduction occupies around one-fifteenth (two pages in a 30-page document or 700 words in a 10,000 word document), the review occupies about four-tenths (13 pages in a 30-page document or 4,000 words in a 10,000 word document), the test occupies around four tenths, and the conclusion occupies around one fifteenth.

A document could include many more than these parts. For instance, your introduction might introduce a new material or concept or policy that deserves a part that simply describes current knowledge to the reader. Your review of the theories might be complex enough that you should assign one part for reviewing one type of theories, followed by another part reviewing another type. Your test might involve several different methods, each with its own part. Your test might involve only case studies, but each case study might be so rich that each case study needs its own part. Your results and findings from the test might be so extensive that you need separate parts there as well.

In a fully presentable document, these parts should be collected with other matter that supports the parts and makes sense of the whole—matter such as a table of contents at the start, and a bibliography or list of references at the end.

The document might be specified by an external authority, such as an academic program that demands a certain document in fulfillment of an academic degree, a client who demands a report, or a publisher who offers to publish your research but only in a certain format. These specifications can affect the structure of your product.

The first specification to note is any restriction on length, usually specified by total words or pages. Many undergraduate theses and journal articles are limited to around 10,000 words. Many reports must be shorter—around 3,000 words—while publishers want around 100,000 words to justify a book. Usually these limits are strict, meaning that a failure to comply could lead to failure or rejection. Some specifications allow some leeway, such as plus or minus 5% of the limit.

The other specifications are likely to describe formatting standards, such as the page layout, font, margins, and so forth.

The other specifications could be structural, such as specifications of the parts. For instance, an undergraduate thesis might be specified with a theoretical section, a report might be specified with an executive summary, and a publishing contract might specify the chapters.

The following subsections will explain how to write the:

- Introduction
- Theory or knowledge review sections
- Methodological sections
- Conclusion
- Other matter, especially the front matter, negative space, and back matter

Introduction

Your first section is always an **introduction** to the project, containing a description of the project, a justification of the project and of the rest of the document, and a preview of the rest of the document.

Your first section is always an introduction in this sense, but does not need to be titled an "Introduction." It could be titled with the research question or some term indicating the scope.

After the section's title, state the research question, describe the scope, and justify why it is interesting, important, improving, challenging, and resolving a gap in our knowledge.

Summarize your project: your upcoming review of the theories, the method of your test, the test's results, your findings, and your conclusion.

Preview the structure of the rest of the document. Sometimes the preview of the structure can be conflated with the summary of your project. This conflation makes sense where you are short of space and the structure of your document exactly maps a conventional project (theory review, test, conclusion).

You should separate the summary of your project from the preview of the structure if the structure of the document is more complicated than a conventional project. For instance, your theory review might be spread across several sections, each dedicated to a review of a particular class of theories. Similarly, your test could be spread across several sections, each dedicated to a particular case study.

Projects vary, so some projects deserve shorter or longer introductions. A good rule of thumb is that the introduction should not be longer than one-fifteenth of the whole document, so in a 30-page document the introduction should not be longer than two pages; in a 10,000 word document, the introduction should not be longer than 700 words.

Theory and Knowledge Review Sections

The ideal introduction explains the research question, the scope, and its justification without need for further explication. In rare cases, the scope is so novel that it deserves its own section; similarly, the scope's boundaries could be so unconventional, disputed, or complicated that they need a longer review than would fit comfortably in the introduction.

Sometimes you should devote a section to reviewing knowledge about something. For instance, we might review the facts, if they are complicated enough, before reviewing the theories that could explain the facts. In applied research, we might review the issue or the problem before reviewing theories about the best solutions. In action research, we should review applied research that suggests that change is needed, before reviewing theories about how to implement that change.

All scientific documents should have a section reviewing theories. It should review theories that could help to answer the research question, argue for a preferred theory or develop a new preferred theory, and conclude with at least one hypothesis.

A theory review might include some modeling, but if the modeling is complicated you might justify a separate section dedicated to modeling your preferred theory. For instance, this would be justified in a project that reviews the theories and then models a preferred theory as a long formal theory.

Methodological Sections

Given a hypothesis, at least one section must be devoted to a test of the hypothesis. It should review the methodological options before you declare your choice, describe how you implemented your test, describe the results, and summarize the findings.

A separate section might be justified to review the methods if they are many or are highly contested in your field.

Another section might be justified if the results are very long or complicated— this is likely for long historical cases, where the author must describe what happened and justify interpretations. Separate sections might be justified for several cases. Even one case might need several sections to explain each period of a long story.

Two separate sections might be justified for the findings and the results, if the results were very long and the findings were not obvious from the results. The results of a survey would include a summary of the responses and an analysis of the response. The findings are whatever meanings the author finds in the results. For instance, the results of a survey might include two results: two thirds of respondents want grocers to offer organic food, and one third of respondents reported that they routinely buy organic food. A simple finding from these two results is that more people favor organic food than actually buy it. Other results might show that most respondents find organic food expensive, and that most respondents find nonorganic food easier to find. We could put together all these results to find that organic food is too inaccessible for people to buy as much organic food as they want.

Conclusion

The final section is always a *conclusion*. It summarizes everything that came before: the research question, the scope, its justification, the theories, your preferred theory, your hypotheses, your test, your results, and your findings.

The conclusion is your final opportunity to admit any failures or limitations—failures such as a failure to prove your hypothesis, or a failure to finish the test as designed, and limitations such as your inability to access the primary sources that would show conclusively whether an interpretation is correct.

You should state clearly the implications of your research, such as the implication that theorists should abandon a theory that you have disproven, or adopt a policy or practice that you have shown to be best.

Finally, you should suggest further research. For instance, perhaps you have proven a theory; you could suggest a different method that further researchers should use to test the theory and thereby triangulate your proof. Perhaps you have proven a theory of why people buy unhealthy foods; you could suggest applied research into how government can encourage people to buy healthier foods. Perhaps you have proven a best policy or best practice; you could suggest action research to decide how to implement the change.

Other Matter

Other matter supports the parts or sections of a document and contributes to the whole document. This other matter includes:

- **Front matter** (also known as **preliminaries**)

- **Negative space**, such as blank pages

- **Back matter** (also known as **reference matter**)

Front Matter

The front matter appears before the introduction. The front matter consists of a page, or a part of a page, dedicated to any or every one of the following things:

- A **title page** shows the whole document's title, the author's name, a date, and perhaps the intended use or audience of this document, together with any restrictions on use or audience. For instance, when distributing a draft that you do not intend to be further distributed or published or cited, you might state so on the title page.

- An **acknowledgment** is an opportunity to thank sponsors of your research, people or organizations that especially permitted access to or reproduction of any information that was useful to your research, or people or organizations that gave you time to complete the project or otherwise supported it.

- A **foreword** is an introduction written by somebody other than the authors of the rest of the document.

- A **preface** is an introduction written by the primary authors of the rest of the document. It is often used somewhat redundantly to preview or summarize a larger introduction. A preface is more appropriate as an insert to a new edition, or to acknowledge some change since the introduction was written.

- A **table of contents** lists the sections to come, usually with page numbers corresponding to the start of each section. Sometimes, when the overall document's structure is complicated, a simple table of contents shows only the major sections, and is followed by a detailed table of contents showing the major sections and subordinate sections.

- A **list of illustrations** is like a table of contents for only the illustrations in the rest of the document.

- A **list of tables** is a table listing the tables in the rest of the document.

- A **list of abbreviations** is a list of abbreviations used in the rest of the document—this is only warranted if a lot of abbreviations are used.

- A **glossary** is a list of terms and their definitions. A glossary might be warranted if the book uses a lot of unfamiliar terms.

- An **abstract** might be specified by the authority demanding the document. An abstract is a very short summary of the document, normally up to 100 words.

- A **dedication** is a statement by the author in honor of someone. This is not normally appropriate in social scientific work.

- An **epigraph** is some text, such as a quotation, separated from any other part in the document. An epigraph is not normally appropriate in social scientific work, but could be used to show a quotation from which you might have derived the title, or to illustrate some conventional or entertaining view of your document's subject.

Negative Space

Negative space is unfilled space. It is negative in the sense that it is the opposite of the text, images, and whatever else fills the space (the **positive space**). Negative space actually gives meaning to positive space. The negative spaces around these letters and words allow you to see the positive ink-filled spaces as letters and words. Likely your publisher or whatever authority demands your document also specifies the font, the size of the font, the size of the space between lines, and the size of the breaks between paragraphs, between sections, and so forth.

Negative space is used to separate front matter too. A title page is normally followed by a blank page before any other front matter is printed. Other important front matter could be separated by blank pages. With or without a blank page, the importance or differentiation of the front matter can be indicated by leaving blank the rest of the page (a **page break**).

Margins around the text on a page are further examples of negative space. Your publisher or other authority is likely to specify the size of the margins along the sides of the page, the negative spaces at the top of the page (the **header**) and the bottom (the **footer**), and whether you can or should write anything in the header or footer—such as the document's title, section title, or page number.

Back Matter

Back matter comes after the conclusion. Likely you will be expected to provide a list of sources. If the list is of sources that were useful but not necessarily cited, the list is a **bibliography**. If the list is of sources that are cited, the list is a **reference list**.

If you have chosen or been ordered to use endnotes instead of footnotes, your endnotes need their own section in the back matter.

Appendices also appear within the back matter. Appendices are used to include information that would be too disruptive to the main sections of the document—information such as all the content of a survey instrument that you used during your test, all the responses to a survey that you analyze in the results section, or the content of a particularly important primary document that you cite in the main sections.

Style

The subsections below will explain how to get started on your writing, the implications for editing, how to find your own style, and how to write fewer words while communicating more.

Getting Started

Writing can be intimidating. You could have lots of ideas about different things that you want to write or a general idea of the whole, but have difficulty expressing anything in particular.

A common problem is knowing the subject of your writing, in which case you should remind yourself of your scoping (Chapter 4) or pick one particular argument that you think would be easiest to describe or create (see Table 7.3).

Source: ©iStockphoto.com/AmmentorpDK

A common problem is knowing how to start. This problem is paralyzing when writers want to work linearly (from start to end) and are uncomfortable writing later parts before earlier parts. However, do not be afraid to write later parts before earlier parts if the information is readier for those later parts. At the least, you should be writing notes about what you intend to write, and you should be writing down technical information such as findings—which otherwise would be easy to forget, even before you are ready to complete anything.

Yet you still need to write the start of the whole document and the start of any section. The starting sentence can be difficult to find. This can be infuriating—fretting about one sentence while the rest of the document remains unwritten!

If you are stuck on what it is that you should be writing—the content—then you should remind yourself of your plan and shift your mind around executing the plan.

If you know what you want to say but are stuck on how to say it—the style rather than the substance—just write it down immediately as you would think it or say it out loud, and then you can edit it later. Truly, something is better than nothing.

Moreover, writing itself is a helpful process. Seeing words can be more helpful than thinking of the words when developing the perfect sentence. Writing words is an active cognitive and biolocomotive process that is stimulating and in itself helps you work out what you want to write. By the way, this is truer when writing by hand (with a pen or pencil) than when typing, because writing is a more complex biolocomotive activity than typing; speaking is less active; thinking is even less active. Thus, if you find yourself routinely struggling to start, abandon whatever is your mode, such as talking it out, and get in the habit of writing it down by hand first. You can always discuss it, type it up, and edit it later.

Try changing your mode if you find that you frequently get stuck in a particular mode. Try switching between writing by hand, typing, speaking into speech recognition software, speaking out loud in a mirror, and engaging in discussion with a trusted peer.

If you are still stuck, write down something, however imperfect, so that you have something to work with. Perfectionism can be paralyzing.

Perfectionism also can be the false justification for procrastination. Sometimes we walk around claiming that we are not ready to start writing because the perfect sentence has not occurred to us yet. This pretension is encouraged by popular cultural expectations for inspiration. Most people seem to think that good writing comes naturally to some people. Movies and novels often portray great artists looking wistfully into the distance before suddenly producing a masterpiece. While some people truly are more gifted than others, all writers must revise what they write. Great writers include those who aggressively correct themselves as well as those who wait for inspiration. Sometimes you are inspired to write the perfect thing, but inspiration is not routine and can be misleading—just because it occurs to you does not make it perfect. Most writing is work. Treat it as work, schedule time for it, discipline yourself, get on with it, and expect to edit it later.

Learn to evaluate your writing as you go along, as in Practical Advice Box 11.1.

Editing

As you should realize by now, your initial approach toward writing should be to get on with it, even though your first attempt is likely to be imperfect. Inevitably, this approach implies later editing. Thus, this approach becomes a trade-off: You are trading off speed against perfection. Freeing up your writing so that it becomes quicker implies that it also becomes more imperfect. This trade-off has extremes: You could be writing too slowly in search of perfection; you could be writing nonsense quickly. By writing quickly, you must expect imperfections, and commit to thorough editing. All writing involves editing—nobody could ever write a first draft that is both substantive and perfect.

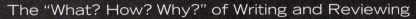

Practical Advice Box 11.1
The "What? How? Why?" of Writing and Reviewing

Source: ©iStockphoto.com/apomares.

As you write (anything from a sentence to a section), ask yourself, from the reader's perspective, these three questions:

1. What am I trying to communicate?
2. How am I accomplishing Number 1?
3. Why are my choices in Number 1 and Number 2 important?

When you edit your own writing, ask the same questions:

1. What do you notice about the text? That is, what stands out or grabs your attention? It could be the use of certain content, grammar, syntax, or rhetorical or structural choices. For an example, imagine that the writing characterizes a "depressed" economy or an economy that is "down." This is the "what."

2. Once you have identified the element that you find interesting (the "what"), try to explain how it is working within the text. How does it influence your interaction with the text? Imagine that the metaphor of a depressed economy helps to suggest the psychological consequences as well as the economic consequences.

3. Now ask, why is it important? What are the implications of it on the text? You could imagine that a reference to depression helps the reader to connect emotionally with the event.

Sometimes you will be uncertain about whether what you have written is good or needs to be edited. This is partly inherent, because as writers we are biased readers; we knew what we meant when we wrote it, so our own writing is easier for us to understand, whereas another person could know only what we actually wrote. You should get in the habit of writing for a strange reader: When you read your own work, get in the habit of posing as an ignorant reader. Learn to empathize with other readers and realize some humility about your own writing.

If you are still uncertain about whether something needs editing, you might follow a rule commonly stated as "When in doubt, throw it out." Uncertainty is a good sign that something is wrong with what you wrote, but you cannot yet determine exactly what is wrong. You should spend some time trying to determine what is wrong. If you are still struggling to work it out, rather than struggle further, you could just scrap it and write it anew. One of the most mature skills in any project is knowing when to scrap one approach in order to try another approach, even while you feel committed to sunk effort. This can be a cathartic and liberating approach to not just a single sentence but also whole paragraphs and even sections.

Of course, you could take this too far and delete content that is fine, perhaps because you are overly self-critical or lacking in self-efficacy, but this attitude is less likely than overprotection of what you have written.

Find Your Style

Now that you are writing something, you can devote more attention to developing your *style*—a distinctive manner. One of the skills that almost all researchers must develop is to write well, with a style that communicates substantive information, yet is easy to read, engaging, unambiguous, unoffensive, and even entertaining.

Try reading freely, comparing different styles, and thinking about what makes good writing. Perhaps you have been in the habit of reading poor writing or basing your own language on bad music lyrics or television scripts. Try to imitate other writing that you like or that has been described to you as good writing. Reading bad writing while benchmarking good writing should help you to develop more humility about your own writing, and to develop your own preferred style.

Try writing freely; try experimenting with new styles. However, do not indulge in experimentation just to be different.

> It's easy to use grammar tricks to make things "different," but as so often happens, the results are long on technique and short on substance. We admire our inventiveness, but the reader is left to ponder the sense of it. It's far better to develop style through word usage than to reach for grammar tricks. (Noble, 1993, p. 49)

Raise your own standards. Routinely correct your own writing, even where it does not matter, such as in emails to casual friends. Conversations, too, are opportunities to practice your style.

Be aware of how different stereotypes write, and how to write better than they. Politicians obfuscate and spin information in order to avoid blame, to maximize credit, or to hedge against future events. Journalists face very tight word limits and need to grab attention, so they use grammatical shortcuts, conflate information, and sensationalize. Traditional historians value good writing and entertaining stories over substantive information. Artists and entertainers value style over substance. Scientists value substance over style, and are accused of boring communications (Olson, 2009).

Write Less, Mean More

You should write as succinctly and as meaningfully as possible. You should learn to communicate more meaning with fewer words. This is somewhat of a trade-off: The fewer words you use, the less you can communicate, all other things being equal. However, most people tend to wordiness and ambiguity—they tend to write too much and communicate less clearly than they could. You should learn to communicate more with fewer words.

To write succinctly, cut out any superfluous words and flowery turns of phrase. For a start, stop using unnecessary qualifiers and modifiers. Qualifiers and modifiers include adjectives that add meaning to a noun or restrictive clauses that add meaning to an independent clause. The following modifiers and qualifiers are never necessary: *really*, *sort of*, *quite*, *much*, *very*, and *just the same*.

Cut redundant words. Grammatical redundancies are tautologies. They occur when a word is used that is unnecessary given another word in the sentence, as in "humiliating embarrassment," "seize control," "free gift," and "major disaster."

As well as redundancies, avoid self-contradictions, such as "I am sure it will probably happen"—a phrase that leaves unclear whether my expectation is certain or probable.

Choose the fewest words for the same meaning. For instance, write *few* instead of *not much*, *to return* instead of *to come back*, and *to view* instead of *to look at*.

Choose more precise words, such as *must* instead of *have to* and *will* instead of *going to*.

Try to write as literally as possible. Use the most literal of a group of synonyms. If you mean to describe someone as "angry," avoid metaphors with other useful meanings such as "apoplectic." Avoid unnecessarily complex or poorly founded synonyms; for instance, don't use the word *unconscionable* to mean "thoughtless" or "unethical."

Limit your use of clichés and metaphors, such as "perfect storm" or "shot across the bows," except in the rare circumstance where the meaning is clear and appropriate.

Some metaphors are meaningful because they remain in routine use in academic discourse, such as:

- Your research should not set up a straw man against a panacea.

- Don't myopically scope explanations.

- You should unpack your assumptions.

- You can finesse ambiguity or criticism.

- You should prefer the least noisy data.

- If disproven, you should fall on your sword.

Check that you properly understand the literal meanings of words that typically are used loosely. For instance, *massive* means something of high mass, not something that is "large," so a "massive fire" makes no sense. Check the differences between, for instance, *abroad* and *overseas*, *nation* and *state*, and *American* and *North American*.

Learn more vocabulary so that you have more choices when searching for the most precise term. Some websites specialize in words; some regularly introduce words or terms and discuss meanings and uses.

Sometimes you do need to add words to clarify ambiguous words. For instance, what is a year? Depending on your meaning, the first use of the term *year* might need to be clarified as the "calendar year," "fiscal year," "tax year," or "academic year." Similarly, when you use the word *oil*, do you mean crude oil, fuel oil, lubricating oil, or another type of oil?

Structure

The subsections below will explain how to structure your writing in general, a paragraph, a sentence, the start of a sentence, the clauses within a sentence, and each clause.

Structuring Your Writing in General

Your writing style should be engaging and even entertaining, but it must be substantive too. Proper structure will help you to achieve both style and substance. A structure breaks up your text into a collection of more manageable parts. A structure indicates subjects—each section of the whole should discuss something differentiated from the previous section. Structuring and restructuring your writing helps you to realize your subjects, and how to relate subjects to each other. If you realize that some subjects are parts of a larger or higher subject, those subjects should become subsections of a section on the larger or higher subject. How you structure your document as a whole helps to direct you as to how to structure each part and each lower level (subsection). Reconsider Exercise 5.1.

Whatever the part or level of your document, your writing should benefit from the following nine steps:

1. Link back

2. Scope

3. Preview

4. Categorize

5. Macro to micro

6. Compare and contrast

7. Justify

8. Conclude

9. Link forward

Link Back

Often, a new part of your document should start with some link back to the preceding part. For instance, an author could use a first section to describe the history of the "food movement" (the general campaign to improve the quality of food). The author could start the next section by reminding the reader of the food movement's aims in the past, before promising to examine whether the food movement could achieve its aims in the future.

Scope

Begin by bounding the scope of each part. At the start of a section, you should declare any boundary that differentiates this section from any otherwise similar section. For instance, one section could be about the healthy food movement in

Michigan, before a section that is about the healthy food movement in Montana. At the start of a paragraph, you should indicate whatever the paragraph will be limited to, using a contextual sentence. For instance, you could begin a paragraph with a sentence to the effect of "Now let us consider the food movement in Detroit." Even a sentence should begin by making clear the boundaries of the rest of the sentence, for instance: "In neighboring counties, at the time the food movement reached the capital . . ."

Preview

For major parts, preview the rest of the part. For instance, at the start of a section you should indicate what the section is about, indicate any subsections, or preview what the section will argue or find.

Categorize

You can structure your writing around any classes, categories, or cases of whatever information is the subject at the time within the current subject. For instance, you could bound a section to the food movement in Michigan. You could preview the section by explaining that it will explain the food movement in each of Michigan's major cities. Then subsections could examine each city in turn. Your disaggregation of the information would have guided you to the structure.

Similarly, you could structure parts of the writing by different theories, different methods, different sources, different types of data, or anything that can be justifiably categorized separately.

Macro to Micro

Generally you should write from the macro to the micro of the subject; from the general to the specific; from the least complicated to the most complicated.

Beginning with the macro helps indicate the whole or the context, and is less burdensome to communicate. From the macro, the micro is easier to disaggregate, justify, and communicate.

You should begin from the most general propositions and work your way down to the most detailed propositions; from the most general or broadest observations to the most detailed; from the most parsimonious theories to the narrowest; from the simplest summary of the data to the detailed analysis; and so forth.

Compare and Contrast

You can find structure in your writing by seeking to compare or contrast different information. For instance, you might want to describe the food movement in

Michigan's different cities. A least interesting way would be to describe each city, in turn, without linking any case. Instead, you should seek to find comparisons or contrasts between each case. For instance, we could note that the food movement is strongest in one particular city. This would give us the opportunity to begin our description of the food movement in another city by writing, "By contrast, the food movement in this other city is weak."

Even if we cannot find contrasts, we should look for comparisons. We could describe the food movement in that other city as more recent, more youthful, or something else.

Sometimes your comparisons and contrasts warrant clarifications about your intended meaning—these are sometimes known as **meta-commentary**. You could begin such clarifications with such familiar phrases as:

- In other words . . .

- To clarify . . .

- The gist of the matter is . . .

- I do not mean to imply that . . .

When comparing and contrasting arguments, remember what you learned in Chapter 7 about how to create an argument (see Table 7.3). Arguments can be reviewed in three main ways:

1. Opposing sides: Present all the arguments in favor of one position or one side of an argument, then present all the opposing arguments. Conclude by declaring your preference.

2. Argument by argument (also known as block by block): Review one argument in its entirety, followed by another argument in its entirety. Repeat for each argument. Conclude by declaring your preference.

3. Point by point: Review one argument's point before comparing another argument's counterpoint, declaring your preferences along the way. Repeat for each point.

Justify

You can structure your writing around observations, propositions, and justifications. For instance, I could begin by observing that the food movement is youthful. Then I should write some justification for my observation, essentially with data: "The average age of the participants is 20 years of age, considerably younger than the average of the participants in the other city." Given this statement of fact, I could propose something further: "Such youthful movements are less sustainable because such young members are more likely to migrate out of the city for work, and to lack their own resources to sustain their campaign." Some people refer to the connection between a proposition and its support as a **link** or **linkage**.

Notice that your presentation of facts should be empirical enough to persuade the reader. If your presentation of facts is unclear or vague, you will be less persuasive. For instance, if you wrote that most of the world's ice has melted due to global warming, that would make your reader ponder: How much ice? Where in particular? Over what period of time? In fact, a more accurate and supportable statement would be that most of the world's surface ice sheets have shrunk in the last 100 years.

Do not forget to cite external information (see the section on plagiarism in Chapter 3 for advice on citations). Citations add credibility to your own writing. Quotations add authenticity to your representations of other sources. However, you do not want your own text to be taken over by external texts—this is sometimes known as **quilting** or **patchwriting**, which can feel like an incoherent quilt of unrelated items. You must use external information to support your own writing, not overtake it.

When using long quotes, remember the "ICE" acronym:

1. Introduce the quote (perhaps with information about the author or a summary of what is in the quote).

2. Cite the quote.

3. Explain the significance of the quote for your argument or for upcoming text.

Conclude

Whatever part you are writing, whether a section or a paragraph, it should conclude in some way. For instance, if you were writing a section about the food movement in Michigan's cities, you would proceed through descriptions of the food movements in each of the cities, and then you would have the opportunity to conclude the section with a summary or finding. Perhaps you should summarize the strength or weakness of the food movement in each city. Perhaps you found that the food movement is weaker in Michigan's cities than in Montana's cities.

Method	Distinguishing feature	Good use	Bad use
Summary	In your own words	• Brief but accurate review of a source • Differentiation of other research from your own research	• A long summary that could be shorter as a paraphrase or quote • Misrepresentation of the source • Unacknowledged source
Paraphrase	Your rewording of the original text	• A shorter but equally accurate representation of a text	• An inaccurate rewording
Quote	The original text is reproduced verbatim	• The author's writing adds authenticity to the information • The author's writing is interesting or entertaining in its own right • You could not summarize or paraphrase without losing accuracy	• Quoting narrowly out of context • Long quotes that seem burdensome to read • Long quotes that would need special permission from the author

Table 11.1 A quick guide to summarizing, paraphrasing, and quoting a source

Link Forward

When you reach the end of any part of the document, you should try to link it with the next part. For instance, after summarizing a section about the food movement in Michigan, your final sentence could state that the next section will find that the food movement is dissimilar in Montana.

Structuring a Paragraph

A **paragraph** contains at least one sentence. Spatially, each paragraph is differentiated from the next by some additional space, such as a line break (additional to the space break between sentences).

A paragraph is a discrete unit of text, so its structure can follow the general rules in the preceding section. This section gives you some more particular advice for writing a paragraph.

The first sentence should segue from any previous paragraph, and establish the current paragraph's main subject or claim. Its subject could be the geology beneath your city, in which case your first sentence should segue from the subject of any previous paragraph (such as "While the other city was built on clay . . .") and establish the forthcoming subject ("this city has very different soils, including . . .").

If you do not need to segue from any previous paragraph, you should start by bounding the scope of the paragraph or with a premise or an observation.

If you start by bounding the scope, you should proceed to further explain whatever is the subject within the scope. If you bound the scope of the paragraph as the geology of your city, your subsequent sentences should simply describe the geology, from macro to micro or general to specific.

If you start with a premise, the paragraph's subsequent sentences should be propositions given the premise.

If you start with an observation, the paragraph's subsequent sentences should justify the observation, or explain the observation in more detail.

Each subsequent sentence should build on the previous sentence, or refine the point of the previous sentence. Each sentence builds on its precedents.

Your final sentence should conclude the theme of the paragraph. You know when a paragraph absolutely should end when you have exhausted the subject. If you started the paragraph talking about geology in this city and find yourself with nothing else to say about the geology in this city, your paragraph is over and you should begin a new paragraph.

Alternatively, you could find that you have much more to say about the subject of the paragraph as you started it, but that the paragraph is getting too long. The length of paragraphs is a personal, subjective choice, but paragraphs rarely should reach a page long, and rarely should be as short as one sentence. If you find yourself writing a paragraph longer than a dozen sentences, consider whether you could disaggregate the current subject into subordinate subjects that deserve their own paragraphs. For instance, you might begin a paragraph about the geology of your city, but find that you could write a paragraph about its sandy soils, another paragraph about its bedrock, and another about its aquifers.

Structuring a Sentence

A **sentence** is a contiguous set of words with a discrete meaning. Sentences include statements, propositions, questions, declarations, exclamations, and commands/ orders (imperatives). In casual speech, sentences mix all these things because speakers tend to run on and on, sometimes without end, until interrupted. Writing should be more structured. For instance, a sentence should not both propose something and ask a question. Here is an example of two sentences conflated as one sentence: "I propose that I should do it and what should I do?" A written sentence should not be more than a statement, a proposition, question, or something similar, unless you are attempting something stylistically exotic or creative, or your sentence includes a quote of another sentence. For instance, an allowable sentence could state that a person shouted. A sentence could state that a person shouted a question. A sentence could state that a person shouted, "What should I do?"

Other than quoting another sentence, and outside of creative work or casual speech, each of your sentences should make only one point. Given that first point, you could make a second point in the following sentence.

Each time you complete a point, consider ending the sentence immediately. Resist the urge to continue the sentence. Resist the urge to add any conjunction, especially the word *and*. A **conjunction** is a part of a sentence that links phrases or clauses. The word *and* is a conjunction best used to link items in a list. The following sentence includes an appropriate use of *and*: "The architect was applauded for her sense of aestheticism and her use of sustainable materials." The word *and* should not be used to link two clauses that do not belong in the same list, as in "The architect was applauded and today a new architect is in town."

Similarly, your sentence should not conflate too much information. It should make one point and include only enough information to make that point. Conflation of information is typical in journalism, where the journalist is facing a very tight word limit. An example of such "journalese" is "Despite recent setbacks, the keen athlete and mother was upbeat about the future." The main point of this sentence is "Despite recent setbacks, she is upbeat about the future." The other information in the journalese is that the subject is a keen athlete, and she is a mother. On the face of it, the relevance of this other information to the main point is unclear. Perhaps the woman's athleticism or motherhood helps her to be upbeat. If so, this relevance needs to be made clear. Be aware of the main point of a sentence, and be aware of whatever other information you are starting to put in the sentence, and then keep it in the sentence only if it is relevant to the main point.

Starting a Sentence

Unless the sentence is a very simple clause, such as "They rested," start the sentence with its scope, especially any boundaries of time or space. If the sentence is restricted in time or space, start the sentence by specifying when or where the sentence applies: "In the past in this region . . ."; "Currently at home . . ."; "In 18th-century Bolivia . . ."; "In 1969 in America . . ." For instance, we would bind the sentence's time and space if we started it by writing, "During the 1920s, American women found new freedoms." The new freedoms that are meant by the sentence are only the freedoms that emerged in the 1920s in America for women. They are not the freedoms that emerged before or after the 1920s, or in any location but America, or for men.

Do not mistake the scope for the point of the sentence. Information about time or space might bound the sentence, or it might bind only part of the sentence, perhaps only one noun, in which case you should not lead with the time or space but keep it near the thing it affects. For instance, your sentence could read, "American women found new freedoms in the 1920s." Here the space and subject are still bound (America is the spatial scope; the subject is restricted to women, not men), but the sentence is not bound in time. These particular freedoms emerged in the 1920s, but others could have emerged before or after; the sentence could run on to include freedoms that are not bound by the 1920s, as in the following: "American women found new freedoms in the 1920s and the 1930s."

Time

You can use prepositions to help to bound time. The word *in* implies a discrete event within an imprecise period, such as, "In the 1930s, she was born."

The word *during* implies change within a period, such as, "During the 1930s, she grew up."

The words *from* and *to* can be used to designate a period of time or a change or flow, such as, "From the 1920s to the 1930s, she matured."

The word *around* implies uncertainty about the time, as in, "She was born around the 1930s, but possibly as early as the 1920s or as late as the 1940s."

The word *through* should be used to clarify that the whole period is meant, not just sometime within the period. The clause "She lived in America in the 1930s" implies that she lived in America at some point in the 1930s, but not necessarily throughout the 1930s. The clause "She lived in America through the 1930s" implies that she lived in America at all times throughout the 1930s.

The word *by* implies that something was certainly true at a particular point, and possibly before and after, as in, "She was married by the 1930s."

Be prepared to use a subordinate clause to clarify or contextualize time or add useful additional information about the time, as in, "By the 1930s, after the economic great depression, she was poorest."

Words that give more exclusive senses of time include *always* (as in "It is always true), *never* ("It never happened"), *sometimes* (some of the time but not all the time), *rarely* (most of the time it did not occur), *often* (not rarely, but not always), *regularly* (at regular intervals of time), and *routinely* (as a matter of course).

Space

Most of the same prepositions are used to scope space as well as time, although some are nuanced. When used to scope space, the word *in* implies somewhere within a contiguous place, as in, "In America, she traveled widely."

The word *within* implies a contrast with something that is *without*, and vice versa. For instance, saying that she was happiest living in America implies that she was less happy living somewhere else.

The words *from* and *to* imply a flow across space, as in, "She moved from America to Asia."

The word *around* implies some space outside of, but close to, something, as in, "Her travels skirted around America, through Canada, Bermuda, and Mexico."

Be prepared to use a subordinate clause to clarify or contextualize space, as in, "In Canada, where she met various tourists from Bermuda, she arranged to travel to Mexico via Bermuda."

Structuring a Sentence With Clauses

A **clause** is the smallest part of a sentence that can express a complete proposition. A small sentence can consist of a single clause. At minimum a clause consists of a subject and predicate (at its simplest, a verb), to which you could add an object and modifiers. At the end of the clause, you could end the sentence, or you could add another clause, where each clause is usually separated by a comma or hyphen.

Remember that in casual speech we run on clause after clause without ending a sentence, but this is not acceptable in writing, so be cautious about sentences with too many clauses. Two or three clauses can work, but more is usually a sign that you should attempt to separate a new sentence. Where you find a clause that can stand alone, you have found an **independent clause**—a candidate for standing alone as a sentence.

Where you choose to add another clause to an independent clause, but the new clause cannot stand alone as a sentence, you are adding a **dependent clause** or **subordinate clause**.

Be mindful of whether the dependent clause is an unrestrictive clause or restrictive clause. An **unrestrictive clause** depends on the rest of the sentence for its existence but does not change the meaning of the rest of the sentence. An unrestrictive clause contains information that is useful to know but is not essential to the meaning of the rest of the sentence. Use unrestrictive clauses to clarify what you meant by a particular word or term in the main clause, or to contextualize the main clause, but do not use unrestrictive clauses to change the meaning of anything else. For instance, a sentence might include an unusual term, such as *unrestrictive clause*, which could be usefully defined in an unrestrictive clause. A sentence might discuss something unusual, which would be better understood with some context as given in a dependent cause.

An unrestrictive clause should be clarified by placing a comma after the main clause and beginning the dependent clause with the word *which*, which is what I am doing here. You could choose either of two other words more appropriate to the referent, such as *who* if the referent is a person ("She met travelers, who . . .") or *when* if the referent is a time ("In the 1930s, when . . ."). Be aware that *who* is one of the few words in English that has a different form when used as a direct object (*whom*), indirect object (*to whom*), or possessive (*of whom*). Keep the preposition with the word rather than strand the preposition at the end of the sentence. Thus, "She met travelers, with whom she had nothing in common" is preferred to "She met travelers, whom she had nothing in common with."

Keep the clause as close to the referent as possible. For instance, if my sentence were describing the impact of a negotiator's stormy personality on the negotiations, I could note that "this particular negotiator's personality, which was stormy, did not help the negotiations." I should not write that "the negotiator's personality did not help the negotiation, which was stormy"—this latter sentence has a different meaning from the other.

Do not split a clause with another clause. For instance, "He remembered that the negotiator's stormy personality did not help the negotiations" is a smooth single clause and clearly smoother than "The negotiator's stormy personality, he remembered, did not help the negotiations."

A **restrictive clause** changes or restricts the meaning of the independent clause and is designated in most American English usage by avoiding a comma between clauses and using the word *that* instead of *which* (although followers of British English still use *which* without a comma in restrictive clauses). Here is an example of an independent clause and an unrestrictive dependent clause: "She met travelers, whom she did not like." Here is an example with a restrictive dependent clause: "The travelers that bothered her were the ones she avoided."

Be aware that the word *that* is used not only to designate restrictive clauses but also to suggest a process, as in "She decided that . . ." and "He said that . . ."

Structuring Each Clause

The subject is the main part of the clause—usually denoted by a noun (such as *people*) or pronoun (*they*). The predicate is almost always a verb, such as *to speak*, as in "The people spoke" or "They spoke." The predicate can include a verb and an object.

The object is acted upon or affected by the subject, as in "They spoke to me." In this clause, the subject is *they*, the predicate is *spoke*, and the object is *me*. You should remember that sometimes different words are required to convey something as a subject (such as *I*) and an object (*me*).

To the verb you can add an **adverb**, which modifies the meaning of the verb, as in "carefully spoke." To the subject or the object, you could add an adjective, as in "little me."

Ideally, place the adverb after the verb that it modifies, because the verb is more fundamental to the clause than is the adverb (so the verb should come first) and the adverb modifies only the verb (so the two should be as close together as possible). Thus, "He reacted quickly to the news" is preferred to "He reacted to the news quickly."

You can place the adverb before the verb where you want to increase emphasis on the adverb or the verb is expected. For instance, if you are describing a long conversation, in which the reader surely expects that the next clause will describe a response in that conversation, you should expect the reader to expect a verb such as *replied* or *answered*, so you should lead with the adverb, which will be more interesting or meaningful. Thus, "They quickly replied" is preferred to "They replied quickly" if you can take for granted that the reader expects a verb like *replied* but is not expecting the adverb *quickly*. You should choose the latter construction if you want to emphasize *quickly*, because one might expect that they replied slowly, but surprisingly they replied quickly.

Note that the order affects meaning, because adverbs can be used to qualify a sentence as a whole rather than just the verb alone. For instance, "He acted quickly, probably because he had reacted slowly the day before" means that his action was quick (the adverb *quickly* modifies the verb), but not that his action was probable (*probably* does not modify the verb, but modifies the subsequent clause). We should add a comma to make the two clauses clearer: "He acted quickly, probably because he had reacted slowly the day before." Here *probably* modifies the second clause and does not modify either verb. Now consider this alternative: "Probably he acted quickly, because we know that he was asleep within the hour." Here, *probably* modifies the first clause, not the second clause.

The above use of *probably* is as a **sentential adverb**—it modifies the meaning of the whole sentence. Some sentential adverbs are used too often; you should avoid them except in special circumstances. Examples are *naturally* and *of course*—these are used nonliterally to mean that the rest of the sentence is obvious or to be expected, but *naturally* literally refers to something of nature ("arising naturally") while *of course* refers to something procedural ("arising as a matter of course").

A conventional order of subject-verb-object gives most attention to the subject. For instance, the phrase "They chose Richard" emphasizes that Richard was chosen, not someone else; "they" did the choosing. This is the most familiar word order. You can change the order to emphasize the object, as in "Richard they chose over every other candidate," which implies that Richard's selection is a surprise.

Prepositions indicate relationships between things, usually verbs and nouns. The most used prepositions are *of*, *to*, *in*, *for*, *with*, and *on*. Place the preposition between the related things, not after, which could leave the preposition stranded at the end of your clause. Thus, "He slept through the night" is preferred to "He slept the night through," and "He cut down the opposition" is preferred to "He cut the opposition down."

Adverbs can be used to modify not just verbs but also nouns/pronouns and even other adverbs. **Adjectives** modify nouns and pronouns. The adjective should be placed as close to the noun as possible, because the adjective is modifying the noun, not anything else. The adjective is almost always placed before the noun. Where you have lots of adjectives before a noun, you might be left wondering about the proper order of adjectives. Long chains of adjectives are inadvisable because the reader is forced to read a lot of modifiers before knowing what is the thing that is being modified. When ordering a chain of adjectives, start with the most general or inclusive adjective and end with the most specific or exclusive adjective. Thus, "a better environmental policy" is easier to read than "an environmental better policy."

CHAPTER SUMMARY

This chapter has explained how to:

- Plan your whole written product
- Write your introduction
- Write your review sections
- Write your methodological sections
- Write your conclusion
- Choose front matter, negative space, and back matter
- Get started on your initial writing
- Edit
- Find your style
- Write fewer words while communicating more
- Structure your writing in general through the following steps:
  - Link back
  - Scope
  - Preview
  - Categorize
  - Macro to micro
  - Compare and contrast
  - Justify
  - Conclude
  - Link forward
- Structure a paragraph
- Structure a sentence
- Start a sentence
- Structure a sentence with clauses
- Structure a clause

KEY TERMS

QUESTIONS AND EXERCISES

1. Choose a short social scientific book.

   a. Identify its introductory part.

   b. Identify its knowledge review and/or theory review.

   c. Identify its methodological parts.

   d. Identify its conclusion.

   e. Identify its front matter.

   f. Identify its negative space.

   g. Identify its back matter.

2. Now read the introduction.

   a. How could it have been edited better?

   b. How could its style have been improved?

   c. How could the author have written less while communicating more?

3. Now choose a long paragraph.

   a. What is the subject of the paragraph as a whole?

   b. Could it have been better linked back to its predecessor or linked forward to its successor?

   c. How could this paragraph have been broken up into new paragraphs?

   d. How could this paragraph have been aggregated with its predecessor or successor?

   e. Should any sentence have been broken up into new sentences?

   f. Identify the scope of a sentence.

   g. Identify an independent clause.

   h. Identify a dependent clause.

   i. Identify a subject, object, preposition, adverb, and adjective.

GLOSSARY

Abstract. A very short summary of a document, normally up to 100 words.

Acknowledgment. An opportunity to thank sponsors of your research, people or organizations that especially permitted access to or reproduction of any information that was useful to your research, or people or organizations that gave you time to complete the project or otherwise supported it.

Action research. Research that improves understanding of how to implement change, such as how to change the leadership or the culture of an organization.

Adjective. A word that modifies nouns and pronouns.

Adverb. A word or phrase that modifies the meaning of another word, usually a verb.

Alternative history. A term for a counterfactual within the discipline of history.

Analogue. Something similar to but not the same as the target.

Analogy. Claiming that an analogue helps to understand the target.

Analysis. Examination of something in order to better understand it.

Analytical research. Research that aims to analyze something.

Anchoring. Becoming more psychologically sensitive to something due to experiencing it.

Anecdote. A story, usually from personal experience, that can be used to illustrate or entertain.

Antecedent. A variable added as a modeled cause of another variable.

Antipositivists. Those who allow knowledge to be derived from largely subjective or other similarly unreplicable observations.

Antinomy. A proposition that contradicts another even though they are both deduced from the same propositions or induced from the same observations.

Antithesis. One of the opposing elements in a dialectic.

Appendix. A section after the main text used to include information that would be too disruptive to the main sections of the document.

Applicable. Able to be used in the real world.

Applicatory method. Telling history from the point of view of the most prominent person.

Application. Something meant to be of practical use or relevance.

Applied research. Research that improves practical solutions to a problem, such as how an organization should be managed. Also called *practice research*.

Archaeologist. A person who professionally studies human history by examining physical artifacts.

Archaeology. A collection of artifacts or the study of artifacts.

Argument. An exchange of dissimilar views between parties, or the content of one party's attempt to persuade.

Argumentum ad hominem. An attack on the author of the opposing argument rather than on the opposing argument.

Argumentum ex silentio. An induction from an absence of evidence.

Art. The expression or application of creative skill and imagination, especially through a visual medium such as painting or sculpture, or an activity with an aesthetic component requiring knowledge and skill.

Article. A discrete writing in a newspaper or magazine.

Artifacts. The physical and material things left over from some process.

Assessment. A relatively objective measurement of something.

Assumption. A premise that is treated as if it is true without there being a claim that it is necessarily true.

Attributes data. Observations of the attributes, characteristics, or qualities of entities at some point in time, such as national population at the time of a census.

Authoritative. Derived from a higher authority.

Authority. An entity with the right or capacity to make decisions, judgments, or orders.

Availability bias. (See Cognitive availability bias).

Back matter. The writing that comes after the conclusion, such as an appendix or a bibliography.

Bad assumption. An untrue assumption.

Base-rate neglect. Reacting to the most available and proximate events rather than checking the longer-term rate or trend.

Basic research. Research that improves knowledge about something, such as how organizations have been managed in the past. Also called *pure research*.

Behavioralist. A researcher who focuses on behaviors as the most tangible subjects of study.

Behaviors. Activities or actions, such as enforcement of the law, mechanical movement, biolocomotive travel, production, feeding, reproducing, and so forth.

Belief. A proposition held as true but not necessarily proven as true.

Bell curve (see Normal distribution).

Benchmarking. Comparative analysis.

Bias. Favor toward something.

Bibliography. A list of sources that were useful but not necessarily cited.

Bimodal. A distribution with two modes.

Bivariate analysis. Examination of only two variables or several independent pairs of variables.

Bivariate fallacy. The claim to causation given correlation between just two variables.

Book. A written or printed work consisting of pages glued or sewn together along one side and bound in covers.

Capacity. The potential for something; usually the potential to achieve something, deliver resources, acquire capabilities, or perform.

Cardinal data. Data that indicate the count or number of something.

Case. One of many examples of a thing.

Case study. Research that aims to explain one case in particular; a study of one among many.

Categorical proposition. Some expectation about all members of some category, class, or group.

Categorical scale. Scale with mutually exclusive categories but no implied relativity.

Categorization. The separation of things into distinct categories.

Category. A holding of things as different to things in other categories.

Causal relationship. A relationship that has a cause, an effect, and a causal direction from the cause to the effect.

Causation. The process by which a cause has an effect.

Cause. Something that affects something else, perhaps by creating it or changing it.

Circular argument. An argument that concludes with a premise.

Citation. A reference to the source.

Class. A category.

Classification. The separation of things into distinct categories.

Clause. The smallest part of a sentence that can express a complete proposition.

Coding rule. An instruction as to how to judge the observation.

Cogent. The quality of an argument that guarantees that the conclusion is probably true.

Cognitive availability bias. The overestimation of the things most available to our senses or memory.

Common Rule. A United States federal policy for the protection of human subjects.

Communications analysis. A specialized form of flow analysis where (a) the nodes are the origins and terminals of communications flows and (b) the flows between nodes are the relations.

Comparing. Examining the similarities and/or differences between things within the same category or along the same scale or dimension.

Comparison group (see Control group).

Competitive intelligence. The comparison of one competitor against another.

Concept. An abstract idea or symbol.

Conceptual analysis. Analysis that measures how many times particular concepts and related things appear in the content.

Conceptual correlate. Something that conceptually is close to the target.

Conceptual model. A model that is less observable than a tangible model, such as a written, formulaic, or statistical description of something.

Conclusion. The final section of a paper that summarizes everything that came before; the last proposition in an argument.

Conclusive research. Research that aims at something conclusive, such as an answer to a question, proof, a recommended policy, or a recommended practice.

Conditional proposition. A proposition that proposes some expectation if something else were true.

Conjunction. A part of a sentence that links phrases or clauses.

Consensus. Majority agreement.

Consequent. A variable added as a modeled effect of another variable.

Consequential. Having consequences that would affect a lot of other things or would dramatically affect one important thing.

Constancy. Components are effectively the same and their sameness remains constant, apart from any experimental treatment.

Constant. A representation of an attribute whose value does not change.

Content analysis. A systematic examination of the content of a source.

Continuous unit. A unit that is reducible to fractions.

Control. Something used to maintain or change a condition.

Control group. The group in an experiment not exposed to the treatment.

Controlled experiment. An experiment under largely controlled conditions.

Correlates. Things that vary together.

Correlation. The extent to which two variables vary together.

Counterfactual. Imagined alternative to the facts.

Counterfactual argument. An argument that compares what actually happened with what could have happened.

Credible opinion. An opinion derived from a credible witness or expert.

Credibility. The extent to which a source should be believed.

Critical analysis (see Critical thinking).

Critical thinking. Fair engagement without any predetermined favor or disfavor; the process of clarifying knowledge by critical consideration of the arguments and evidence.

Culture. Collectively held norms, beliefs, or values.

Curvilinear. A model or distribution with both linear and nonlinear relationships.

Cycle. A process through the end of one thing to the start of another of the same type of thing, without end.

Data. Items of information.

Datum. One item of information.

Dedication. A statement by the author in honor of someone.

Deduction. A proposition guaranteed by preceding propositions.

Deductive research. Purely theoretical research, in which deductions are made from premises for the purposes of developing theory.

Definition. A description of meaning.

Delphi survey. A survey that asks respondents to re-forecast a few times, each time after a revelation of the previous round's forecasts.

Dependent clause. A clause added to an independent clause that cannot stand alone as a sentence.

Dependent variable. A variable that models the effect, product, or output.

Description. A declaration of what something is.

Descriptive argument. An argument that aims to describe how things are.

Descriptive model. A model that describes something.

Descriptive research. Research that aims to produce a description of something, such as the material composition of ancient pottery or the process of an animal's reproduction, and is usually analytical.

Design. A scheme for how to achieve something

Deterministic. Term describing a deduction that is certain given the categorical premises.

Deterministic argument. An argument whose conclusions claim something as certain.

Deterministic model. A model that does not allow for uncertainty; given the same inputs, the model would produce the same outputs every time.

Deterministic proposition. A proposition that proposes things as certain and does not allow for chance or randomness.

Developmental relation. Something derived from another thing, such as a derivative of a product or a child of a parent.

Dialectic. A model of something as the result of a clash between opposing or inversely related other things.

Dialectic argument. An argument that models each thing as the result of a clash between opposing or inversely related things.

Differential attrition. When certain subjects drop out of the group at a higher rate than other types, leaving the group biased to the types that remain.

Diminishing returns. When outputs decelerate with increasing inputs.

Direct evidence. An observation of the thing itself.

Direct relationship. A relationship in which one variable increases in value as the other variable increases.

Direct survey. The direct observation of lots of cases.

Direction. An expression of the way from one thing to another; in causal models, the direction is from the independent to the dependent variable.

Disaggregation. Breaking something into its parts.

Disciplines. Defined areas of study or work.

Discrete unit. A unit that is not reducible.

Distribution. A statistical description of all the values in a population.

Distrust. Doubt about whether something positive would be fulfilled.

Driver. Something that is directing something else.

Dynamic model. A model that allows for changes in the inputs and thus changes in the outputs.

Ecological fallacy. Inference from higher-level units about lower-level units.

Effect. A change or the thing that is changed by the cause.

Empirical. Replicable observations of the real world for the purpose of obtaining knowledge.

Empirical data. Data produced by verifiable observations.

Empirical research. Research that focuses on replicable observations of the real world in order to gain knowledge.

Employable. Useful in the real world; able to earn pay.

Endogenous. Things within the model.

Epigraph. Text, such as a quotation, separated from any other part in the document.

Epistemological approaches. Approaches that aim to understand what is understood.

Epistemology. A branch of philosophy dealing with how knowledge is understood.

Error of commission. An action that misleads.

Error of omission. A failure to share information that the consumer needs in order to understand your subject.

Estimation. A measurement, especially one that is more judgmental.

Ethics. Considerations of what is right or wrong.

Ethnocentric bias. Projecting one's own cultural beliefs and expectations on others.

Ethnography. Research where the observer is participating in the thing under observation.

Event data. Observations of discrete happenings.

Evidence. Information used to support some proposition.

Ex post facto. A Latin phrase meaning "after the fact."

Ex post facto research. Further research into something after it has happened.

Exogenous. Anything without the model.

Experiment. A comparison of two cases, one of which is exposed to something, the other of which is not, and everything else ideally is the same for both cases; research performed under controlled conditions (often termed "laboratory conditions").

Experimental research. Research performed under controlled conditions (often termed "laboratory conditions").

Expert opinion. See Expert panels.

Expert panels. Surveys of experts or selected subpopulations.

Explanatory variable. A variable that models the cause, driver, or input.

Exploratory research. Research aimed at finding a new research project.

Exponential model. A model in which the output changes at an accelerating rate.

Extraneous. A term to describe anything outside the model.

Fact. An item of information that is true.

Faith. Belief or trust without evidence.

Fallacious argument. An argument containing a fallacy.

Fallacy. A flaw in an argument.

False analogy. An unfair induction across dissimilar categories, such as apples and oranges, as if they were the same.

False-positive result. A result that claims to prove something but does not.

Falsifiable. Able to be disproven.

Fashionable. More popular than normal.

Feasible. Possible but not necessarily probable or improbable.

Field. Commonly agreed-upon part of a discipline; an uncontrolled environment.

Field research. Research performed in less-controlled, more natural conditions (often termed "field conditions").

Figure of merit. The most valid measure.

Flow. Some exchange, movement, or communication, such as trade, migration, and diplomatic communications between two regions.

Flows data. Information about movements, communications, or changes over a period of time.

Footer. Negative space at the bottom of the page.

Foreword. An introduction written by somebody other than the authors of the rest of the document.

Formal fallacy. An unguaranteed or false deduction.

Formal theory. A mathematical representation of a logical process.

Frame of reference. The context within which you place the things you plan to compare, such as the environmental, biographical, or historical context.

Framing. The context or tone chosen for a subject.

Frequency. The number of events per defined unit of time.

Frequency data. Rates of the same event over a period of time.

Front matter. Everything before the introduction.

Fundamental attribution error. The attribution of another person's behavior to intrinsic reasons while attributing one's own behavior to extrinsic reasons.

Fungible. Easily converted into other resources.

Generalizability. The ability of something to be made more general rather than just personal.

Glossary. A list of terms and their definitions.

Grouped data. Data that are differentiated by being placed in separate groups, without necessarily implying that they are categorically different.

Hard sciences. The natural sciences such as physics, chemistry, and biology.

Header. Negative space at the top of the page.

Hierarchy. A structure of levels from the lowest or most inferior to the highest or most superior.

Hindsight bias (see Narrative fallacy).

Historian's fallacy. An argument that assumes that a person in the past had the same information or perspective as the historian.

Historical fiction. Fiction set in real historical contexts.

Historical research. Research that aims to produce knowledge about things from the past; research that collects past observations.

Hopeful. An expectation of improvement.

Humanities. Academic disciplines that study human culture.

Hypothesis. A proposition that is subject to testing.

Hypothetical. Anything imagined without the assertion that it is true.

Hypothetical argument. An argument based on something imagined.

Hypothetical history. A counterfactual in the discipline of history.

Hypothetical proposition. A proposition that proposes something without claiming that it is true.

Hypothetical soundness. The argument is sound outside of its hypothetical propositions.

Identification. Determining which entity to examine.

Important case. A case that is more important than the average case.

Independent clause. A clause that can stand alone.

Independent variable. A variable that models the cause, driver, or input.

Index of measures. A statistical combination of multiple measures.

Indirect evidence. An observation of something consistent with the thing.

Induction. A proposition suggested by an individual observation.

Inductive research. Research that induces theory from observations.

Informal fallacy. A flawed but not necessarily illogical argument.

Input. Something that enters a system; the thing you must invest in to be productive, such as effort, skills, or time.

Institution. A body such as an organization; may also refer to an informal grouping, norm, culture, belief, or value.

Instrument. Something used to measure something else.

Instrumentalism. A view of theory as useful in itself, without proving that a theory actually fits observations.

Intellectual property. Intellectual creations claimed by a stakeholder.

Intelligence. Analyzed information.

Intentional. Stating how the author intends to behave.

Internal validity. When an experiment's intended independent variable is the only thing that could explain the effect.

Interval scale. An ordinal scale where each point on the scale is equidistant in scale.

Intervening variable. A variable between other variables.

Introduction. The first section of a document, containing a description of the project, a justification of the project and of the rest of the document, and a preview of the rest of the document.

Invalid operationalization. Measuring something other than the target.

Inverse relationship. A relationship in which one variable increases as the other decreases.

Inversely related (see Negatively correlated).

Judgmental correlate. A correlate subjectively coded, meaning somebody (the coder) must make a judgment as to what the code should be.

Justification. Something offered to justify something else.

Key case. A case that is more important than the average case.

Knowledge. Acquired awareness and understanding.

Knowledge worker. Someone whose main value is his or her knowledge, such as an academic, lawyer, or medical consultant.

Laboratory. An artificially controlled environment.

Large-n. Large datasets that imply more statistical confidence.

Leading question. A question that leads the respondent to answer in a certain way.

Least-likely case. A case selected by attributes that make it least like the sort of case that the theory is best at explaining.

Level of analysis. One step in a hierarchy.

Liberal arts. Traditional core disciplines.

Liberalism. A long political philosophical tradition that expects trading states to avoid war lest war interrupt the economic benefits of trade.

License. A formal consent.

Life cycle. A process through the life of one project before the life of another project, without end.

Linear model. A model in which two variables change at a constant rate in proportion to each other.

Link. The connection between a preposition and its support.

Linkage (see Link).

Link analysis. Relational analysis.

List of abbreviations. A list of abbreviations used in the rest of the document and their full definitions.

List of illustrations. A table of contents for the illustrations in the rest of the document.

List of tables. A table of contents for the tables in the rest of the document.

Literature. A collection of related but discrete writings.

Logic. Reason; an argument that follows certain rules.

Logical argument. An argument that follows certain rules and concepts.

Manipulated group. The case or group of subjects exposed to the intended independent variable in an experiment.

Manipulation. Anything deliberately applied to the subject in expectation of some effect

Maturation. The process of change in the subject during the experiment; a process of improvement or aging.

Measurement. The process of collecting observations.

Mediator. A variable between other variables.

Medium. A vehicle for the content.

Message. Whatever the content is communicating.

Meta-analysis. The combination of results from several studies of the same thing, without gathering new results.

Meta-commentary. Clarifications about your intended meaning.

Metaphysical approaches. Largely nonempirical claims to understanding the physical world.

Metaphysics. A late ancient branch of philosophy examining the physical world.

Method. A technique for investigating or testing.

Methodology. A collection of methods that is prescribed or used as appropriate for particular conditions.

Misrepresentation. Any inaccurate representation.

Mode. The commonest value or item in a particular population.

Model. A representation of something.

Moderator. Something that moderates the direction or strength of a relationship.

Mood purism. The decision not to challenge moods.

Motivation. The conscious or unconscious stimulus for action toward a desired goal.

Multidimensionality. The measurement of more than the intended phenomenon.

Multiple measures. Measuring the same phenomenon in multiple ways.

Narrative fallacy. A causal explanation for the narrative as a whole that does not admit that some events could have had independent causes that have been lost to history or were practically random.

Natural. Existing in nature without humans affecting it.

Natural experiment. A situation that arose naturally with the attributes of a desired experiment.

Naturalist fallacy. The claim that something must be better just because it is natural, or that something must be worse just because it is unnatural.

Necessary cause. A cause that must be present for the effect to occur.

Negative relationship. A relationship in which one variable increases as the other decreases.

Negative space. Unfilled space.

Negatively correlated. Varying in opposite directions.

Net assessment. Comparative analysis of one entity's capabilities against another's.

Nominal scale. A scale with mutually exclusive categories but no implied relativity.

Non sequitur. A conclusion that is not guaranteed by the argument's propositions.

Nonlinear relationship. A relationship in which two variables change without any constant rate.

Nonparticipant observation. The direct observation of natural phenomena without participating in the subject.

Nonsystematic measurement errors. Random errors.

Norm. A normal value, expectation, or behavior; something that a majority accepts as true; a behavior that a majority practices.

Normal distribution. A distribution in which the outputs do not increase much for a while, dramatically increase like an exponential curve, flatten off like diminishing returns, dramatically decrease, then flatten off.

Normative. Whatever normally should occur or does occur.

Normative argument. An argument that describes how things normally are or prescribes how things normally should be.

Null. Neither positive nor negative.

Objective correlate. A correlate collected without subjective involvement.

Objective research. Research not based on personal experiences and judgments.

Observation. The process of closely observing or monitoring and gaining information through the senses or instruments, or one item of information produced from the observing process.

Observation error. The difference between the measured value and the true value.

Observational approaches. Approaches that attempt to understand something as it is without interpretation.

Ontological approaches. Approaches that develop ways to classify the objects of research. See also Ontology.

Ontology. A branch of philosophy dealing with existence.

Operable conditions. The conditions under which the cause operates or is dominant

Operationalization. The process of defining how we could observe something that is not perfectly observable.

Opinion. A subjective proposition.

Optimistic. Expecting the best; accounting for failures by situational factors rather than blaming an enduring dispositional trait.

Ordinal scale. A categorical scale on the same dimension, but in which the categories are not necessarily of equal size.

Organization. A formal group with members.

Output. Something that exits a system; the result of productivity.

Page break. Blank space before a new page.

Paragraph. A discrete unit of text that contains at least one sentence.

Parental relation (see Developmental relation).

Participant observation. Research where the observer is participating in the thing under observation.

Patchwriting. When your own text is taken over by external texts.

Peer. A person of similar rank, training, or expertise.

Peer pressure. Group encouragement of a member toward a certain behavior.

Peer review. A review by the author's peers prior to passing the product for release.

People's histories. The past from the perspective of the common people.

Permit. Formal consent.

Phenomenological approaches. Attempts to explain how something is interpreted by humans.

Phenomenology. A branch of philosophy focusing on how observations are interpreted by humans.

Phenomenon. Anything observable, such as an event, behavior, or entity.

Philosophy. Reasoning about fundamental issues, such as ethics, rights, and aesthetics, and reasoning itself without it necessarily being replicable or even factual.

Physical approaches. Approaches based on observations of physical things.

Physical model (see Tangible model).

Placebo. Something as similar as possible to the treatment without being the same as the treatment.

Plagiarism. The reuse of work without due attribution.

Plan. A scheme for how to achieve something.

Policy. Guidance for behavior.

Positive relationship. A relationship in which one variable increases in value as the other variable increases.

Positive space. Whatever fills space on a page.

Positively correlated. Varying in the same direction.

Positivism. A branch of philosophy that denies that anything can be known unless it is observed in a replicable way.

Practice. Doing things.

Practice research. Research that improves practical solutions to a problem, such as how an organization should be managed. Also called *applied research*.

Preface. An introduction written by the primary authors of the rest of the document.

Prejudice. A premature judgment not justified by observation or reason.

Preliminaries. The content of a document before the introduction (also known as front matter).

Premise. A proposition that founds the argument without being guaranteed by a preceding proposition.

Preposition. A word that indicates relationships between things, usually verbs and nouns.

Prescription. Advice, guidance, or even an obligation regarding how something should be done.

Prescriptive. Stating how specified actors are supposed to be behave.

Prescriptive argument. An argument that prescribes how things should be.

Prescriptive model. A model that shows how the user should behave.

Prescriptive research. Research that aims to conclude with a prescription.

Presentism. The projection of present-day things, such as current morality or political ideology, onto the past.

Pretest. A test of something before it is implemented for its intended purpose.

Primary source. A source of information not derived from other sources.

Probabilistic. More likely than not.

Probabilistic argument. An argument whose conclusion is likely or happens most of the time, but not necessarily all the time.

Probabilistic model. A model that includes uncertainty.

Probabilistic proposition. A proposition that proposes something as likely, but not necessarily certain.

Process. A sequence of actions or changes; a series of activities or steps by which something occurs or is produced.

Process tracing. Identifying variables to add to the modeled process.

Product. Something created from or by inputs or drivers; the final output or result of productivity; the finished item that is sold or exchanged.

Productivity. A measure of how much is being produced.

Project. An enterprise carefully planned to achieve a particular aim.

Proof. Indisputable evidence.

Proposition. A declaration or assertion.

Proven hypothesis. A hypothesis that has evidence it is true.

Provisional evidence. Evidence that does not disprove the proposition but is not yet indisputable proof of it.

Provisionally accepted hypothesis. A hypothesis that is not yet proven, but that has not been falsified by the tests to date.

Proximity bias. When people feel more sensitive to something when it is more proximate in time or space than when it is remote.

Psychologist's fallacy. The projection of the subjective self onto someone else.

Public opinion. An opinion held by the majority of the public.

Pure research. Research that improves knowledge about something, such as how organizations have been managed in the past. Also called *basic research*.

Questionnaire. A survey instrument with questions that the subjects are meant to answer.

Quilting (see Patchwriting).

Rate. A ratio of one thing to another.

Ratio scale. An interval scale starting from zero.

Rationality. A self-interested or optimal decision.

Reader. The one who attends to a text to process its information.

Reading. An interpretation or understanding of a word that is considered a separate sense.

Realism. A paradigm of international relations whose central argument is that states naturally struggle for power in an anarchical world without recourse to a higher authority.

Recorded. Measurements are stored just as they were produced by the process.

Reductionism. The process of reducing something to a part or a much simpler version.

Reference list. A list of sources that were cited.

Reference matter (see Back matter).

Regression to the mean. The tendency of members of a group to adjust behavior to fit the average member or the dominant member of the group.

Relating. Describing the relationship between things.

Relation. The connection between two things or the thing that has a connection with another thing.

Relational analysis. Analysis that examines the relationships between things.

Relationship. A connection or comparison between things, such as a trade agreement or a signal.

Relationship of authority or responsibility. A relationship based on the authority and/or responsibility of one of the parties in regard to the other.

Relativists. Those who deny the existence of replicable observations.

Reliable. When measurements do not vary between different measurements.

Replicable. When researchers can reproduce a measurement with the same processes and instruments; able to be confirmed or checked by others.

Reported. When the process and the products are reported accurately in sufficient detail so that consumers can understand and reproduce whatever was done.

Repository. Wherever artifacts from the past or past observations are deposited or reposed.

Representative. Term describing something whose attributes are matched by everything else in the same class.

Research. The process of acquiring knowledge or the product of the research process.

Research ethics. Considerations of what is right or wrong in the conduct of research.

Research proposal. A plan of research submitted as a petition for external approval or support.

Review. The process of examination, or a report on something examined.

Rhetoric. The art of persuasive communication.

Rigorous. Prepared carefully or in accordance with applicable standards.

Robust. Able to survive challenges or new tests.

Robust argument. An argument that has been re-proven by different testers or methods.

Salient. Particularly pronounced or important.

Sample content. The part of the content sampled as representative of the whole.

Science. A replicable way to verify knowledge.

Scope. The number or variety of things affected or considered.

Scoping. Defining what you intend to examine.

Secondary source. A source that derives its information from primary sources or other secondary sources.

Selection bias. Biased selection of one thing over another.

Self-efficacy. The belief that the self controls destiny and thus that the self can achieve something.

Self-selection bias. Where subjects choose to join a group so that the group is not the same as it would have been otherwise.

Sentence. A contiguous set of words with a discrete meaning.

Sentential adverb. An adverb that modifies the meaning of the whole sentence.

Sign. Whether the relationship could be positive, negative, or null.

Simulation. An operable model, meaning that it can be operated like a machine.

Skills. Learned abilities.

Small-n. Small datasets that allow deeper study of each case and the gathering of more data about each case.

Social and organizational psychology. The psychology of groups and of people within groups.

Social network analysis. Analysis of entities and their social relations.

Social science. The application of science to the study of human society.

Solvable model. A model that describes something in a formal way that can be solved logically or mathematically.

Sophist. A person who argues cleverly but deceptively.

Sound. The argument is valid and all of its propositions are true.

Source. A person or document that provides information.

Spatial analysis. Analysis that relates things such as events and actors to their locations.

Specific. Clearly defined or identified.

Spurious relationship. When a third thing is causing two other things to be statistically correlated.

Stake. An interest in something.

Stakeholder. An entity with a stake in something.

State. A sovereign country; one of the constituent states within the United States of America; the particular condition or situation that something is in at a particular time.

Static model. A model that has no variables, only constants. All inputs are fixed and do not vary, and thus the outputs cannot vary.

Statistical correlate. Something that statistically varies with the target.

Stochastic model. A model that includes uncertainty, usually in the form of some random variation or some variation of probability.

Stoicism. A philosophy of accepting the way things are.

Structural data. Observations of authoritative relationships at some point in time, such as the number of international organizations to which a state belongs at the start of the year.

Structure. A pattern of relationships, such as a network of friendships or a hierarchy of authority; or discrete parts of a written work, some superior or subordinate to others.

Style. A distinctive manner.

Subfield. A part of a field, which is a part of a discipline.

Subject-matter expert. Someone with extra knowledge within a certain scope.

Subjective research. Research based on personal experiences and judgments.

Subjects of research. The things under study.

Subordinate clause. A clause added to an independent clause that cannot stand alone as a sentence.

Sufficient cause. A cause that is sufficient on its own to have an effect.

Survey. A study of lots of cases from the same category.

Survey instrument. An instrument that prompts for observations and controls the responses.

Survey item. Whatever is used to generate an item of information.

Survey research. Research that aims to assess many things, such as the behaviors of one animal, the attributes of a building, or the attitudes of a group of people.

Syllogism. A valid three-proposition argument that has at least one premise and one conclusion.

Synthesis. The product of the thesis and the antithesis in a dialectic.

System. A set of entities that interact, such as countries in an international system.

Systematic measurement errors. Errors that are inherent to the process or instrument.

Table of contents. A list of the sections of the document, usually with page numbers corresponding to the start of each section.

Tangible model. A model that observably represents something.

Tautology. Something that is inherently always true.

Temporal. Defined by time.

Tertiary sources. Guides to other sources.

Test. Any attempt to establish something.

Theoretical. Explanatory but not necessarily practical.

Theoretical research. Research that focuses on explaining facts.

Theory. An explanation for the facts.

Thesis. One of the elements of a dialectic; an argument.

Threshold model. A model in which the outputs change only once the inputs have breached some threshold.

Title page. A page that shows the whole document's title, the author's name, a date, and perhaps the intended use or audience of this document, together with any restrictions on use or audience.

Traditional research. Research that views theory as useful in itself, without proving that a theory actually fits observations.

Treated group. The group of subjects who are exposed to the independent variable.

Treatment. Anything deliberately applied to the subject in expectation of some effect.

Triangulation. The use of more than one thing in the study of something.

Trust. Confident expectation of something positive being fulfilled.

Truth. The accurate understanding of things as they really are.

Unfalsifiable proposition. A proposition that cannot be proven or disproven.

Unimodal. Term describing a distribution with a single most common value or item.

Unit of analysis. The discrete entity that is being measured.

Unrepresentative. Not consistent with the whole.

Utilitarian history. Study of the past that honors sacrifice and perpetuates pride.

Utilitarianism. Harm in return for a greater good.

Valid. Term that characterizes an argument whose deductions are each guaranteed by the preceding propositions.

Valid operationalization. Measuring something as similar as possible to the thing that we want to measure.

Value. The worth of something from a given perspective; something held as worthy.

Variable. Something used to represent a real attribute with varied values.

Verifiably observable. Able to be observed by someone else, given the same method.

Virtual history. Inaccurate or inferior term for a counterfactual within the discipline of history.

Vivisection. Experimentation on live animals.

Weak argument. An argument that is unlikely to be true.

Wishful thinking. Excessive optimism or avoidance of unpleasant choices.

Working hypothesis. A hypothesis that is not yet proven but has not been falsified by the tests to date.

Writing. The process of recording what one means to communicate.

REFERENCES

Abrahms, M. (2014). Suicide terrorism is a political failure. In S. Gottlieb (Ed.), *Debating terrorism and counterterrorism: Conflicting perspectives on causes, contexts, and responses* (2nd ed., pp. 152–165). Thousand Oaks, CA: SAGE.

Alger, J. I. (1982). *The quest for victory: The history of the principles of war.* Westport, CT: Greenwood Press.

Arena, P. (2010). Why not guns and butter: Responses to economic turmoil. *Foreign Policy Analysis, 6*(4), 339–348.

Axelrod, R. (1984). *The evolution of cooperation.* New York, NY: Basic Books.

Baldwin, D. A. (1989). *Paradoxes of power.* New York, NY: Basil Blackwell.

Baylis, J., & Wirtz, J. J. (2002). Introduction. In J. Baylis, J. Wirtz, E. Cohen, & C. S. Gray (Eds.), *Strategy in the contemporary world* (pp. 1–14). Oxford, UK: Oxford University Press.

Betts, R. K. (1995). *Military readiness: Concepts, choices, consequences.* Washington, DC: Brookings Institution.

Borofski, R. (2005). *Yanomami: The fierce controversy and what we can learn from it.* University of California Press.

Brandon, S. (2013). "The Myths of Foreign Affairs School," Fair Observer. Retrieved from http://www.fairobserver.com/article/myths-foreign-affairs-school-part-1.

Bui, Y. N. (2014). *How to write a master's thesis* (2nd ed.). Thousand Oaks, CA: SAGE.

Campbell, B., & Porzucki, N. (2013). *The 6 highly effective habits of the creative genius.* Retrieved from http://www.pri.org/stories/2013-10-28/6-highly-effective-habits-creative-genius

Campbell, P., & Desch, M. C. (2013). *Rank irrelevance: How academia lost its way.* Retrieved from http://www.foreignaffairs.com/articles/139925/peter-campbell-and-michael-c-desch/rank-irrelevance

Carnevale, A. P., & Cheah, B. (2013). *Hard times: College majors, unemployment and earnings.* Georgetown University Center on Education and the Workforce.

Carnevale, A. P., Strohl, J., & Melton M. (2011). *What's it worth? The economic value of college majors.* Georgetown University Center on Education and the Workforce.

Clark, R. M. (2013). *Intelligence analysis: A target-centric approach* (4th ed.). Thousand Oaks, CA: SAGE/CQ Press.

Claude, I. L. (1962). *Power and international relations.* New York, NY: Random House.

Cohen, E. A., & Gooch, J. (1990). *Military misfortunes: The anatomy of failure in war.* New York, NY: Free Press.

Copeland, D. C. (1996, Spring). Economic interdependence and war: A theory of trade expectations. *International Security, 20*(4).

Crosier, S. (n.d.). *John Snow: The London cholera epidemic of 1854.* Retrieved from the Center for Spatially Integrated Science website: http://csiss.ncgia.ucsb.edu/classics/content/8/

Davis, P. M. (2013). *Journal usage half-life.* Retrieved from http://www.publishers.org/_attachments/docs/journalusagehalflife.pdf

Dawkins, R. (2011). *The magic of reality: How we know what's really true.* New York, NY: Free Press.

Dershowitz, A. M. (2014). There is a need to bring an unfortunate practice within the bounds of law. In S. Gottlieb (Ed.), *Debating terrorism and counterterrorism: Conflicting perspectives on causes, contexts, and responses* (2nd ed., pp. 329–340). Thousand Oaks, CA: SAGE.

Desch, M. C. (2002). Democracy and victory: Why regime type hardly matters. *International Security, 27*(2), 5–47.

Desch, M. (2008). *Power and military effectiveness: The fallacy of democratic triumphalism.* Baltimore, MD: Johns Hopkins University Press.

Deutsch, D., & Ekert, A. (2013). Beyond the quantum horizon. *Scientific American Special, 22*(2), 102–107.

Downes, A. B. (2011). The myth of choosy democracies: Examining the selection effects theory of democratic victory in war. *H-Diplo/ISSF Roundtable Reviews, 2*(11), 64.

Federal Bureau of Investigation. (n.d.). *Intelligence cycle.* Retrieved from http://www.fbi.gov/about-us/intelligence/intelligence-cycle

Ferris, W. H. (1973). *The power capabilities of nation-states: international conflict and war.* Lexington, MA: Lexington Books.

Fisher, T. D. (2013). Gender roles and pressure to be truthful: The bogus pipeline modifies gender differences in sexual but not nonsexual behavior. *Sex Roles, 68*(7-8), 401–414.

Greenberg, M. D., Chalk, P., Willis, H. H., Khilko, I., & Ortiz, D. S. (2006). *Maritime terrorism: Risk and liability.* Santa Monica, CA: RAND.

Guilhot, N. (2008). The realist gambit: Postwar American political science and the birth of IR theory. *International Political Sociology, 2*(4), 281–304.

Hawking, S., & Mlodinow, L. (2013). The (elusive) theory of everything. *Scientific American Special, 22*(2), 91–93.

Hollywood, J., Snyder, D., McKay, K. N., & Boon, J. E., Jr. (2004). *Out of the ordinary:*

Finding hidden threats by analyzing unusual behavior. Santa Monica, CA: RAND.

Hughes, S. (2013). The anatomist of crime. *The Pennsylvania Gazette, 112*(2), 28–35.

Hughes, S. (2011). LSE criticized for links with Gaddafi regime in Libya. *BBC News.* Retrieved from http://www.bbc.co.uk/news/education-15966132

Institute for Economics and Peace. (2012). *Global Peace Index 2012.* Sydney, Australia: Author. Retrieved from http://economicsandpeace.org/wp-content/uploads/2011/09/2012-Global-Peace-Index-Report.pdf

Jones, S. G., & Libicki, M. C. (2008). *How terrorist groups end: Lessons for countering al Qa'ida.* Santa Monica, CA: RAND.

Kennedy, L. W., & Van Brunschot, E. (2009). *The risk in crime.* Lanham, MD: Rowman & Littlefield.

Ketcham, C. (2014). *The troubling case of Chris Hedges.* Retrieved from http://www.newrepublic.com/article/118114/chris-hedges-pulitzer-winner-lefty-hero-plagiarist

Krueger, A. B., & Laitin, D. D. (2004). Misunderstanding terrorism. *Foreign Affairs, 83*(5), 8–13.

Levy, J. S. (1988). Domestic politics and war. *Journal of Interdisciplinary History, 18*(4), 661–662.

Lowenthal, M. W. (2011). *Intelligence: From secrets to policy* (5th ed.). Thousand Oaks, CA: SAGE/CQ Press.

Luker, K. (2008). *Salsa dancing into the social sciences: Research in an age of info-glut.* Cambridge, MA: Harvard University Press.

Luttwak, E. N. (2001). *Strategy: The logic of war and peace* (Rev. ed.). Cambridge, MA: Belknap Press of Harvard University Press.

Makel, M. C., & Plucker, J. A. (2014). Facts re more important than novelty: Replication in the education sciences. *Educational Researched.* Retrieved from http://edr.sagepub.com/content/early/2014/07/23/0013189X14545513

Markovits, A. S., & Rensmann, L. (2013). *Gaming the world: How sports are reshaping global politics and culture.* Princeton, NJ: Princeton University Press.

McCormick, G. H., & Fritz, L. (2014). Suicide terrorism is a pragmatic choice. In S. Gottlieb (Ed.), *Debating terrorism and counterterrorism: Conflicting perspectives on causes, contexts, and responses* (2nd ed., pp. 139–152). Thousand Oaks, CA: SAGE.

McNabb, D. E. (2010). *Research methods for political science: Quantitative and qualitative approaches.* Armonk, NY: M. E. Sharpe.

Mowday, R. T., & Sutton, R. I. (1993). Organization behavior:

Linking individuals and groups to organizational contexts. *Annual Review of Psychology, 44,* 195–229.

Nagel, T. (1991). *Equality and partiality*. Oxford, UK: Oxford University Press.

Newsome, B. (2003). Don't get your mass kicked: A management theory of military capability. *Defence and Security Analysis, 19*(2), 131–148.

Newsome, B. (2006). Expatriate games: Interorganizational coordination and international counterterrorism. *Studies in Conflict and Terrorism, 1*(29), 75–89.

Newsome, B. (2007). *Made, not born: Why some soldiers are better than others*. Westport, CT: Praeger Security International/ABC-CLIO.

Newsome, B. (2014). *A practical introduction to security and risk management*. Thousand Oaks, CA: SAGE.

Nisbett, R. E., & Cohen, D. (1996). *Culture of honor: The psychology of violence in the south*. Boulder, CO: Westview Press.

Noble, W. (1993). *The 28 biggest writing blunders (and how to avoid them)*. Cincinnati, OH: Writer's Digest.

Nozick, R. (1974). *Anarchy, state, and utopia*. New York, NY: Basic Books.

Olson, R. (2009). *Don't be such a scientist: Talking substance in an age of style*. Washington, DC: Island Press.

O'Reilly, C. A., III. (1991). Organizational behavior: Where we've been, where were going. *Annual Review of Psychology, 42,* 427–458.

Overy, R. J. (1996). *Why the allies won*. New York, NY: W. W. Norton.

Overy, R. J. (1998). *Russia's war: A history of the Soviet WAR Effort, 1941–1945*. New York, NY: Penguin.

Paret, P. (1989). Military power. *Journal of Military History, 53*(3), 239–256.

Pennington, L. A., Hough, R. B., & Case, H. W. (1943). *The psychology of military leadership*. New York, NY: Prentice Hall.

Pew Research Center. (2013, April 30). *The world's Muslims: Religion, politics, society*. Washington, DC: Pew Research Center. Retrieved from http://www.pewforum .org/uploadedFiles/Topics/ Religious_Affiliation/ Muslim/worlds-muslims -religion-politics-society -full-report.pdf

Pfeffer, J. (1998). Understanding organizations: Concepts and controversies. In D. T. Gilbert, S. T. Fiske, & G. Linzey (Eds.), *The handbook of social psychology* (pp. 733–777). Boston, MA: McGraw-Hill.

Pherson, K. H., & Pherson, R. H. (2013). *Critical thinking for strategic intelligence*. Thousand Oaks, CA: SAGE.

Public Broadcasting Service, Frontline. (2014). *Modern meat: Industrial meat*. Retrieved from http:// www.pbs.org/wgbh/pages/ frontline/shows/meat/ industrial/consolidation .html

Rawls, J. (1971). *A theory of justice*. Boston, MA: Belknap Press.

Rayner, R. (2010). Channeling Ike. *The New Yorker*. Retrieved from http://www.newyorker.com/ talk/2010/04/26/100426ta_ talk_rayner

Reiter, D., & Stam, A. C., III. (1998). Democracy and battlefield military effectiveness. *Journal of Conflict Resolution, 42*(3), 259–277.

Reiter, D., & Stam, A. C., III. (2002). *Democracies at war*. Princeton, NY: Princeton University Press.

Reynolds, D. (2004). In *Command of history: Churchill fighting and writing the Second World War*. London, UK: Allen Lane.

Rothgeb, J. M. (1993). *Defining power: Influence and force in the contemporary international system*. New York, NY: St. Martin's Press.

Sagan, C. (1997). *The demon-haunted world: Science as a candle in the dark*. New York, NY: Ballantine Books.

Simmons, J. P., Nelson, L. D., & Simonsohn, U. (2011). False-positive psychology: Undisclosed flexibility in data collection and analysis allows presenting anything as significant. *Psychological Science, 22*(11), 1359–1366.

Simon, H. A. (1947). *Administrative behavior*. New York, NY: Macmillan.

Suder, G. G. S. (Ed.). (2004). *Terrorism and the international business environment: The security-business nexus*. Cheltenham, UK: Edward Elgar.

Taleb, N. N. (2007). *The Black Swan: The impact of the highly improbable*. London, UK: Allen Lane.

Tetlock, P. E. (2006). *Expert political judgment: How good is it? How can we know?* Princeton, NJ: Princeton University Press.

United Nations, Department of Peacekeeping Operations. (2008). *United Nations peacekeeping operations: Principles and guidelines*. New York, NY: Author.

University of Minnesota, Charles Babbage Institute. (n.d.). *Who was Charles Babbage?* Retrieved from http://www.cbi.umn.edu/about/babbage.html

U.S. Department of Defense. (2012). *Dictionary of military and associated terms* (Joint Publication 1-02). Retrieved from http://www.dtic.mil/doctrine/new_pubs/jp1_02.pdf

U.S. Department of Health and Human Services. (1979). *The Belmont report*. Retrieved from http://www.hhs.gov/ohrp/humansubjects/guidance/belmont.html

Volkman, E. (2007). *The history of espionage: The clandestine world of surveillance, spying and intelligence, from ancient times to the post-9/11 world*. London, UK: Carlton.

Waltz, K. N. (1979). *Theory of international politics*. Reading, MA: Addison-Wesley.

White, C. T. (2005). *Intelligence/counterintelligence: Operation trade craft*. Bloomington, IN: Author House.

Wilkinson, R., & Pickett, K. (2009). *The spirit level: Why more equal societies almost always do better*. London, UK: Allen Lane.

INDEX

Logic
  paradoxical, 166
  rhetoric and, 152, 157
  truth and, 167–168
Logical arguments, 157–167
  antimony, 165–167
  building arguments from propositions,
      160–162
  deduction, 158–159
  defined, 157
  induction, 159–160, 161
  non sequitur, 165
  premises, 157–158
  propositions, 157
  syllogism, 162–163
  validity, 163–165
Logical fallacy, 221
Logos, 152
Lombroso, Cesare, 68
London School of Economics, 41–42
Lowenthal, Mark, on intelligence process, 25–26,
      26–27
Luker, Kristin, 230
Luttwak, Edward, 166

Macro to micro, writing, 302
Majority as evidence, 280–281
Manipulated group, 249
Manipulation, 249, 254
Margins, 294
Marketing and marketing research major,
      popularity of, 7
Mark up text, 115
Marx, Karl, 193–194
Material resources, 81
Material thing, disaggregation of, 139
Mathematics, forms of analysis, 132
Maturation, 191, 252
Mean, regression to the, 252
Meanings in similarities and differences, 141,
      143–144
Measurement, 262–266
  judgmental correlates, 263–264
  meta-analysis, 266

multiple measures, 264–266
objective correlates, 263
triangulation, 264
Mediators, 212, 220
Medium, 117
  of response, 243
Memoirs, 232
  as primary sources, 102, 104
  time of completion, 105
Message, 118
Meta-analysis, 266
Meta-commentary, 303
Metaphors, 300
Metaphysical approaches, 19
Metaphysics, 19
  dialectic and, 193–194
Methodological sections, 291
Methodology, 227
Methods, 227–231
  case study, 233
  challenging, 72
  content analysis, 118–122
  control, 230–231
  defined, 227
  direct observation in the field, 244–247
  experimental research, 247–254
  historical research, 231–232
  naturalness, 230–231
  qualitative, 229–230
  quantitative, 229–230
  replicability, 228
  triangulation, 231
  See also Survey research
Micro organizational behavior, 61
Military, forms of analysis, 132
Military technologies major, 8
Minutes, as primary sources, 102
Misrepresentation
  avoiding, 49
  Stephen Ambrose and, 50
Mitochondrial inheritance, 209
MLA (Modern Language Association)
    style, 51
Mode, 220

participant, 246–247
structuring writing around, 303–304
See also Measurement
Observational approaches, 20
Observation error, 262
Occupations, research, 3
OECD. *See* Organization for Economic
Cooperation and Development (OECD)
of, 312
of course, 312
often, 309
of whom, 310
on, 312
Ontological approaches, 20
Ontology, 20
Open response, 243
Operable conditions, 204–205
Operationalization, 260–262
invalid, 259, 261
valid, 261
Opinion, 169–170
Opposing sides, reviewing, 303
Optimistic, 32
OR, in Boolean logic, 99
Ordinal scale, 244, 267, 268
Organization, 62
Organizational behavior, 61
Organization for Economic
Cooperation and Development
(OECD), 46, 47
Output, 204
productivity and, 35–36
Overy, Richard, 183–184

Page break, 294
Paintings, as primary sources, 103
Paradoxical logic, 166
Paragraph, structuring, 305–307
Paraphrases
choosing among summaries, quotes,
and, 306
citation of, 51
Paraphrasing, guide to, 305
Parental relation, 145
Parentheses, in Boolean logic, 99
Parochial interests, 181
Parsimony, 63, 205–206

Participant observation, 246–247
ethnography *vs.,* 247
Patchwriting, 304
Pathos, 152
Patterns of Global Terrorism, 273
Peer pressure, 192
Peer review, 71, 108–109, 110
Peers, 108
People's histories, 183
Perfectionism, procrastination
and, 296
Permissions, 48
Permit, 48
Personality, content analysis and, 121
Persuasion. *See* Argument
Pertinent readings, 112
Pharmacology major, popularity of, 8
Phenomenological approaches, 20
Phenomenology, 20
Phenomenon(a), 138, 260
Philadelphia Inquirer, 52
Philosophy, 6, 90
dialectic and, 193–194
positivism *vs.* traditional, 18
prescriptive arguments and, 155
quantum physics *vs.* bad, 21
reductionism, 182
theory and, 204
Photographs, as primary sources, 103
Physical approaches, 19
Physical model, 217
Pickett, Kate, 282
Placebo, 251
Plagiarism, 42
avoiding, 50–52
example of, 52
Plan, research, 92
Planning, managing motivations
and, 30
Point-by-point analysis, 143–144, 303
Policy, 70
challenging, 72
research question and, 88
Policy-relevant research, 70–71
Political science and government
major, employment rate and
earnings in, 9

Robust argument, 175
Robust research, 108–109
routinely, 309

Sagan, Carl, 227
Salient research, 66
Sample, 239
Sample content, 119
Scale(s), 243–244, 267–268
  types of, 267–268
Schedules, as primary sources, 102
Scheutz, George, 84
School student counseling major, popularity of, 8
Science, 6
  hard, 6
Science Museum (London), 84
Scientific skills, 6
Scope
  answering questions about, 59
  defined, 55
  describing, 91–92
  efficient reading and, 114
  sentence and, 308
  writing and, 301–302
Scoping, 55–63
  academic and professional boundaries and,
    60–61
  benefits of, 56–58
  defined, 55
  focusing within the boundaries, 62–63
  geographical or spatial boundaries and, 61–62
  human and social subjects and, 62
  research question specificity and, 87–89
  setting boundaries, 58–62
  time and, 62
  writing and, 295
Secondary sources, 98, 100–101
  time of completion, 105–106
The Second World War (Churchill), 104
Security, data protection and, 46
Selection bias, 111, 116, 251–252
  surveys and, 240
Self-contradictions, avoiding, 299
Self-discipline, 30–31
  external disciplines *vs.,* 84–85
  scoping and, 56

Self-efficacy, 32–33
Self-guidance, scoping and, 56
Self-selection bias, 251–252
Sentence
  defined, 307
  order of, 312
  starting, 308–309
  structuring, 307–308
  structuring with clauses, 310–311
Sentential adverb, 312
Sign, 119
Similarities, comparisons and, 141, 142
Simplicity, of theory, 205–206
Simulation, 218–219, 248–249
Skill management, 28–30
Skills
  advanced, 29
  basic, 29, 131
  defined, 28
  managing, 28–30
  scientific, 6
  social scientific, 22
Skimming readings, 115
Small-*n* dataset, 270–272
Smith, Adam, 74
Snow, John, 83
Social and organizational psychology, 61
Social contagion, 192
Social expectations, questionnaires
    and, 237
Social network analysis, 145–146
Social resources, capacity and, 78–81
Social sciences, 6
Social science writing, 287
Social scientific, 6
Social scientific majors, employment rate and
    earnings in, 9
Social scientific methods, expectations
    for, 227
Social scientific skills, 22
Social subjects, research boundaries and, 62
Society, disaggregation of, 139
Socioeconomic mobilization theory of victory in
    war, 183–184
Sociology major, employment rate and earnings
    in, 9